Maurits of Nassau and the Survival of the Dutch __

This book describes the crucial period in the monumental 80-year Dutch struggle against the Spanish Empire, through which a small nation gained its independence from one of the mightiest European powers. Dr. Ridley shows how, even though the Dutch Revolt was at its lowest point, Maurits of Nassau and the Dutch fought on and the Revolt survived. It was a turbulent time, with complex diplomacy and shifting alliances, assassination plots, France torn by civil war, Spain spearheading the Counter-Reformation, England facing invasion, and Europe eventually convulsed with the Thirty Years' War. In all these, the Dutch Revolt was a significant factor.

The book also explores subsequent insurgencies over the following 3 centuries, when nationalist groups revolted against European powers, and analyses and identifies essential factors for a successful insurgency. The key roles of finance and international relations in insurgencies are emphasised. This volume will be informative and compelling reading for readers and students of history, international relations, and insurgencies.

Nick Ridley, is currently Visiting Lecturer at Liverpool John Moores University. He has formerly worked as an intelligence analyst with the Metropolitan Police and Europol, has taught at several European universities, and has trained police and security forces in Africa and at NATO Centres of Excellence-Defence against Terrorism.

Routledge Research in Early Modern History

Series editor:
Renato Lancelotta

For more information about this series, please visit: https://www.
routledge.com/Routledge-Research-in-Early-Modern-History/
book-series/RREMH

Maurits of Nassau and the Survival of the Dutch Revolt

Comparative Insurgences

Nick Ridley

Routledge
Taylor & Francis Group

NEW YORK AND LONDON

First published 2020
by Routledge
52 Vanderbilt Avenue, New York, NY 10017

and by Routledge
2 Park Square, Milton Park, Abingdon, Oxon, OX14 4RN

Routledge is an imprint of the Taylor & Francis Group, an informa business

© 2020 Taylor & Francis

Library of Congress Cataloging-in-Publication Data
A catalog record for this book has been requested

ISBN 13: 978-0-367-34608-9 (pbk)
ISBN 13: 978-0-367-34607-2 (hbk)
ISBN 13: 978-0-429-32683-7 (ebk)

Typeset in Sabon
by Apex CoVantage, LLC

Contents

Acknowledgements

The author is particularly grateful for the kind advice and guidance of Professor Martin Prak of the University of Utrecht and for the kind advice of Professor Judith Pollman of the University of Leiden.

In addition, the author wishes to thank the staff of the Netherlands National Library in The Hague and the Netherlands National Archives in The Hague for their assistance, valuable assistance which was given with unfailing courtesy, friendliness, and efficiency.

Most importantly. the author owes a large debt of gratitude for the translations, for the preliminary proofreadings and for the advice, constant support and patience of Ingrid.

Introduction
The Dutch Revolt and Other Revolts

This book is about Maurits of Nassau and the survival of the Dutch Revolt, with comparisons to other revolts and insurgences. The principal subject of the book, Maurits of Nassau, was a remarkable individual during a period of intense struggle in which a remarkable people gained their independence. The struggle for independence lasted for over 3 generations and is known to history as the Eighty Years' War. At its end, the Dutch Republic was officially acknowledged as a sovereign and independent nation state by Spain, which, although declining, was still an empire. The 7 northern provinces of the Spanish Netherlands had successfully revolted and had won their independence from one of the greatest European powers of the era. As part of this struggle, Maurits of Nassau had ensured the survival and continuation of the Revolt.

There has been and is much scholarship by eminent historians of this period and of the long event of the Dutch struggle. Some historians have designated it the "Eighty Years' War". The author has drawn upon and has taken guidance from the works of these eminent scholars and historians, particularly the older but still valuable works of H.T. Colenbrander, drawn from groundbreaking archival documentation techniques, the works of C.V. Wedgwood and of Peiter Geyl, as well as those of the more modern works of Geoffrey Parker, the monumental works of Jonathan Israel, those of Arnaud van Cruyningen and of Theo van Deusen. Geoffrey Parker, in his trenchant account of the Revolt containing incisive analysis, points to one school of historians who insist that the Dutch Revolt was not one but several revolts, each with different causes. Accordingly, he divides his work into 3 revolts spanning the respective periods 1565–1568, 1568–1576, and 1576–1581 This current book, whilst fully respecting and acknowledging their scholarship, will take the traditional term of the singular "Dutch Revolt". Significantly, Parker, in his *The Dutch Revolt*, entitles one of his chapters, chapter 5, covering the period of much of Maurits's activities as "Independence and *Survival*" (italics mine). There are many factors affecting the success or failure of revolts, rebellions, and insurgencies and to what extent one single factor is important varies from struggle to struggle. However, for the purpose of considering the survival of the Dutch Revolt and comparing its success to later insurgencies, 4 important factors form a backdrop and will be considered:

National identity, the revolt or insurgency having a clear identity of and constancy in the national cause

Adequate armed forces, having adequate armed forces to engage in, sustain, and survive the armed conflict against the forces deployed to suppress the revolt

The international dimension. This involves the insurgent leadership fully comprehending and understanding the contemporary international affairs situation. From this the insurgent leadership turns and exploits developments in the international situation to the advantage of the insurgency, or at least prevents such developments from adversely impacting against the insurgency.

Finance, "the sinews of war", ensuring adequate and sustained financial support

This book will emphasise the financial aspects of the Revolt, particularly the finances involved in the Dutch Revolt and the economic achievement of the Dutch Republic, itself a tribute to the steadfast determination of the Dutch during this period. Also, Maurits has a well justified reputation for his military abilities. However, this book will also highlight his shrewdness and perception at vital periods of the contemporary international situation and at turning this to good effect for the Revolt.

Overall, this book is a modest contribution to the knowledge of insurgencies and revolts and of its principal subject, Maurits of Nassau. As such, the book acknowledges and adds to the tributes to both him and the Dutch people for their achievement in their successful revolt that resulted in their gaining their independence.

Part I

The Revolt

1 Early Days

The Sixteenth Century saw much change in the Hapsburg Netherlands. In the late mediaeval era, the Hapsburg Netherlands were part of and semi-autonomous within the Duchy of Burgundy. When they were acquired by the Hapsburgs they were a complex patchwork quilt of lordships and jurisdictions and of local privileges and customs of various nobility and landowners, a hangover from mediaeval times. Since 1516, during the reign of Emperor Charles V, governmental changes in the Hapsburg Netherlands resulted in reform and more unification. Standardised laws administered by provincial high courts, a newly created state service of highly trained bureaucrats with responsibility for unified jurisdictions, all were creating a more unified Hapsburg Netherlands. But at the same time these changes were antagonising the traditional nobility, who saw their local powers and privileges being increasingly eroded. Holland and Zeeland nobility in particular were upset about the practice of the new trend of officials from the other and—to the Holland and Zeeland nobility—lesser provinces being appointed to governmental and administrative posts in Holland and Zeeland.

Religious changes were also occurring. In 1559 and 1561, papal bulls, fully supported by Philip II, reorganised the bishopric structure throughout the Hapsburg Netherlands. These reforms created several new bishoprics under 3 archbishoprics whose seats were at Utrecht, Cambrai, and Mechelen, the archbishop of Mechelen becoming Primate of the Netherlands. Philip II fully supported these reforms, calculating that more bishops, provided they were zealous, would be effective in combating the growing heresies of Lutheranism and Calvinism. The reorganisation was opposed by the abbots of the wealthier monasteries, who would lose their independence as they would come under closer supervision of the new bishoprics, and the reorganisation also harmed their close relationships with the local nobility. The mandatory qualification of a high level of religious scholarship for the new bishops and the clergy under them upset the nobility, who previously had a say in the appointments of bishops and local clergy and had used the positions for placement of junior members of their family. The rural workers and peasants were confused and suspicious of the perceived upheaval within the church. One Dutch historian states that all classes of the Netherlands were united in their opposition to the new bishoprics.[1]

There were also adverse financial changes. Charles V's various wars, all fought on behalf of the Holy Roman Empire, had proven extremely costly, and much of the financial burden had fallen on the Netherlands's provinces. Collectively, the Netherlands were a comparatively rich part of the Hapsburg's domains, and they were looked to by Charles to furnish the needed revenues. By 1545, the deficit in Charles's central treasury was over 700,000 florins. To offset this, the short-term remedy was heavy borrowing on the Antwerp market, with interest rates to service the debt as high as 30%. By 1556 the debt stood at over 7 million florins.[2] To meet and service these rising debts and to finance further wars, imperial taxation on various parts of the Netherlands increased, causing bitter resentment amongst the Netherlanders.

The States-General, the representative body of the various provinces as well as the States of the individual provinces voiced increasing opposition to the taxes and financial demands called upon them. After Philip II succeeded to the throne of the Spanish Empire[3] and he finished his tour of the Netherlands, he returned to Spain. His first fiscal decisions in Madrid were that no more revenues were to be sent to the Netherlands from Spain; the governance and maintenance of order there had to be paid for by revenues raised within the Netherlands. This meant that the States-General had to be convened to raise the revenues. However the States-General proved extremely recalcitrant, being resentful and weary of the financial demands. Also, they were encouraged by the States of Brabant, which included the powerful representatives from Brussels and which in 1566 had refused to blindly and obediently grant the amounts demanded; the Spanish had backed down. On 3 August 1557, the States-General convened and discussed and debated. In 1559 they agreed to provide for a period of revenues, or the so-called Nine Years' Aid. However, it was to be facilitated, collected, and distributed under the orders and authority of the States-General. This meant that the States-General had at any time the power to withhold funds, should they so choose. Philip II had left the Netherlands for Spain in 1559, leaving the government of the Netherlands in the hands of Regent Margaret of Parma. Margaret, the sister of Philip and illegitimate daughter of the former Emperor Charles V, was sensible, moderate, and well meaning. However, she had little practical experience in government. Philip had also ensured that 3,000 experienced Spanish troops were based in the Netherlands. In 1561, the States-General refused to grant any more money and halted the Nine Years' Aid programme until there were no Spanish troops in the Netherlands. Margaret, seeing the potential collapse of government through a lack of funds, acquiesced.

To assist and guide Margaret of Parma as regent, Philip created 3 advisory councils as part of the government, each one staffed by experienced councillors. However, also part of the government at Brussels was Antoine de Perronet, later Cardinal Granvelle. It was Granvelle who was the originator of the reorganisation of the bishoprics. Opposition in the Netherlands centred around hostility to Granvelle. It was led by a group of nobles who held lands inside and outside of the Netherlands. This group included a distinguished soldier and Catholic noble, Count van Egmont, William of Nassau—the future William of Orange and soon to gain the immortal epithet "the Silent"—and Philip de Montmorency, Count Hoorn. Hoorn was captain of Philip II's bodyguards and had returned with Philip in 1559 to Spain. Disturbed by developments in the Netherlands, he left Spain and returned in 1561, joining the opposition to Granvelle. All 3 nobles made it clear to Margaret that they were loyal to Spain—and Egmont that he was loyal to Spain and a devout Catholic—that they wished to assist her in governing, and that their opposition to Granvelle was that of opposing toxic policies, detrimental to all in the Netherlands. In their opposition, they were supported by all the other principal nobility of the Netherlands, all of whom were part of the nobility of the Knights of the Golden Fleece, a traditional and high-ranking order created by Hapsburg rulers and bestowed upon trusted nobles. Margaret saw the validity of their arguments and sent despatches to Philip, advising that Granvelle be recalled. In 1564, Granvelle was ordered to leave Brussels on a face-saving pretext. Spanish rule had encountered more opposition and had again backed down.

The religious reorganisation of the bishoprics was accompanied by a more repressive policy against heresy. By the 1550s, the Reformation had impacted upon the Netherlands and upon both Lutheran and Calvinist doctrines, and the more extreme Anabaptist creeds had taken root in several parts of the Netherlands. Since 1520 there had been a series of imperial anti-heresy laws passed relating to the Netherlands; an inquisitorial system authorised by the Pope and fully supported by Charles V had been set up in 1522. However, enforcement of the anti-heresy laws had been light, and only a small number of prosecutions had been pursued. In 1540 the inquisitorial system had been expanded, given extra resources, and granted increased powers of investigation and interrogation. Its activity increased in the 1550s, and by the 1560s, prosecutions, fines and confiscations, and executions by burning had dramatically increased. These caused resentment and discontent amongst wide sections of the population, with open demonstrations in favour of heresy and heretics. There were hostile demonstrations when individuals were condemned for heresy and while they were led to their execution. Condemned heretics were rescued by mobs from execution escorts and from jails in which they were being held. Against this rising tide, it was decided that van Egmont, of Margaret's Council, should travel to Spain and plead for a relaxation of the heresy laws. Egmont did so in early 1565. In Spain, van Egmont was treated courteously and was given some assurances there would be some form of revision and relaxation. He returned to the Netherlands in April 1565 and reported this to the nobles, including William of Orange, Hoorn, and Brederode. In fact, Egmont had been completely deceived. Philip II had had no intention of relaxing any policies. A month after Egmont returned and reported the good news, orders came from Madrid to Margaret and her Council that Anabaptist heretics who had repented had nonetheless to be executed. Further instruction letters addressed to Margaret stated that there was to be no change in any policies, that the powers of the Council remained, and that the heresy laws remained as they were and were to be enforced. To William of Orange, this was clear proof of Spanish intransigence, and from then on he never trusted Spain or Philip. Egmont and Hoorn remained trusting, and Margaret of Parma attempted to keep overall control. Furtive meetings among many of the nobles followed. The lesser nobility signed a petition urging Margaret to adopt a policy of leniency; most of the higher nobility avoided signing but did voice their concerns and stated the need for the Brussels government to be lenient. William of Orange did not sign but asked to be relieved of his position in the Council. Egmont and Hoorn, sincere and anxious, warned Margaret that they could not guarantee restoring order.

Margaret agreed and issued instructions to government officials and magistrates that heresy laws were not to be fully enforced and that a policy of a level of tolerance adopted. Back in Madrid, Philip and his councillors and ministers remained implacable and openly fulminated against William of Orange and the other nobles whom he deemed to be misleading his Regent Margaret. Against Margaret herself the King was increasingly angry, fulminating against her and her council for granting unacceptable concessions to subversives and heretics.

Despite Margaret and her councillors' adopting a more flexible policy in dealing with heresy, the situation remained unstable. Indeed, Calvinist groups and other Anabaptist groups gained confidence from this policy, conducted mass open air services, and organised themselves into "consisteries" whose attitude and actions were militant. A meeting of Margaret's Council advocated more compromising measures including full toleration of non-Catholics. However, this was overtaken by militant demonstrations, riots, and rapidly spreading outbreaks of church invasions, iconoclasm, and destruction, centring at first in Ypres and Antwerp and spreading out, the latter as far as s'Hertogenbosch. Iconoclasm, riots, and destruction also hit individual towns in the north, including Groningen, Amsterdam, and Utrecht. In some areas the militia, or *schutters*, stood idly by and refused to act against the rioters. Margaret and her councillors tried further policies of compromise and negotiations with leaders of the nobility, the lesser nobility, and the Calvinist leaders but made little progress.

By late 1566, Philip II and his ministers in Spain were determined on robust action. The decision was made to send the Duke of Alva and Spanish troops. (All Spanish troops had left the Netherlands under the terms of the financial agreement of the States-General in 1561 for their continuation to implement the Nine Years' Aid.) Egmont, Hoorn, and William of Orange were identified by Philip as the instigators of the disturbances and were marked men. Meanwhile in the Netherlands, an uprising had begun, with groups of Calvinists supported and led by the Calvinist nobles such as Henry, baron van Brederode, and Louis of Nassau, William's brother. Egmont, loyal to the government, refused to join, refused point-blank to raise troops against Spain, and retired to his estates; Hoorn also refused and retired to his estates. William remained undecided, alarmed by the excesses of the iconoclastic mobs. The two main armies of rebels materialised, one in the north-west under Louis of Nassau, backed by forces from German Protestants and mercenaries, and another in the south backed by French Huguenot forces. Also, some individual towns such as Tournai and Valenciennes declared for the Revolt and made ready for siege.

Margaret quickly acted, adopting a robust policy. She and her commanders raised troops and levies from the many towns still loyal and declared the towns and populaces of Tournai and Valenciennes guilty of treason unless they surrendered and accepted a royal garrison. Forces were deployed and besieged these towns. The Calvinist forces moved to relieve Tournai, plundering and destroying churches and villages as they went. They were defeated at an engagement at Wattreloos, just north of Lille, and then when they tried to obtain access to the town of Lannoy the cowed town population refused them entry. Outside Lannoy they were completely defeated by Margaret's forces. These two victories ended the revolt in Flanders. Still some towns defied the government, and van Brederode was mustering rebel forces in Brabant and around Antwerp. Margaret's government troops advanced upon them. Significantly, a large contingent of these government forces had been raised by Egmont, fully loyal to the government on Brussels; also, William of Orange intervened to stop a Calvinist force being raised in Antwerp. The rebel main base in Flanders was attacked by government forces and completely defeated. Some Calvinist leaders, including the nobles who had sided with them, were killed (but not van Brederode who survived to rebel another day). The town of Valenciennes surrendered and submitted to Margaret and Brussels. The town of Maastricht expelled the Calvinist clergy and rebellious councillors and declared itself loyal in March 1567; in April 1567 the Calvinist rebels in s'Hertogenbosch fled, and at the end of this month in 1567, Antwerp accepted a garrison of government troops. Apart from some pockets of resistance and groups of rebels who laid low, the revolt had been effectively suppressed. It had been suppressed due to prompt action by Margaret's government at Brussels and the loyalty of most of the nobles including William of Orange, van Egmont, and Hoorn.

Margaret of Parma had proven herself fully capable of decisive action. In Aalst, she had sanctioned troops being sent to apprehend—and strangle in public—a Calvinist preacher who was inciting the crowds. She supported firm action in Furnes, facing down the Calvinists who threatened to bring in 15,000 of their own forces. Haarlem, Leiden Brielle, and Delft had all appeared to be heading towards insurrection, yet eventually pacified themselves and arranged a rapprochement with the Brussels government. By a combination of quick action and restraint, she had managed to restore peaceful rule. On 27 April 1567 Margaret sent a letter to Philip II of Spain stating that the disturbances had been effectively suppressed and were at an end and that no Spanish troops were needed.

It was too late. Philip II, fanatically sincere in his Catholicism and the Catholic mission of the Spanish Empire, was incensed at the outbreaks of Calvinism and at their iconoclasm. He was angry that the Brussels government had adopted policies of compromise and leniency, even though these policies had been later replaced by decisive and robust action that had quelled the disturbances. From distant Madrid he was convinced of the complicity of the Netherlands nobles, especially William of Orange, Egmont, and Hoorn, and he was unable to differentiate between the varying loyalties amongst the nobles. Both he and his councillors were always conscious of the value and strategic importance of the Netherlands within the Spanish Empire, so that there could be absolutely no risk of its loyalty to Spain. Alva, implacable, was on his way with 8,000 Spanish troops based in Milan to make sure that any further revolt would be impossible.

Alva set out, and he and his forces made for the Netherlands via the Spanish Road of Milan, up through the Valtelline passes and following the Rhine, arriving in the Netherlands on 3 August 1567 and in Brussels on 22 August. Brussels, Ghent, and other towns in Brabant and Flanders were garrisoned with Spanish troops. These troops were billeted and fed, with no payment to the population. The government forces that had been raised by Margaret and the loyal nobles stood down and were disbanded. The disbanded Brussels government troops, even those loyal veteran units who had served for years, were not paid.[4]

Alva presented his credentials to Margaret and effectively took power. Direct rule from Madrid, through Alva, was to be the way the Spanish Netherlands were governed. And ruthless repression was to be the policy.

Notes

1. Geyl, P *A History of the Dutch Speaking Peoples* p 71
2. Parker, G *The Dutch Revolt* p 38
3. When Charles V, weary of wars and the burdens of the Holy Roman Empire, abdicated in 1555, he divided the Hapsburg possessions in two. The Austrian Hapsburgs retained the bulk of the land empire of the German and central European provinces and the throne of the Holy Roman Empire, whilst the Spanish Hapsburgs retained Spain, Portugal, the overseas possessions of Spain and Portugal, the territories and duchies in northern Italy, and the Netherlands
4. Stein, CR *Margaret of Parma—A Life* p 278

2   William of Orange Forges
a Nation

As effective governor of the Netherlands, Alva intensified enforcing Spanish rule with the anti-heresy laws. Within days of his arrival in Brussels,
he set up a tribunal to investigate, identify, and punish all rebels. This
tribunal was named the Council of the Troubles but became infamously
known as the "Council of Blood". Alva's mindset in his task of quelling
the Revolt is epitomised in two of his communications. In establishing
the Council of Blood, he loyally wrote to Philp II:

> [L]awyers are only accustomed to pass sentence on a crime being
> proved: that will never do here.[1]

And in a letter of 1571 to the city authorities in Delft, he was to order:

> I understand that you are holding a certain Commer Euwotsj from
> Briel. . . . If he continues to be stubborn in his heresy you shall burn
> him alive; strike out his tongue with a hot ire on prior to his leaving
> the prison to deny him opportunity to speak out against our Catholic
> faith.[2]

In formulating policy for dealing with heretics and rebels, moderation
was not part of Alva's vocabulary. Some 12,000 individuals were brought
before the tribunal, of which just over 1,000 were executed, and a further
9,000 were condemned with fines or total confiscation of their goods and
assets. Two of those arrested and executed were Egmont and Hoorn.
Alva had set up the Council of the Troubles on arriving in Brussels, but
its existence and true remit had been kept secret for a period in order not
to alert or alarm the perceived ringleaders of the recent troubles. During
this period, several of the nobles, including Egmont, Hoorn, and William of Orange, were summoned by Alva to Brussels to confer with him.
William, cautious and mistrustful, avoided going; Hoorn travelled and
attended, and Egmont, ever trusting and confident in his loyalty to Spain,
made himself available. The following day both Egmont and Hoorn were
arrested and interrogated. In June 1568, after lengthy interrogations,

they were publicly executed in Brussels' central square. The executions shocked moderate public opinion, and the subsequent trials and executions caused further resentment and anger. The executions of Egmont and Hoorn left William of Orange at large and the only prominent focal point for any further opposition to Alva.

William had not heeded Alva's summons but instead had moved to Heidelberg, at the court of the elector Palatine, a Calvinist, the brother-in-law of Count Egmont and an elector of the Holy Roman Empire. The elector Palatine was offering sanctuary to all those fleeing Alva's harsh regime. William of Orange had issued his *Justification*, a document that was produced, printed, and distributed widely, despite Alva's penalties against any and all those who distributed or were found in possession of the document. The *Justification* implied William's rejection of Catholicism— or its use of the extreme inquisition—but still proclaimed his loyalty to Spain and to King Philip II but declaring against the mistaken and malicious councillors and ministers.[3] It was an assertion of loyalty but also an effective propaganda technique for continuing the struggle.

William then moved across the border to Strasbourg, still keeping out of Alva's reach and raising funds for the Revolt. Later in the Revolt in 1571, William was to move to the safer location of Delft, which was to remain his headquarters. Significantly, one of his first acts was to issue a decree through the city authorities imposing religious toleration.

Meanwhile William's brother Louis of Nassau, impetuous and always ready for action, organised an invasion from the north through Friesland. Alva moved troops out of Brussels and speedily marched north to meet them and engaged. Louis's forces retreated and fell back to Jemmingen on the river Ems. The Spanish forces under Alva followed, overwhelmed the defensive positions of the insurgents, and soundly defeated Louis and his forces.

Jemmingen effectively quelled this Dutch Revolt. William had also made an unsuccessful foray into Brabant and had also been defeated. He retreated across the border into France, where he disbanded his forces. He paid them and settled their pay arrears. This was costly but prudent; he was now extremely short of funds, but had he not settled the payment of his troops, he would have great difficulty in recruiting in future. Spain was later to learn the lesson of paying troops.

Alva had quelled the Revolt. His military actions had been ruthlessly successful. His policy as Captain General and effective ruler had been dictatorial, reactionary and violent. The Council of Blood tribunal had been appalling in its practice. However Alva also inaugurated reforms in that he unified and standardised the criminal law—the non-seditious, non-treasonable offences—throughout the provinces and codified financial law and practice. This last brought a measure of gratitude and appreciation from the merchants of Antwerp and the commercial interests of other towns. But Alva's reorganisation of government, and its institutions and administration which eradicated traditional customary practice and local laws was to be wide-sweeping and radical; it caused upheaval and further resentment. Indeed:

> "the King planned to force upon the Netherlands uniformity unprecedented in the governments of the time.[4]

Also, finances were to come to the fore.

Philip II, whilst fully appreciating and praising Alva's draconian efficiency in re-establishing order, also made it quite clear, in a direct despatch for Alva's view only, that the troops based and operating in the Netherlands could not be paid by the Spanish central treasury. Revenues to pay for Spanish forces in the Netherlands had to be raised from and within the Netherlands. Alva was nothing loathe to comply. He consulted with tax officials and financial experts within his entourage. Then in 1569 he convened—or confronted—representatives of the States of the different provinces of the Netherlands, and, following the advice of his officials with whom he had consulted, he requested that the States authorise 3 new taxes. These 3 new taxes were the Hundredth Penny, the Twentieth Penny, and the Tenth Penny. The Tenth Penny was a 5% tax on all property sales; the Tenth Penny was a 10% tax on all other sales, a small amount but wide-sweeping, for the well off and poor alike; the Hundredth Penny was a single, one-occasion 1% tax on all capital, with the capital of an individual being assessed in a sliding scale depending on the revenue gained from that capital.

Initially there was some room for negotiation. The States consented to the Hundredth Penny, and it was collected, bringing in a revenue for Alva's administration of 3,628,507 florins.[5] The States were concerned about the other two taxes, the Twentieth Penny and the Hundredth Penny, as these were to be permanent. The States offered to Alva, instead of these two taxes, a single grant of 4 million florins to be raised over a two-year period, the whole sum to be collected and given over by late 1571. Alva accepted this. By 1570 he had achieved a repression of the Revolt, and by 1571, for what would be the only period in the whole decade of 1566–1576, for a whole year the troops of the Spanish administration in the Netherlands were maintained entirely by revenues raised from the Netherlands. This contrasted with every other year, when the proportions were to be between 4 and 6 times as much monies sent by Spain to the Netherlands as those raised in the Netherlands.[6]

Alva did accept the single grant from the States-General but only as a compromise, and a temporary one at that. He calculated that this, together with the revenues raised from the Hundredth Penny tax, would maintain his forces in the Netherlands up to 1571. However, he insisted that the Twentieth and Tenth Penny taxes must be implemented and collected eventually. Further attempts at negotiations took place, and the States accepted the Twentieth but refused point blank to pay the Tenth Penny tax.

By mid-1571 Alva resolved again on force. He rode roughshod over the States-General and appointed his own tax collectors, and in early 1572 troops were deployed in the intimidation of shopkeepers and merchants in Brussels and other big towns, forcing them to open for business and pay the taxes on their takings. By this time, large sections of the population were active in a general tax strike, or a refusal to pay taxes; this took place over large parts of the Netherlands. The Antwerp exchange closed. The weavers of Valenciennes went on strike. In Namur, residents loosed dogs on tax collectors. In various towns, rather than buy and sell food and incur a tax, people resorted to direct bartering of food. The States of Flanders, Brabant, and Hainault sent delegates to Spain to remonstrate with King Philip, whilst in the north there was open hostility to any government officials. Groups of rebels were discreetly arming, but there appeared little that they could achieve and little prospect of success.

Alva had apparently achieved everything King Philip had ordered. He had ruthlessly repressed the Revolt, chased down and executed suspected subversives and heretics, and imposed financial measures to pay for the Spanish forces in the Netherlands. However, two fatal misjudgements had been made, one by Philip and one by Alva. Philip II, at a distance in Madrid, underestimated how much Margaret had restored and stabilised the situation, and Alva *in situ* had failed to recognise how much opposition he had caused in his follow-through measures.

Anti-Catholic sentiment remained strong in many parts of the country, Calvinism remained strong, and anti-Spanish anger and resentment remained strong. However, in terms of effective opposition by force, there were only remnants of insurgent forces. But one unit of the remnants of the insurgent forces remained active.

During Louis of Nassau's disastrous attempted invasion through Friedsland, he had hired a small fleet to safeguard his seaborne supply lines of provisions and munitions. These freelance sailors came from a variety of backgrounds—anti-Spanish patriots, Calvinists, freebooters, or outright criminal pirates—but all were hardened and experienced seamen. Louis had at his disposal a small fleet of 15 ships, but after Jemmingen they had no paymaster and returned to freebooting. William, anxious to build and maintain a war fleet, adopted these so-called Gueux de Mer (Sea Beggars) and in his capacity as the sovereign prince of Orange, issued the captains with official letters of marque and reinforced them with seamen from England who had fled Alva's persecution. Queen Elizabeth of England, supportive of the Revolt, allowed the Sea Beggars fleet to use English ports to refit, to take on provisions, and to recruit and expand. They were under the command of a minor noble, William Lumey van Marque, a fervent Calvinist and implacably anti-Spanish. His zeal did not discriminate between Spanish and neutral shipping, if the latter were deemed supplying the Spanish occupiers (or if they were good plunder).

The indiscriminate attacks backfired. The Spanish organised a seaborne counteroffensive and managed to locate 8 of the Sea Beggars ships, frosted and ice bound off Friesland, and destroyed them with cannon fire. By this time, the neutral powers, including the Hanseatic League, had made loud and repeated representations and protests to Queen Elizabeth of England about the Sea Beggars' constant attacks, and in March 1572 Elizabeth closed the English ports to them, specifying that her withdrawal of support was withdrawal specifically to the fleet of William of Orange.[7] Elizabeth was careful, however. The official proclamations in March 1572 of the Special Commissioners of Kent, Sussex, Southampton, and the Isle of Wight stated that the offences of the Gueux de Mer (Sea Beggars) were "acts of war" for which they could be arrested—but there were no grounds for their apprehension and arrest as pirates or as rebels. And Elizabeth did ensure that every Gueux de Mer (Sea Beggars) ship and crew were allowed to leave (i.e. escape) the ports unmolested. Nonetheless, the English south coast ports, the only real safe haven of the Gueux de Mer were now closed to them.

The Sea Beggars' fleet cruised in low morale up and down the English Channel, looking for coastal targets to attack. Brielle in Holland was a small fishing port. When the Sea Beggars under their naval commander, van Marque, approached, it had been temporarily left without a Spanish garrison, Alva concentrating his forces along the French frontier to guard against an attempted rebel invasion from the south. Brielle had one main street, lined with simple dwellings and buildings, and a small inner harbor. The inner harbor was a good sheltered area for refuge, repairing, and refitting ships. The layout of the small port made the plundering raid under van Marque's second in command, William de Treslong, easy and speedy. However, not only could the port itself be taken speedily; more importantly, given the support of the small population, it could effectively be held. This became apparent to de Treslong, who persuaded van Marque to take, occupy, and hold Brielle. It was taken, the small population welcomed the occupiers, and detachments of Sea Beggars were posted. The Dutch Revolt had gained control of its first piece of territory. Five days later the population of Vlissingen, a fishing port to the south in Zeeland, openly rebelled, declaring that they would accept only a garrison of William's troops. The Brussels-appointed tax collector was murdered by a mob. Brussels' government troops in Vlissingen were expelled, and the Revolt had gained its second port. In May the port of Enkhuizen declared for William. The sentiment was anti-Spanish, but the wealthier inhabitants were also appealing to William restore order in ports in turmoil with mob violence. Between June and July, other towns inland in Holland defected from Spanish rule and declared for William. Dordrecht, Bommel, Buren, Delft, Leiden, Naarden, Medemblik, Gouda,

Oudewater, and the ports of Alkmaar and Hoorn all placed themselves under William and the Revolt. By August 1572 a large part of Holland and Zeeland was under the control of William.

Alva attempted to restore the situation by inviting—or summoning—all the main towns of the province of Holland to send representatives to a meeting of the States of Holland in The Hague. The rebel council of Dordrecht countered by inviting all the towns in Holland to send representatives to a meeting in Dordrecht. Twelve of the 18 towns in Holland responded to Dordrecht, sending representatives there and shunning Alva's projected meeting. Most of the nobility of Holland also attended Dordrecht. William of Orange, as count of Nassau and prince of Orange, sent Philip Marnix as his representative to Dordrecht.

In a historic meeting on 19 July 1572, Philip Marnix addressed the meeting, and after discussions it was agreed[8] that all recognised William of Orange as the king's stadhouder in Holland, Zeeland, and Utrecht. A common budget was to be available to pay for troops and sailors and ships currently fighting in the prince's name. Broad-based religious toleration was agreed, including Catholicism. Some days later, governmental structures and institutions were agreed. The individual provinces of the States were to retain their Accounting Offices (Rekenkamer) and High Courts, but coming under the States-General were the Admiralty Colleges and the Finance College. A Gecomimittererde Raad, or States Committee, was to advise and support the Prince. A *de facto* constitution and government of the nation had come into being.

The Spanish made a vigorous counterinsurgency advance. The towns of Mons, Ost, Mechelen, Zutphen, Naarden were taken. In December 1572 Haarlem had been reached by the advancing Spanish forces. Haarlem's defences were not strong, but it was surrounded by a network of small canals that were fed by two major canal ways. The defenders used these and built up strong defence works inside the older dilapidated ones and strengthened the gateways. These were vigorously held against Spanish attacks, the Dutch being led by the resourceful commander van Hogensteyn. There was heavy fighting around the Jansenpoort, leading to the centre, which held. However, by July 1573 the lack of supplies and food affected the defenders, and the Spanish finally broke through, firing the Kruispoort gate and quickly overwhelming the emaciated defenders.[9] The commander of the Spanish troops was Alva's son, Don Fernando de Toledo.

> By straining the quality of mercy through the hair-shirt of his own judgement,[10]

he ordered that the surviving, half-starved civilians from Haarlem should be allowed to go free but at the same time ordered that the surrendering Dutch troops to be executed. He assumed that news of this would be favourably received by the Dutch as evidence of clemency. Compared to the previous massacres committed by the Spanish troops in the surrendering Dutch towns they had besieged, it was—but the Dutch population failed to appreciate the gesture as showing mercy.

The capture of Haarlem, combined with the previous towns taken, threatened to cut in two the territory controlled by the Dutch, dividing Zeeland and parts of southern Holland on the one hand and northern Holland on the other. However, Don Fernando de Toledo next struck north, besieging Alkmaar in the north-west. Also, Dutch forces in the south-west blockaded the port of Middleburg. Now it was the Spaniards' turn to be besieged, by land and by sea, and in the latter the Gueux de Mer were past masters at coastal naval warfare. Middelburg surrendered to the Dutch in February 1574. Up north, the defenders of Alkmaar held out, and the Dutch flooded the surrounding countryside. Don Fernando abandoned the siege. Alkmaar was a check, a setback, but the siege was abandoned only because it was more trouble than it was worth. In failing to take Alkmaar, the Spanish had not suffered a significant defeat; they could always return at later stage and deal with Alkmaar.[11]

In the south in the provinces who remained loyal to Spain, there had been a change of government. Alva was ordered home, much to his surprise and bewilderment, to be replaced in 1573 by don Luis de Requesens. Reserved by nature, Requesens was a career diplomat and a former Spanish governor of Milan. This post was normally taken by one of the great noble families of Spain, amongst whom Requesens did not belong. However, his ability in diplomacy caused Philip to appoint him to govern Milan, and his moderate rule there had resulted in benefitting both the Milanese and Spain. Arriving in the Netherlands in November 1573, he took post in Brussels as governor-general. He spoke neither French nor Dutch. However, despite his taciturn nature and lack of languages, he counselled a more moderate approach to the Dutch Revolt than the repressive Alva, and Philip sent him with the full authority to reach some sort of settlement, provided Requesens did not yield on the heresy edicts and Spanish sovereignty.[12]

Meanwhile, military operations against the Revolt continued. The fledgling Dutch Army led by William's brother Louis of Nassau was entirely defeated in a pitched battle with the Spanish at Mook, near Nijmegen in April 1574. Louis was amongst those killed. The main thrust of the Spanish through the centre of Holland was continued.

However, the capture of Middelburg had gained the Dutch an important stretch of Zeeland coastal territory in the south-west, with access to ports and the sea—Brielle to Vlissingen to Middelburg, all under Dutch control. Also, they had held out in north-west Holland. However, all this would be seriously offset if the Dutch territory was split by the surrender of the towns as a result of a series of Spanish victories—Mons

Ost, Mechelen, Zutphen, Naarden, Haarlem, and now Leiden, which was besieged in May 1574.

The Spanish advance appeared inexorable, unstoppable. But Leiden brought this to a halt; it held out, and it was relieved. William had persuaded the States of Holland to flood the area by opening the dykes. In the massive floods that followed, Dutch relieving forces, led and assisted by the Sea Beggars, were able to float relief troops and supplies on barges, and the besieging Spanish forces, waist deep in rising waters, broke and fled. Leiden held.

The failure to capture Leiden resulted in an outbreak of indiscipline in the Spanish armies. As more of these disturbances occurred and indisciplined Spanish troops committed further riots, Requesens was pressured by the State-General to withdraw all forces, negotiate, and restore the provinces' former rights and privileges. He attempted to mediate with the States-General. He offered to withdraw all troops in return for the restoration and primacy of the Catholic religion. However, such a restoration was long past possible in the northern provinces. Calvinism had taken an iron hold, especially in Holland and Zeeland. Negotiations broke down. Requesens attempted to renew hostilities by advancing upon Breda, but then in February 1576 William of Orange and his supporters gained ground in the States-General. William himself attempted to broker negotiations between the representatives of Holland and Zeeland, and the Catholic nobility of the south (who, though they were against Spanish rule, were strongly Catholic). There were significant differences between the two parties, the Catholic nobility in the south and the provinces of Holland and Zeeland in the north, which made any agreement difficult. However, in November 1576 an event occurred that overshadowed and put aside differences.

In that month, Spanish troops in Antwerp, whose pay was years in arrears, mutinied and ran amok. In a horrific period of 11 days, the city was sacked, causing 7,000 civilian deaths, victims of pillaging, plundering, and murder. This focused both the north and the south on the need for common urgent action, action that would also be an expression of rejection of Spanish rule. By an agreement, the Pacification of Ghent, delegates from the southern provinces of the States-General, delegates from the States of Holland and Zeeland, and delegates from William of Orange all agreed to full cooperation in expelling Spanish forces from the Netherlands. The Pacification of Ghent also included in its terms a form of freedom of worship whereby the practice of Calvinism in the provinces of Holland and Zeeland would be fully permitted, provided Calvinists did not interfere with the practice of Catholic worship elsewhere in the Netherlands. This last effectively nullified Philip II's edicts against heresy; Calvinism remained the religious dynamic of the Revolt. In the midst of these tumultuous events and changes in politics, Requesens died suddenly. His replacement was Don Juan of Austria, who arrived in the Netherlands as the new governor-general.

Don Juan of Austria was an illegitimate son of Charles V. He was of a warlike, fiery disposition that masked an inner sense of deep insecurity. He had been prominent as a leader of the anti-Turkish coalition of Venice, Genoa, and Spain and had led—literally—from the front at the naval Battle of Lepanto in 1571. He was in the first of the large galleys forming the van of the coalition's fleet that defeated the Turkish fleet at this battle. One historian sums up his personality when he arrived in the Netherlands as governor-general:

> In 1571 he had virtually driven the Turks out of the western Mediterranean at Lepanto and had been insufferable ever since.[13]

His mission to the Netherlands was to pacify but with restraint. This stance contradicted his own personal, grandiose mission in which he saw himself as the eventual conqueror of the Netherlands Revolt and then going on to lead the Spanish troops in invading England and restoring the true faith.

Confronted with a virtually united opposition to Spanish rule, in the midst of mutinous units of *tercios* rampaging, Don Juan signed the Perpetual Edict with the States-General in June 1577. This agreed to Spanish troops leaving the Netherlands. However, the Perpetual Edict also stipulated the restoration of the Catholic faith throughout the Netherlands. The Catholic provinces of the south had achieved their main objective to be free from Spanish troops. But the provinces of Holland and Zeeland and William had been frustrated in one of their most important priorities, freedom of worship. Don Juan had driven an ideological wedge through the anti-Spanish unity of the north and south Netherlands.

Don Juan's remit as governor-general was, as a victorious general, to represent Spain in its grandeur and as such to pacify the rebellious subjects but also to be magnanimous and to reconcile both sides. His personality, his perception of being deprived of total authority, which he considered Spain should have granted him, and a lack of funds militated against his pacifying with restraint. In July 1577 he seized Namur. The States-General reacted by withdrawing their allegiance to Don Juan and defiantly proclaiming allegiance to the Archduke Matthias. The Archduke Matthias was the third son of the Holy Roman Emperor Maximilien II, of the Austrian branch of the Hapsburg family. In doing this the States-General renounced the right of Spain to appoint the governor-general of the Netherlands. Don Juan reorganised units of the Army of Flanders positioned in Luxembourg. He excelled in this with his expertise of military command. He and his forces moved on and defeated the Dutch rebel forces at Gembloux.

The Spanish victory brought out into the open the elements in the Netherlands opposing William of Orange. These were the young Catholic nobility, representatives in the States and provinces of the south.

These self-styled "Malcontents" were concerned for the payment of their troops, who were essential for enforcing the Pacification of Ghent. They also increasingly feared, as representatives in the southern States, as nobility, and as landowner classes, the rapid growth of popular "extremism" of the lower classes and their militant Calvinism. Don Juan, despite his clumsiness and his lack of restraint and conciliatory policies, by his victory at Gembloux had exposed divisions within the Revolt.

Don Juan was congratulated by Philip on his victory. But changes in the alignments in the politics of the Spanish Court had resulted in Don Juan losing influence. Philip had always been frustrated by Don Juan's failure to conciliate and bring about a form of settlement with the Dutch. Isolated, disillusioned, and fatigued by his duties, Don Juan caught typhus and died in 1578.

The rebels were divided by class and religion and in the extent to which they wished to repudiate Spanish rule. They were short of funds and militarily overawed and outclassed by their encounters with the Spanish *tercios*. Yet the Revolt continued. Three governor-generals had come and gone—Alva with brutal repression, Requesens with attempted conciliation but fatally disrupted by the violent mutinies of the Spanish troops, and Don Juan with spasmodic military action instead of following instructions to end the Revolt in a peaceful settlement. What would the next governor-general attempt?

The next governor-general was a combination of great military ability and astute diplomacy, in the form of Alexander Farnese, Duke of Parma. Being the son of Margaret of Parma, Philip's regent in the Netherlands before the Revolt began, he was of an extremely practical nature. Margaret was ordered by Philip to return to the Netherlands. Farnese was fond and fully respectful of his mother, but he insisted that he govern alone and would be the sole authority. Margaret, ill and aging, finally withdrew and left the Netherlands. Divided command was not part of Parma's vocabulary.

Parma maintained an astute appreciation of the geostrategic situation in Europe, no matter how complex it became. Soon after taking his post, he grasped the potential solution to the situation, which was to exploit the differences between the southern and the northern provinces. He realised the rifts amongst the rebels in their attitude to a united Netherlands and their differing views on totally breaking with Spain; with timing, these could be exploited. He also realised that the end solution—be it suppressing the whole Revolt or damage limitation if the Dutch Revolt succeeded—lay in the Catholic Walloon provinces and in the necessity of regaining their trust, if not their loyalty to Spain. Later he also realised— unlike Philip and many of the Court in distant Spain—that the defeat of England, even its conquest, lay in pacifying the Netherlands. Therefore, he resolved to concentrate upon the southern provinces and save for Spain all that could be saved. In the words of historian in a work taking a long-ranging view of imperial Spain over the fifteenth, sixteenth, and seventeenth centuries:

> The Catholic provinces of the south, for him they were a smaller but more secure patrimony for the Spanish Hapsburgs.[14]

He realised the importance of good relations with the southern provinces. Since the Pacification of Ghent, Calvinism in the north was spreading over into the southern provinces, into the cities of Ghent, and even into Brussels. The Catholic Malcontents had made moves to offer their allegiance to Archduke Matthias. Now they turned from Matthias and offered their allegiance to a French prince, the Duke of Alencon. There was already a widening of the division between the northern and southern provinces, despite William of Orange's frequent attempts to mediate and heal these. In January 1579, the Walloon, or southern, provinces formed their own union, the Union of Arras. The northern provinces also formed their own union (Holland and Zeeland had formally united in a union in 1576), the Union of Utrecht.

Two years later in July 1581, the provinces of the Union of Utrecht made their union firmer by the Edict of Abjuration by which they formally deposed Philip II of Spain as sovereign of the Netherlands. The States of Holland and Zeeland formally offered the title of count of Holland and Zeeland to William of Orange, and on its being accepted, bestowed the title, thus firming up their own dual union of 1576. Up to now, William had carefully maintained the legal fiction that he and the Dutch rebels were loyal to Philip II,[15] that they were fighting only against the mistaken policies and bad royal councillors, and that he, William, remained—outwardly at least—conciliatory and anxious for peace and for maintaining the unity of the 17 provinces. This legal fiction was no longer feasible or necessary. In the early stages of the Revolt, "patrie", or fatherland, was to William a historical entity, equated with upholding the ancient rights and privileges over which Philip II was riding roughshod. As the struggle continued and became more widespread, "patrie" had solidified into liberty and freedom and a collective hatred of Spain and its rule. With the Union of Utrecht and the Edict of Abjuration, the Revolt was irrevocable. However it was also vulnerable.

Parma made a treaty, also at Arras, with the representatives from the States of Artois, Hainault, and Flanders, whereby these States—in effect the southern Walloon provinces—recognised the sovereignty of Philip of Spain, and the primacy of the Catholic religion as the form of worship in these provinces was guaranteed. The Pacification of Ghent and Don Juan's Perpetual Edict were confirmed. By this, Parma was deprived of Spanish troops in the Netherlands, for he had undertaken by this treaty to ensure that the remaining *tercios* departed and that he would form an army within the southern Walloon provinces with Flanders levies.

However, the lack of Spanish troops was a good price for Parma to pay for the achievement of reconciling the southern Walloon provinces to Spanish rule and in effect perpetuating the divisions within the Dutch Revolt. The Flanders levies under Parma, well trained, well led, and regularly paid, were deployed on campaign, and in June 1579 he captured the great city of Maastricht from the Dutch. To the surrendering troops and civilians of the Maastricht garrison, Parma was magnanimous and merciful and gave lenient surrender terms, avoiding the mistake of massacres committed after the surrenders of Haarlem and Naarden. In December 1579, the city of Groningen was betrayed to Parma's troops by its Catholic governor, who was pressurised into the surrender by the Catholic inhabitants, anxious for a "reconciliation" with such an apparently reasonable and merciful Parma.

The following year, a minor plot, which could have escalated, was discovered in which one of the Malcontent nobility was attempting to overthrow Parma's authority. The perpetrator was executed, but no retribution was made against his family, who kept their estates. Again, the mistake of not showing mercy and carrying out extreme retribution, especially when meted out to the nobility, was avoided. Parma's forces moved on from Maastricht and in 1581, and the town of Tournai was taken. Again, the surrendering forces were treated with generous terms.

These military gains were followed by another successful, indeed invaluable, coup in diplomacy. Parma convened a meeting at Tournai of the representatives of the provinces who had signed the Union of Arras. There, Parma convinced them of the unquestioned need of the return of Spanish troops to the Netherlands; the *tercios*, he assured them, would all fall under his strict command, and they would be paid regularly which would guarantee that order would be maintained. The representatives of the provinces agreed to the return of the Spanish troops. Within a year Parma's command included over 8,000 experienced *tercios* from Spain and the Italian territories.

His subsequent campaign was pursued with a slow but inexorable advance and regaining territory bit by bit.[16] Manoeuvrings and skilfully timed advances were combined with sieges and the use of earthworks, exploiting the topography. His troops complained that they did more fighting with shovels than with musket and pike. Overall, his strategy was that of:

> an intellectual analysis that lifted the art of war to a level the Sixteenth Century saw rarely.[17]

Oudenarde was taken, then Ghent, then Hulst. Then in February 1585, Brussels fell, and 5 months later Mechelen fell. Then, after a long but brilliantly executed siege, the imperial port of Antwerp fell to Parma's forces.[18] Whilst advancing northward through the Walloon provinces,

Parma's forces also took chunks of the northern and eastern extreme limits of territory controlled by Dutch forces. By the time Antwerp had been captured in 1585, Spanish troops were also entrenched outside Groningen, Delfzijl, Coervorden, Oldenzaal, Steenwijk, Zutphen, and Nijmegen. Moreover, in the previous year, a major blow had struck at the heart of the Dutch Republic.

In July 1584 at Delft, William of Orange was assassinated by a Catholic fanatic, spurred on by a reward of 20,000 ecus. Since 1580 Spain had officially declared William of Orange an outlaw and had placed a reward for his capture or death. Parma had objected to the proscription, arguing that his death would increase popular support for William and the Revolt. Other unsuccessful attempts on William's life had indeed drawn the Dutch population closer to him.

With the death of William, the States-General endorsed popular opinion, officially designating him "Father of the country". William's steadfastness and sincerity, his tireless resolving of political issues, and his resilience had been essential for sustaining the Revolt. And, arguably, a country—a national entity—had come into being from the Revolt. Helped and sustained by the wealth of two provinces, Holland and Zeeland, the Dutch rebels had endured and stood against repressive security crackdowns; continued in resistance despite military defeats in battle; had grasped, carved out, and held a territorial area; and had formally declared their independence from foreign rule.

But this new national entity was vulnerable and was severely threatened. The wealth and resources of Holland and Zeeland were finite. Within the United Provinces, disagreements continued, and with the assassination of William of Orange, the Revolt had lost the one individual capable of resolving those differences and keeping the provinces united.[19] The Spanish *tercios*, who outmatched the Dutch rebel levies, had returned to the Netherlands in greater numbers and were now under Parma's brilliant leadership and command.[20] The southern, or Walloon, provinces had been retaken and were reconciled. The territory of the infant northern Dutch state, which was entirely free from Spanish control, had been reduced to 4 provinces.[21] By 1587 the Dutch Revolt was at its nadir.

Notes

1. Oman, C *The XVI Century* p 91
2. Staatsarchief Delft 406
3. 'May his Majesty being instructed by light and by heaven turn and prevent further disasters; may he learn rightly to understand the actions of his good and faithful subjects at present wrongly slandered, persecuted and oppressed'
4. Stein, CR *Margaret of Parma- a life* p 274
5. Parker, G *The Dutch Revolt* p 115
6. Parker, G *The Army of Flanders and the Spanish Road 1597–1659* chapter 6 p 119

7. The Warden of the Cinque Ports—the crucial ports on the south coast of England—ordered that "no matter of victuals from henceforth shall pass to be carried to the sea for the victualling ore relief of the fleet currently serving the Prince of Orange"

8. *Resoluties de Eerste Vrie Statenvergadering gehouden te Dordrecht 19 tot23 July 1572 met instructie voor Marnix van St Aldegonde 14/7/1572* Regional Archives Dordrecht/1076

9. Archives Provincie Noord-Holland KNA006000679

10. Wedgwood, CV *William the Silent* p 133

11. Even though it did not distract Alva from his main thrust through Holland, CV Wedgwood in *William the Silent* pp 134–135 cites the failure to take Alkmaar as the first check to the Spanish onslaught and cites it as a turning point—"the tide of defeat was on the turn". Wedgwood also highlights the Alkmaar defenders' use of flooding the outlying areas of the town against the advancing Spanish, a tactic that would be a crucial factor in the relief of Leiden—which itself was another significant stage in the survival of the Dutch Revolt

12. Kamen in his *Spain 1469–1714*, which covers a wide, long-term view of Spain, states that Alva's fanaticism against heresy and his constantly emphasising the alleged heretical nature of the Dutch rebels, was viewed by many Spaniards, including Requesens, as so deliberately exaggerated as to distract from the real issue of the constitutional issues, to which the Dutch were reasonable and justified in aspiring

13. Wedgwood, CV *William the Silent* p 167

14. Ballesteros y Beretta, A *Figuras imperieles—Alfonso VII el Emperador. Colon, Fernando el Catolico, Carlos V, Felipe II* pp 72–82

15. The popular song *Willhelminus*, widespread amongst the rebellious Dutch populace after the taking of Brielle and Vlissingen, contained the line in which William states, "To the King of Spain I have been and am always loyal". The song became the official national anthem of the Netherlands and still contains this line

16. Geyl, P *History of the Low Countries—Episodes and Problems* p 13

17. Mattingly, G *The Defeat of the Spanish Armada* p 55

18. Arnold, T *The Renaissance at War* pp 204–205. Elliott, JH *Europe Divided 1558–1598* p 298

19. Prak, M *The Dutch Republic in the Seventeenth Century* p 20

20. Elliott, JH *Europe Divided 1559–1598* p 298

21. Lesaffer, R (ed) *The XII Year Truce*

Part II

Maurits of Nassau and the Survival of the Dutch Revolt

3 Sufficient Armed Forces

Maurits was one of the sons of William of Nassau, a son by William and William's unfortunate wife Anna. His mother was Anna, Princess of Saxony, whom William married both out of affection and as a useful political alliance. The marriage was not a happy one, and after some affairs Anna became involved in an adulterous relationship in Siegen on the Rhine with an already married lawyer. They were apprehended. Siegen lay within the estates of William's brother Jan van Nassau, and whilst William suffered his wife's infidelities with tolerance and passivity—he was occupied with the Revolt—Jan saw no reason why his brother should have to be humiliated and had the couple arrested. William, though a prince whose wife had committed adultery, acted with restraint. Anna lived for the rest of her life in genteel seclusion, and no revenge was taken upon her lover, who returned to his wife, settled down, and had more children, one of whom was to become a famous painter. Partially thanks to William's forebearance, the world enjoys the works of Peter Paul Rubens.

To spare his first son, Philip William (whose godfather was Philip II of Spain), and his daughter the unpleasant family atmosphere as William and Anna's relationship rapidly deteriorated, William sent his daughter to serve at the court of the regent of the Spanish Netherlands, Margaret of Parma, and he sent his son to study at the University of Louvain. When the Revolt escalated and Alva's severe security regime fastened itself on the Netherlands, both son and daughter were out of the safety reach of their father. Philip William and his university tutor were taken into custody and shipped to Spain, where he was detained in comfortable but guarded accommodation. Some years after his father's death, he was released and returned to the Netherlands, retaining his title as the Count of Buren. He became a member of the Archduke Albert's court in the Spanish Netherlands, free but still watched.

After the assassination of William of Orange, for the House of Nassau to continue the Revolt, it was up to the second son, Maurits. Maurits had been brought up out of the reach of any Spanish action. He grew up at Dillenburg and was taken under the wing of Jan van Nassau's large family. Jan's eldest son Willem Lodewijk became very loyal to his cousin, and they both studied at the university of Heidelburg, then an eminent institution of European scholarship and a pillar of Lutheranism (much to Jan's chagrin, as he would have the preferred the young men to have studied at a Calvinist seat of learning). Maurits and William Lodewijk both completed their studies at Heidelburg and the cousins were to work closely together throughout their lives and share successful military campaigns. After Heidelburg, between 1584 and 1585, Maurits studied at the University of Leiden. His father by that time had been assassinated, and the young Maurits's studies and upkeep were paid for by the States-General as one form of gratitude to his father, who had spent almost the entire family fortune in maintaining the Revolt.

A profile of Maurits in later life is revealing. He was of middle height (probably in our modern terms of small height, as people were shorter in the Sixteenth Century than in the Twentieth and Twenty-First Centuries), with a light-coloured beard and hair and small bright eyes. His voice is described as not particularly pleasant in tone but firm. His resolve and character were strong; he was quick-witted and grasped situations rapidly. He is said to hardly ever laugh and spoke little, had little time for conversation or small talk, and tended to keep his own counsel. Invariably polite in dealing with people, he was nonetheless conscious of and insisted upon due dignity and deference to his status as a prince of the House of Nassau. With his immediate family, he showed warmth and wisdom, and his family admired him. Amongst his advisors, ministers, and commanders, he would respond to flattery with instant and abject rudeness and encouraged frank advice and counsel.[1]

As a boy of 15, Maurits had already shown initiative and a calm head in 1582, when one of the attempted assassinations on his father occurred at an official banquet. Whilst the guests were entering, a young man emerged from a group of servants and handed William a petition, and while William examined it, the young man drew a pistol and fired it, wounding William in the mouth, smashing teeth and part of the jawbone and temporarily blinding him. William on being revived, interceded on behalf of the young assassin and forbade that he be killed. Maurits, then just turned 15, took charge and immediately ordered the doors of the building locked and no one permitted to leave. He then ordered that of all the servants present be searched and that all articles and papers found on them to be handed over. Then, accompanied by a trusted old retainer, he left with all the papers and carried out a thorough examination of them. The papers revealed some correspondence in Spanish and details of a conspiracy sponsored by Spain and implicating certain servants.[2]

Maurits, early on in his rule, embarked upon a massive programme of military reforms, which were eventually to change the rebel Dutch forces into a professional army of the Dutch nation.

From the mid-1580s to the 1590s, Maurits worked closely with his cousin Willem Lodewijk. In May 1590, he, as stadhouder of Holland

and Zeeland, had made an official mutual agreement of assistance with Willem Lodewijk, as stadhouder of Friesland, to render each other advice and support. (Even troops from Leeuwarden under the command of Willem Lodewijk were made available to Maurits.)[3] Together, they scoped and implemented radical reforms to the Dutch Army, which were part of a long-term evolution of warfare in Europe occurring over one and a half centuries. Cooperation in the late Sixteenth and early Seventeenth Centuries between Willem Lodewijk and Maurits was a fundamental part of and a principal reason for the survival of the Dutch Republic. (Their close cooperation in political matters, however, especially when they concurred with Oldenbarneveldt, was regarded with great suspicion by the States of Friesland, who viewed it as concerted action with Holland to keep the other States totally subordinated.[4])

Maurits's primary interest was in the army, due to the pressing danger of Parma's victorious advances. However, during his reign, the Dutch navy made an important advance in organisation. In 1597 the States-General pulled together several trends regarding the Dutch naval power and issued the 100 Instructions.[5] These formalised 5 Admiralties, or Admiralty Colleges, which in effect ran 5 differing but hopefully coordinated navies. Despite obvious defects caused by the divided governing structure of the differing admiralties,[6] Maurits devoted comparatively little time to the Dutch Navy. He may have been reassured to certain extent by his relative, Justin van Nassau, illegitimate son of William the Silent, being Lieutenant Admiral of the important Zeeland fleet, who was to give valuable support to the English fleet at a crucial stage against the Spanish Armada. Also, after 1598 there was no direct naval threat from Spain in terms of invasion or destruction of the Dutch fleet (although the economic war involving maritime trade was a major concern), and the various commercial entities, especially the Vereenigde Oostindische Compagnie (the VOC), that in effect sponsored and maintained the fleets were managing well enough. The army needed Maurits's constant attention if it was to be an efficient military force to withstand the might of Spain. The Dutch Army, therefore, was his main concern

The opponents of the Dutch, the Spanish Army, owed its success to adapting and changing its equipment and tactics in response to changing circumstances. The Spanish army, highly professionalised and experienced, was itself a result of continued adaption over the preceding century. Although strategically the Turkish Wars were a distraction to Philip and his advisors, necessitating planning for fighting on several fronts, the Turkish Wars themselves had brought valuable lessons. The same tactics used against the Turkish units, who generally evaded battle and engaged in quick spasmodic fights with small units, were used to good effect against the Dutch rebel insurgent forces. However, the reforms of the Dutch Army were in themselves notable and radical. In a later era, the armies of the Empire and Sweden were influenced by the Dutch Army reforms.[7]

Maurits and Willem Lodewijk took as guidance for general principles the theories and works of Justus Lipsius, the First-Century Greek philosopher Aelian, and the military textbook of the Byzantine Emperor Leo VI. Justus Lipsius was a historian, scholar, and professor at the University of Leiden when Maurits was studying there. Lipsius emphasised the stoical values of Rome and applied them to an army in one of his books, Book V "Military Providence", in his massive work *Politicorum sive civilis doctrine libri sex*. These emphasised that stoical values—obedience, discipline, and calmness in battle—were essential to an army and that infantry was by far the most important part of an army.

Lipsius advocated that infantry must be drilled constantly, trained, and well versed in the use of the shovel for digging trenches and ditches. From Aelian, Maurits and Willem Lodewijk learned the importance of the "lesser", or smaller, units with clear lines of command. Also the commands themselves had to be clear, precise, and logical. One simple example of this was the command "Right face":

> "*Face*" is a general command, therefore I must prefix the specific ("*right*") to the general ("*face*") so that all will do the same together.[8]

This is a small but essential point underlying the need for the clear, unambiguous commands essential for deploying troops in the confusion of battle. The Byzantine Emperor Leo VI's military writings and military manual particularly impressed Willem Lodewijk with its clear tenets and its emphasis on daily training and daily drilling of the troops and on the individual training of the soldier in the handling and use of weapons. All told, Maurits and Willem Lodewijk studied hard and had absorbed much valuable knowledge.

One major, essential reform had already been carried out: paying troops well and regularly. Under Willem Lodewijk's urging, pleading, and cajoling, the States-General in 1588 passed and implemented the system whereby the Dutch Army was paid for by all the provinces who were signatories to the Union of Utrecht, each province's contribution depending on its financial resources and ability to raise a specific sum.

During the period of the Dutch Revolt, the Dutch infantry weapons consisted of the time-honoured pike and the caliver firearm or the musket. Infantry formations, as with other armies, consisted of mixed pikemen and gunmen. Arguably the pike had become a secondary weapon to the firearm as early as the first decades of the Sixteenth Century.[9] The caliver was a lighter weapon than the musket and more portable, but its shot could not penetrate body armour. Maurits and Willem Lodewijk doubled the number of pikemen in each company but tripled the force of musketeers in each company, phasing out the caliver. They realised the simple maxim of a later military leader:

Firepower kills.[10]

This was the first stage of the military reform, namely the standardisation and increase of potential firepower, combined with constant repetitive drilling. Troops were drilled daily in simple exercises, with clear commands so that they could, in battalion formation, turn, wheel, advance, and retreat.

When the discipline of comparatively simple movements and formations was perfected, more complex deployments were introduced and practiced. Musketeers on the battlefield formed blocks akin to smaller versions of the phalanxes of antiquity. When the front rank had fired, it was necessary for them to clear for the next rank to fire. Maurits and Willem Lodewijk reduced the number of musketeers in each rank to no more than six. When the front rank fired, instead of each front rank musketeer doing an about turn and making his way back through the ranks behind, all 6 who had just fired turned in unison to the right or to the left and went rearward in a line moving along the side of the block, to reform as a rank at the rear and to reload and make ready. This resulted in giving the next rank due to fire a clear field of fire more quickly and in speeding up the collective rate of fire of the whole block.

Another advanced manoeuvre that was practised and perfected was the counter-march. This was an orderly retreat performed by the unit *en bloc*. The unit retired but, whilst doing so, still fired by ranks, each rank moving to the rear to reload and make ready, the whole unit moving backwards, giving ground yet totally unscathed. To make an orderly retreat was essential to all contemporary armies, who accomplished this in different ways. Maurits and Willem Lodewijk perfected the Dutch military adaptation of the counter-march that proved highly successful.[11] Given the strength of the well equipped and battle-hardened Spanish forces opposing them, one of the most essential manoeuvres of the Dutch Army was to be able to disengage when the course of battle went adversely yet still have forces intact and in good order.

In addition to drill and intense practice in forming, re-forming, and manoeuvring of ranks and units, much time was spent in practice and drill in the ranks of musketeers firing by volley. With the development of firearms and increasing firepower, the impact of a well- timed volley on the opposite enemy unit could be devastating. From 1594 onward Willem Lodewijk laid down that each well drilled advancing rank that fired and returned to the rear would fire in volleys. The Dutch units were generally smaller than other armies, with battalions being broken down into fighting units of companies. However, after volley fire had been implemented and perfected, on the battlefield several companies were often ordered to come together and form lines of volley-firing musketeers. This tactic was adapted with further drill so that volleys were fired by two ranks firing simultaneously, the frontmost rank kneeling, with both ranks then retiring for the next two ranks to fire a dual volley.

Discipline and constancy, as well as holding positions and formations in battle, were instilled in recruits and veterans alike by constant drill. However, training and drill were intended to be a learning process, beneficial to all. Drill sergeants and captains were ordered by Maurits to give instructions clearly and with patience, not in a denigrating manner and without physical violence. The training of the troops was regular and monitored. In 1598 the council of State appointed 4 inspectors of troops, whose function was to tour the garrisons and strongpoints in order be updated and to make reports on the progress of the troops.[12] The Dutch soldier was expected to be trained, disciplined, and competent, but he was also to be afforded respect as a soldier

Artillery was standardised and gunners trained to improve their skills, especially in the use of short-range mortars, which were essential in sieges. Maurits and Willem Lodewijk took steps to standardise and reduce the number of calibres of guns (though in fully accomplishing standardisation of artillery, it was only Gustavus Adolphus of Sweden later in the century who fully accomplished this, imposing a ruthless standardisation of artillery guns and shot for his Swedish army). In 1590 Maurits laid down that cannon were to be manufactured in only 4 differing dimensions. In 1598 a national artillery foundry supplying cannon was established in The Hague. Short-range mortars were developed, and production of them increased. Also Maurits and Willem Lodewijk made the innovation that every artillery unit must have an adequate supply of wooden and rush mats, long and broad. These prevented guns from slipping out of position when being fired in heavy muddy conditions or on sand dunes.

Maurits worked with students from several universities on improvement in compass bearings and readings and on improvements in cartography, all of which would be beneficial to moving and deploying military units. He consulted with the then eminent scientist Stevin on various soils and their compositions,[13] widening the knowledge needed for future entrenchments. The Dutch Army's diggings and earthwork constructions at the siege of Hulst had been severely hampered by large areas of particularly hard earth. Siege works were to be a vital part of campaigning. According to a Seventeenth-Century biographer of the House of Nassau, Maurits had an impressive siege record. He took by siege 38 towns and 45 sets of fortifications, in addition to a further 5 towns and 109 sets of fortifications by surprise attack.[14]

Accordingly, the infantry diversified their skills, and one important skill was that of digging trenches and constructing earthworks. Each infantryman was issued a spade as part of his equipment. (Parma also extensively trained and exploited his infantry in the use of digging trenches and earth-works.) At the siege of Steenwijk in 1592, Dutch infantry who engaged in digging and constructing earthworks were given a daily bonus payment. In one year alone, 1597, the Raad van Staat expenditure on siege works and diggings came to 90,000 guilders[15]; it was money well spent. Other European armies sought learning from the Dutch. In the 1590s, military representatives from France, Brandenburg, and Denmark and the Haps-burg Empire came to the Low Countries to observe and learn during the course of Maurits's troops besieging towns. The Great Elector Frederick of Prussia was to maintain links with the Dutch stadhouder, and he per-sonally stayed at Dutch Army camps.[16] The Scottish soldier Alexander Leslie served under Maurits as a military clerk engaged in general admin-istration duties, then served as a soldier in the Dutch Army. He thereaf-ter enlisted in the armies of Venice, then in the army of Hesse -Cassel, then rose to a command position in the imperial armies, and eventually became a general in the Scottish armies during the English Civil Wars.[17]

For the past two centuries, the cavalry arm of armies had evolved but was being eclipsed by the infantry as the principal arm of an army. How-ever, they still were an important part of an army and had developed into two basic types, light and heavy, the latter being armed with long lances or long swords. Light cavalry were skilled swordsmen armed with shorter, sharper swords used either for charging against unsupported infantry or as mobile scouts and tactical intelligence gathering. William Lodewijk had served as a young cavalry officer during the Revolt period of William of Orange and could bring to bear practical experience in his and Mau-rits's various changes to the Dutch cavalry units. Maurits was the first European army commander to abolish cavalry units armed with a lance and replacing the lance with a firearm. Another type of cavalry was also developing, the so-called carabineers or dragoons, armed with muskets or pistols. These would slowly trot in formations up against the opposing enemy formations, discharge their firearm by ranks—holding and dis-charging their forearms out to the side to avoid burning the horses' ears with the discharge—then retire by ranks. After firing, each rank would retire with half the rank wheeling to the right-hand side of the formation then back, and half the rank wheeling to the left then back. This was the *caracole*, or cavalry counter-march. Maurits and Willem Lodewijk developed and integrated this type of cavalryman into the Dutch Army, enhancing their priority of increased firepower. Later in the century, Gus-tavus Adolphus of Sweden added to this by having heavy cavalry attack with pistols, then following through with a charge to totally break the opposing lines. The Dutch were content with the *caracole* having as its main object and achievement continuous steady fire.

Maintaining discipline, as we have seen, was paramount. When Gro-ningen was captured by Dutch forces in 1594, only a few contingents of the Dutch Army were allowed entry. They were billeted in specially allocated locations, all together. Pillaging and looting were strictly prohibited.[18]This was to evolve into the garrison system, particularly after 1600 when sieges, taking fortified towns and fixed points, become a cardinal part of Maurits's strategy. During this period and even more so later in the struggle of the Dutch Revolt, units of troops were semi-permanently based in certain towns. Generally, communities, towns, and cities dreaded having troops billeted with them. During the rapacious and near-anarchistic situations in certain regions in the Empire during the Thirty Years' War, such dread was fully justified. However, the Dutch troops were disciplined and had respect for the civilian populations. Maurits's successor Frederick Henry unhesitatingly and without exception hanged soldiers who had committed rape. With such overall, well disciplined troops garrisoned in certain parts of the towns, the local economy improved with the increased demand for goods and services.

All told, the army reforms conceived, planned, and implemented by Maurits and Willem Lodewijk were a remarkable achievement and crucial to the future survival of the Dutch Revolt. An authoritative work on early modern European history trenchantly summarised the whole achievement:

> The reforms of Maurits of Nassau, William's son, made the Dutch army a match for the Spanish.[19]

It was just as well, for Parma's thrusting advance for the total reconquest of the Netherlands was fully under way.

Notes

1. Anonymous visiting Italian nobleman in 1622, cited in GI Hoogerwerff "DeNederlander in 1622 Door Ein Italien Bereist" deel 4 pp 1–42
2. Motley, J *The Rise of the Dutch Republic* p 859
3. Van Deursen, A *Maurtis van Nassau* p 55
4. Israel, J *The Dutch Republic—Its Rise, Greatness, and Fall 1477–1806* p 306
5. Eekhart, L "Het Admiraltly Boek" p 20
6. See also Appendix
7. Wilson, PH *The Thirty Years War* p 141. Wedgewood, CV *The Thirty Years War* p 272. However, Massie, JK, in his monumental *Peter the Great—His Life and World*, holds that the reforms of Gustavus Adolphus constituted a major development in its own right, particularly those changes and adaptations of the artillery p 307. In a general book on early modern warfare by Arnold, T *The Renaissance at War*, Maurits is described as "A Major Military Reformer" p 216. Parker, G in his *Thirty Years War* p 205 ascribes credit to Maurits and Willem Lodewijk in the general context of army reform by stating that the new warfare was "the military reformation wrought by Maurits of Nassau and the Dutch army". A detailed and meticulous account of the army reforms of Maurits and Willem Lodewijk—emphasising the part of Willem Lodewijk—is given in a highly scholarly researched chapter by O van Nimwegen in "Tactical Military Revolution in Dutch Army

Operations During the Era of the Twelve Years Truce 1592–1618" in Lessafer, R (ed) *The Twelve Years Truce*. Perhaps, in order to give due weight to the achievement of Maurits and Willem Lodewijk, the reader should note Parker's terminology of military "reformation" and the title words of the extremely scholarly chapter of van Nimwegen "tactical revolution"

8. Aelian *Tactics* ch 52, translated by Jan Bingham in 1616 in *The Tactics of Aelian or the Art of Embattling an Army After ye Grecian Manner*
9. Brigadier Fuller, JFC in is *Decisive Battles of the Western World, Vol I* argues that as early as 1522 at the Battle of Biccoca, the Marquis of Pescara deployed musketeers in open field and "for the first time pikemen became no more than their auxiliaries" p 471
10. Marshal Petain, in French army planning, First World War
11. Wilson, PH *The XXX Years War* pp 87–88
12. Council of State to States-General 23 July 1598, *Archief de Staaten-General 4889*, National Archives, The Hague
13. Van Deursen, A *Maurits van Nsssau* p 77
14. de la Pise, J *Tableau de l'Historie des princes et principaute d Órange*
15. Van Deusen, A *Maurits van Nassau* p 107
16. Israel, J *The Dutch Republic—Its Rise, Greatness, and Fall 1477–1806* p 270
17. Wilson, PH *The XXX Years War* p 141
18. Israel, J *The Dutch Republic—Its Rise, Greatness, and Fall 1477–1806* p 268
19. Campbell, E *Early Modern Europe* p 130

4 English Support, Leicester's Ambition, Oldenbarneveldt's Steadiness

But we must return to the situation in the Netherlands following the terrible blow of the assassination of William of Orange. After the assassination the States-General considered the 17-year-old Maurits too young and lacking experience for office. Rather than appoint him stadhouder, the Estates of Holland and Zeeland ensured that he was designated head of the newly established Council of State (Raad van State) in August 1584. However, to find a replacement and to counter Parma and Spain's increasing threat, the States-General under Oldenbarneveldt turned to England and offered the sovereignty of the United Provinces to Queen Elizabeth.

England under Queen Elizabeth was becoming increasingly alarmed at Parma's successes. They were threatening the Channel ports, and from a distance it appeared that Parma could possibly complete the reconquest of the provinces of the Union of Utrecht. By March 1985, the vital city of Antwerp was threatened by Parma (and indeed it fell within 6 months). Elizabeth had offered the States-General an alliance, which they initially refused, but with the deteriorating situation, the States-General changed their stance and offered her the sovereignty of the Netherlands and negotiated for England sending regular military aid and assistance.

An agreement was reached in August 1585 whereby England would provide the United Provinces with a governor-general and send immediate aid in the form of 4,000 troops for the defence of Antwerp. The United Provinces agreed to pay England's expenses, and the towns of Brielle, Vlissingen, and Rammekens would be handed over to England for safekeeping and as a guarantee.

Elizabeth realised that the wider implications of the agreement would lead England into eventual conflict with Spain. Accordingly, she initiated a pre-emptive strike strategy, authorizing Sir Francis Drake to start his legitimised piracy against Spanish trade. Drake's first punitive expedition was soon heading for the rich pickings in the West Indies. The whole agreement was ratified in the Treaty of Nonsuch, whose terms stipulated the establishment of a central authority for governing the United Provinces.

Leicester arrived in 1586 and took post as governor-general of the Netherlands. The Earl of Leicester was a controversial figure in England. He was a close favourite of the queen, and his reputation was further damaged when his wife allegedly fell down the stairs of their mansion home and died of her injuries. Well educated, open-minded, and forward-looking, he patronised both traditional institutions such as the legal Inns of Court and new innovations such as investing in the first joint stock companies and in trade and nascent industries. He was conscious of and well informed about the international situation and well aware of the strategic importance of his mission as governor-general of the Netherlands to the interests of both Protestantism and England.

Leicester started working with the provincial States to establish a central government. The land-based States of Friesland, Overijssel, Utrecht, Gelderland, and the Ommelands were content to have such a government, assuming that it would then give them protection from invasion. Not so Holland and Zeeland. They were jealous of their independence and suspicious of any centralisation of power within the United Provinces. Zeeland was particularly resentful of the handing over to the English of Brielle and Vlissingen, whilst Holland had already assumed and possessed a vast amount of political influence due to Holland's regularly providing the greater proportion of the finances necessary for sustaining the Revolt. In November 1585, the States of Holland and Zeeland appointed Maurits as their stadhouder. This was more of a tactic to ensure that some form of restraint was placed on Leicester's authority before he arrived in the Netherlands rather than expecting the young Maurits to be significantly active. However, together with Oldenbarneveldt, he was to play his part during the brief and unsuccessful tenure of the governor-generalship of Leicester

Leicester established a Council of State for the Netherlands, consisting of two English members and representatives from the States, circumventing the States-General as the form of central authority. Unlike the States-General, the proceedings of the Council of State did not permit a single State the power of veto, whereby one representative of one State could nullify a proposal or proposed course of action. Leicester tried to raise continuous funds for the war and to establish a reserve war chest by special taxation. These special taxes would not be authorised by or monitored by the States-General. He also tried to prohibit any trade with the Spanish Netherlands.

Predictably, the province of Holland, through its States, completely opposed the cessation of trade with the Spanish Netherlands and also opposed what they regarded as unconstitutional special taxes. Leicester countered this opposition from the States of Holland by turning to the States of Utrecht. He was supported in this by the elderly stadhouder of Utrecht, the elderly Count van Neuenahr. Leicester tried to make Utrecht his power base. He purged or moved sideways some representatives and ensured that his Dutch supporters gained offices. One of his principal supporters, Prounick, became burgomaster of the city of Utrecht. One of the most outspoken members of the States of Holland, representing Holland on the Council of State (who, in fact, had been a strong supporter of the alliance and Treaty with England) was removed from the Council and imprisoned on Leicester's authority. Leicester also wished to place all naval and maritime matters under a single central authority. This would further weaken the influence of the States of Holland.

The Treaty of Nonsuch stated that henceforth stadhouders were to be appointed by the Council of State and be subordinate to the Council. Maurits had inherited by default, from his assassinated father, being stadhouder of Holland and Zeeland. Only after the Treaty did Holland and Zeeland formally make the appointment, which was confirmed, as was that of Willem Lodewijk of Nassau as stadhouder of Friesland and the Ommelands. The States-General insisted that the appointment of the stadhouder was the decision of the individual provinces, through the individual States. Leicester's attempt to enforce this clause of the Treaty of Nonsuch alerted both Maurits and Willem Lodewijk.

Leicester made some progress in establishing both his authority and in raising taxes for the war effort. However, he was not helped by the attitude and behaviour of some of the English troops. On one occasion, a joint force of Dutch and German mercenaries and English troops were advancing against the Spanish enemy in the Nijmegen area. The English troops, disdainful of their allies, refused to allow the other contingents to advance parallel with them, insisting that they should follow the English and even using their halberds and pikes to keep the others behind them.[1] His attempts to prevent trade with the Spanish Netherlands ran into sustained and determined opposition from the States of Holland. They maintained that the only beneficiaries from this, to whom Flanders and Brabant would readily give favourable trade policy terms, would be their international competitors. As a result Holland maintained that the economy of the Spanish Netherlands, at present devastated by the conflict, would steadily improve and in turn strengthen the enemy, Spain. The States of Holland also pointed out that the revenues they gained from their trade with the Spanish Netherlands were vital as it was used for the upkeep for the Admiralties for which they were responsible. By contrast, the States of Utrecht, which had no such responsibilities, argued that a trade with the Spanish Netherlands would be useful in applying further pressure on them and would inevitably impact upon Parma's ability to recruit troops and sustain his campaign. The States of Utrecht were supported by the other provinces.

However, the States of Holland were extremely powerful, and Leicester could push neither too far nor too fast.[2] Within the States of Holland, a leader had emerged since 1586 who led the opposition to Leicester with skill, eloquence, and determination. The United Provinces were to experience much more from Johan van Oldenbarneveldt. Also Maurits, as stadhouder of Holland and Zeeland and captain general, and his cousin Willem Lodewijk, as stadhouder of Friesland, both had effective control over the Dutch armies. Whilst they were both in accord with the English alliance and the Treaty and recognised the value of Leicester—and the reinforcements of his troops—they would not stand idly by if Leicester became too powerful or dictatorial. Leicester was indeed making progress, but he had to be slow and steady in dealing with the various States.

Unfortunately for him, time was not on his side, for events in England necessitated his recall. In November 1586, he was urgently summoned to Elizabeth's court to be part of the advisory council of ministers to decide on the matter of Mary Queen of Scots. The conspiracy against Elizabeth, patiently and skilfully infiltrated and monitored by Walsingham, was broken and the main conspirators in custody. Given that this had been just one of a series of thwarted conspiracies with Mary at their centre, the only solution appeared to be to speedily eliminate Mary. Such an execution would have international consequences, and Elizabeth demanded wise counsel before taking action. Leicester left the Netherlands, and, when in England and attending the Council, he pressed and cajoled, together with other members of the Council, that Elizabeth authorise Mary's execution. He did not return to the Netherlands until the following March.

During his absence, events had moved at a pace. The English garrison at Deventer and the English troops manning a fortified position near Zutphen surrendered to the Spaniards. The Dutch were further alarmed by several other English garrisons, who were owed arrears of pay, behaving extremely aggressively towards the local population. Oldenbarneveldt was partly alarmed but also, realizing an opportunity, exploited the Dutch indignant reaction and led the States of Holland in nullifying the authority of the governor-general within the province of Holland. The States of Holland gave extra powers to its stadhouder, Maurits, and all soldiers paid by the States of Holland were compelled to take an oath of loyalty to Maurits. The remaining supporters of Leicester within the States of Holland protested but were overruled and outvoted. Then the representatives of the States of Holland to the States-General persuaded the States-General to increase the powers of the States-General and severely curtail the powers of Leicester's Council of States.

Leicester returned to the Netherlands in March 1587, accompanied by fresh troops. This time his remit, still officially as governor-general, was to negotiate with Parma. This caused consternation amongst several representatives of the States-General. When their concern was raised in the States-General, he denied any intention or having any instructions to negotiate with Parma. However, he subsequently admitted that he was to so negotiate[3] and requested the representatives' participation in such negotiations, arguing that negotiations were the best way forward in the current conflict. When faced with further opposition from the States-General, he tried to assert his authority by force. In September he advanced from Utrecht into the province of Holland, and his troops occupied several towns. Maurits, as stadhouder of Holland, forbade any forces in Holland to obey any orders issued by Leicester. Only two towns, the coastal town of Medemblik in the West Friesland area and Leiden, responded to Leicester's authority. In Leiden, some prominent citizens and a small force of troops discreetly made plans to side with Leicester and attempted to mobilise and rouse the town, but the rest of the garrison remained loyal to Maurits and crushed this attempt. Two of the principal pro-Leicester officials fled, but others were hunted down and executed. That left only the small town of Medemblik offering any support and a small unit of Dutch troops to Leicester.

Medemblik in its pro-Leicester stance was tacitly supported by another coastal town, Enkhuizen. Enkhuizen and the area were in dispute with mighty Amsterdam over the administration and jurisdiction—and revenues—of the admiralties. Maurits intervened, using troops from the States of Holland in order to blockade Medemblik. Oldenbarneveldt also intervened with detailed plans and offers of compromise over the admiralties dispute, and together they regained the loyalty of West Friesland. The agreement brokered by Oldenbarneveld was that Amsterdam and West Friesland were both to have their own separate admiralties. The admiralty of West Friesland was to be jointly based, with its own college and administration in the Holland town of Hoorn in Holland's North Quarter and Enkhuizen in West Friesland. The province of Friesland itself was to have its own Admiralty based in Dokkum.

Leicester's efforts to assert a central authority under the governor-general had been effectively halted. In February 1588 Elizabeth recognised Leicester's loss of authority, instructing all commanders of English troops in the Netherlands to cooperate with and be under Maurits as Captain General. Also, Elizabeth, in an attempt to gain time, authorised formal negotiations directly between England and Parma. However, Phillip II of Spain was resolved on war, and preparations were well under way for the Armada and the invasion of England. The Armada was to pick up Parma's troops for invasion. In May 1588, Leicester and his English troops were withdrawn from the Netherlands for defence against the coming invasion.

The two-year attempted governorship of Leicester and his increasing confrontation with the States of Holland reinforced the lesson that, whilst the United Provinces needed foreign support in their struggle, being under foreign sovereignty was not the answer. In future, they were to look to their own. It also reinforced the lesson that there was a need for a more powerful central authority whilst respecting and guarding the rights of the provincial States. Oldenbarneveldt and Maurits had stepped forward and projected the States-General in this role. However, the domination of the States of Holland remained and indeed was to be enhanced by the rise of Oldenbarneveldt.

Johan van Oldenbarneveldt had studied law at several European universities. On the outbreak of the Dutch Revolt, he immediately gave his full support to William of Orange. He was to remain steadfast and loyal to William and to the latter's strategy. He was an official of the States of Holland giving detailed advice and counsel in 1574 regarding the breaking of the dykes, which enabled Boisot's relief "fleet" to raise the siege of Leiden. He then became pensionary of Rotterdam and as such was a delegate from Rotterdam to the States of Holland and became a prominent figure in that assembly. Intensely hard-working and highly efficient, he was part of Holland's mainstay support to William of Orange throughout the latter's struggle against both Spain and those elements in the Netherlands north and south who had wished to remain loyal to Spain. He was one of the delegates from the United Provinces who had negotiated the Treaty of Nonsuch with England. By this time, 1585, he was the principal office holder in the States of Holland, the advocate, and the spokesperson for the States of Holland in the States-General. Longheaded and conscientious, he realised the Dutch Revolt needed foreign allies but was fearful that such an ally—or its governor-general—would become the *de facto* ruler of the Netherlands.

To Oldenbarneveldt, the province of Utrecht, by supporting Leicester, had proven a centre of resistance to the province of Holland; therefore Utrecht had to be nullified. A year after Leicester had finally left the Netherlands, Stadhouder of Utrecht van Neuenahr had died in an accident. Oldenbarneveldt stepped in and arranged for Maurits to be appointed stadhouder. In addition, Maurits was appointed stadhouder of Gelderland. The following year, Oldenbarneveldt ensured that his own nominee was appointed advocate of the States of Utrecht. As a result, for 25 years until 1618, the States of Utrecht were little more than an appendage of those of Holland.[4]

Next Oldenbarneveldt, within and supported by the States-General, arranged that all discussions on military strategy would fall under the States-General, thus depriving the Council of State of this important power. Officially, Oldenbarneveldt was advocate of the States of Holland and merely a representative of Holland in the States-General. However, due to his efficiency and tremendous capacity for hard work, and as advocate of Holland, the most important province, he controlled all the diplomatic correspondence of the United Provinces. The secretary of the States-General, the greffier, was subservient to Oldenbarneveldt and followed his advice and directions.[5] Oldenbarneveldt had dominance of the States-General, a dominance that was unchallenged.[6]

At this time, he enjoyed a good working relationship with Maurits. With Oldenbarneveldt dominating political government through the

States of Holland, and Maurits having military command together with Willem Lodewijk, the partnership augured well for the United Provinces.

Despite Leicester's failure to dominate the Dutch Republic as governor-general, Anglo-Dutch cooperation was firm during the crisis of the Spanish Armada and the projected Spanish invasion of England. During the crisis of the Armada between May and August 1588, when the Armada was sailing to do battle with the English fleet—in a battle that was:

> the longest sea battle ever known[7]

—and link up with Parma, the Dutch fleet too played a role in its defeat. The commander of the English fleet, Lord Howard of Effingham, mistrusted and then became frustrated with the Dutch. However, the true cause was by no means inactivity but lack of communication. As the Spanish fleet, in a massive and disciplined battle formation of reversed half-moon crescent approached the end of the English Channel at the Lizard in late July, Justin of Nassau as Lieutenant Admiral of the Zeeland fleet learned of its progress. His fleets, consisting of small but well-armed ships manned by experienced sailors, had maintained a low presence in north Flanders waters, near Nieuwport, waiting for Parma's ships and barges to venture out of their bases where they could be surprised and picked off. When Justin knew of the Spanish Armada's progress into the Channel with the running battles with the English fleets off Plymouth, then off Weymouth, then off the Isle of Wight, then that the Armada was proceeding up the Calais Roads, he moved his fleets down past Ostend and lay between Ostend and Dunkirk. He effectively prevented Parma's assembled fleet from setting out and attempting any junction with the Spanish Armada. But no one informed Howard. Also during the final engagement between the English fleet and the Spanish, Justin and the Dutch played a part. After the Spanish Armada had been thrown into confusion and out of its haven at Gravelines by English fireships with parts of it engaging with the English fleet, Justin's fleet of small ships took two large damaged Spanish galleons.[8]

Howard and the English may not have been fully aware, but Justin's assistance was celebrated by the Dutch in contemporary song:

> The Netherlands and England were united . . .
> The seamen of Holland and Zeeland were brave . . .
> Saw to it that the Prince of Parma was halted.[9]

For England, the defeat of the Spanish Armada brought relief (though Spain was to make further attempts). However, subsequent events in the Low Countries were to bring both relief and an opportunity for the beleaguered Dutch. Maurits was quick to seize the opportunity and strike.

Notes

1. Van Deursen, A *Maurits van Nassau* p 34
2. Geyl, P in his *History of the Dutch-Speaking Peoples 1555–1648* has a somewhat partisan view, being suspicious of Leicester's ulterior motives.
3. Geyl, P *History of the Dutch-Speaking Peoples 1555–1648* p 214
4. Israel, J *The Dutch Republic—Its Rise, Greatness, and Fall 1477–1806* p 240
5. Grossman, EH Chapter XII "The Low Countries" in *New Cambridge Modern History—The Decline of Spain and the XXX Years War* p 364
6. Israel, J *The Dutch Republic—Its, Greatness, and Fall 1477–1806* p 238
7. Frere-Cooke, G and Macksey, K *The Guinness History of Sea Warfare* p 36. This work fully acknowledges the achievement of the Spanish fleet in maintaining its formation over a long period against repeated English attacks.
8. Mattingly, G *The Defeat of the Spanish Armada* pp 270–272, 286
9. Ghy Nederland met England verbonden . . . Die van Holland en Zeeland seer vermaert . . . Dat de Prince van Parma wert belet. "1588 Ondergang van Onoverwinnelltjke Vloot" in Scheurleer, DDF *Onze Mannen ter Zee in dicht en bled Vol I 1572–1654* p 15

5 Parma's About Turn—And Maurits's Counterstroke

In 1589 the Spanish Council of State received news of the death of Henri III of France. A meeting was convened to consider the situation. French internal affairs during this period of the wars of religion occurring in France were of keen interest to Spain. By an earlier treaty, the Treaty of Joinville in 1584, Philip II had committed to providing finances and discreet military support to the Guise family and to the French Catholic League whenever necessary to assist the Catholic League's internal struggles in France against both the Protestant faction and the forces and supporters of Henri III. With the death of Henri III, there was now a likelihood that the Protestants led by Henri of Navarre would not only be ascendant, but Henri of Navarre himself would gain the throne. (Before his own death by assassination, Henri III had ensured that the leaders of the Catholics, Henri of Guise and his brother Cardinal d'Amboise, were both assassinated. There was no other viable leader in France.) To Philip and the Spanish Council, intervention in France appeared imperative.

In September 1589 Parma was ordered to deploy all available Spanish forces in the Netherlands to the Netherlands–French frontier and to prepare to assist the Catholic League in France. The campaign against the Dutch insurgents was to be reduced to defensive, holding operations. Parma demurred. Whilst seeing that timely intervention in France would be of value, he stressed the overriding necessity and priority of making secure the situation in the Netherlands, which meant settling the Dutch insurgency. Accordingly, a month after receiving Philip's order, Parma sent a proposal to Philip for a peace plan with the Dutch. He argued that at this point in their insurgency the Dutch may possibly accept peace terms if the terms involved recognition of some form of overall, distant Spanish sovereignty in return for full toleration of Calvinist worship in Holland and Zeeland. Parma sent this proposed peace formula through Jean Richardot.

Jean Richardot was a civil servant and diplomat in the Spanish government administration in Brussels, in which he had given long and loyal service. He had been a member of the Privy Council in Requesens's government but then sided with William of Orange and the States-General in various efforts to deal with the Spanish mutinies. Moderate in outlook and constantly assisting in the search for pragmatic solutions, during 1581 he was skilful in negotiations with the States of Artois as part of Parma's successful negotiations with all the States to permit the return of Spanish troops. He was further successful as Parma's emissary to the Court at Madrid in 1582 and 1583, when Parma was pleading for more funds for his Netherlands campaign.

However, Richardot on this mission to Madrid bearing and support-ing Parma's proposed peace plan with the Dutch was unsuccessful. After briefly considering it and discussing it with his Council Philip decided that the original orders stood; Parma was to form a defensive front in the Netherlands and make ready to intervene in France. In other words, Parma was to fight on two fronts. In retrospect, this refusal by Philip II to even contemplate a compromise peace, a decision made in Madrid at a distance from the fighting, was a mistake. When the news reached Madrid that Henry of Navarre was gaining a series of victories and advancing on Paris itself, Philip II ordered Parma in April 1590 to invade. Parma com-plied, invaded, and in September 1590 took Paris in a skilful deployment, preventing Henri of Navarre from taking possession of the capital.

Maurits had anticipated these moves and launched a counter-offensive. Parma's previous campaigns had dramatically reduced the area of the Netherlands under Dutch control. Now:

the Dutch breakout began.[1]

Maurits, together with William Lodewijk, mustered 26,000 troops, which included some English units, and made a surprise lunge south, tak-ing Breda. Then he moved eastward, hastily gathering together 10,000 troops. Maurits made for Zutphen. He transported the troops and the important artillery on small craft, moving through the parallel water-ways and canals. They arrived in the immediate area of Zutphen in only 5 days. Zutphen was a strongly fortified town standing on the east bank of the river IJssel. The main approach to the town from the western bank was via a bridge, and the start of the bridge on the western bank was guarded by a strong fort. A small unit of troops from the English contin-gent of Maurits's infantry gained access to the bridge fort and engaged the garrison in hand-to-hand fighting. Other Dutch units then charged and overpowered the fort garrison. Once this fort was secured, Maurits moved up and sited 3 artillery guns, together with reinforcements and a contingent of Dutch troops from Friesland. The artillery made an intense and sustained bombardment of Zutphen, and the Spanish garrison sur-rendered on 30 May 1591. They were given lenient terms of surrender, being allowed to depart and retreat. Zutphen, a strong and strategically valuable town, was under Dutch control and was to remain under Dutch control for the duration of the Revolt.

Then Maurits moved on Deventer, starting the siege on 1 June 1591, 48 hours after he had taken Zutphen. With a force of just over 10,000, including a strong contingent of English troops, the town was surrounded, and meticulous trenches were carefully dug and siege outworks constructed. Repeated attacks and bombardments resulted in a breach in the walls. After a temporary repulse and withdrawal, and some apprehension about the possibility of a relieving Spanish army, the attack was pressed, and Deventer surrendered on 10 June 1591. As with Zutphen, the Deventer garrison was given lenient terms of surrender, the garrison being allowed to march out and retreat.

The Dutch had rapidly broken out from their restricted control territory to the south, taken Breda, then had moved east, and within 2 months had taken 2 strategically important towns and gained control of a swathe of territory.

Parma realised the significance of this breakout and how essential it was to contain it. With his reduced forces in the Netherlands, he attempted a counteroffensive. However, he was beset by a mutiny of one of his key regiments and so was unable to engage in open battle with Maurits's troops. The most he could do was to detach a force and relieve Nijmegen. Then in late 1591, he travelled hastily to Brussels to arrange for payment of the arrears for the mutineers, who were numerous and whose loyal service was essential. Restoring their loyalty cost 80,000 florins. After dispersing these payments, Parma turned south towards France, being severely cajoled and criticised by Philip II back in Madrid for not having already done so. He advanced into France and manoeuvred, countering a French force that was attempting to relieve Rouen from the besieging Catholic forces. Parma by this time was ill and weary. He had been forced to take leave and spend time taking the waters and resting at a health spa before starting out on his successful relief of Rouen. He returned to the Spanish Netherlands in 1592 but in December of that year died at Arras.

His death may have been welcomed by Philip II. The king had turned against Parma, viewing his achievements as over-costly. Parma constantly had to plead for more funds, stating blatantly to the King in 1586:

In the end we cannot do everything with nothing.[2]

Philip had despatched no less than 32 million florins for Parma's forces in a single year, 1590.[3] He had become increasingly suspicious of Parma's reluctance to divert Spanish forces from the Netherlands to intervene in the French internal wars of religion. Parma's death had spared Philip II the unpleasantness of taking action against him and had spared Parma the humiliation of dismissal. It was a meagre and shabby end for such a gifted and loyal servant of Spain. However, Parma's death also led to a period of confusion as to who would succeed to his command.

The taking of command was contested by Parma's two under-commanders. When Parma had departed for the French invasion, he had deputized the elderly van Mansfeld to command overall in Brussels and a field officer, Francisco Verdugo as Brussels (and Spanish)-appointed governor of Friesland, Groningen, Drenthe, and Overijssel provinces. Both individuals detested the other, and now that Parma was dead, they both claimed overall command of the Spanish armies in the Netherlands. The situation was exacerbated by the representatives of the loyal Spanish Netherlands who were raising objections to any further Spanish involvement in the French wars of religion. Also, mutinies in Spanish units forced the government in Brussels to open negotiations with the different parties in France, leading to a truce with Henri of Navarre. This truce, which lasted through 1593 until late 1594, enabled Henri of Navarre to take Paris—having first converted to Catholicism and uttering the famous pragmatic maxim, "Paris is worth a mass".

Maurits continued his offensive, exploiting the confusion over Parma's successor as commander. From Deventer Maurits took his forces north, originally intending to take Groningen. However, he received reports of an approaching force of Spaniards, and, given the strength of Groningen's defences and this potential threat, he turned and besieged Delfzijl, a port some distance away on the river Ems, which serviced Groningen. He used the waterways and canals to transport both troops and artillery and was in front of Delfzijl by 26 June. The Spanish garrison was out-numbered and, more importantly, heavily outgunned by Maurits's artillery. This artillery had been sited in siege positions directly in front of the town. After 6 days of bombardment, the garrison surrendered. They were allowed lenient terms of surrender, being allowed to depart, and they went to join the Spanish forces in Groningen. Maurits may have been generous to them, but Spain was not. When the surrendering troops arrived at Groningen, Verdugo, acting as the Spanish governor of the province of Groningen, ordered the execution of their commander and imprisoned some of the troops. In securing Delfzijl and later strengthening its fortifications, Maurits ensured that the Dutch Republic had control of the river Ems traffic.

Maurits and his forces then turned southward and headed towards Nijmegen. This area had fallen under Spanish control as a result of Parma's ruthless advance of the mid-1580s. His forces numbered just under 9,000, including a contingent of English troops and troops from Friesland under William Lodewijk. In mid-October he and his forces crossed the Waal and occupied the nearby fort of Knodsenburg, built by the Dutch in 1585 as a counter against the then advancing troops of Parma. Here he sited his artillery and started bombardment. The garrison of Nijmegen was heavily outnumbered by the besieging Dutch but stubbornly refused to surrender. Frontal attacks were made, which took several fortified positions outside Nijmegen. More artillery guns were set up in these captured positions, enabling a heavier bombardment that finally forced surrender on 25 October 1591. Again, as in the sieges of Zutphen and Deventer, generous terms were given to the defenders, who were allowed to march out and depart.

The following year, Maurits continued his campaign. By the first week in May, he and his forces, 6,000 strong, were before Steenwijk. Unlike the other towns Maurits had taken the previous year, Steenwijk was strongly protected with earthworks and well provisioned and had a garrison of well trained and experienced troops.[4] However, overall there was still the divided and quarrelsome Spanish command. Verdugo, realising that Maurits was moving in the region, had asked for reinforcements to be urgently sent, but Mansfeld in Brussels refused to sanction any sending of troops from the southern provinces. The besiegers put much care and planning into the digging and constructing of trenches and siege outworks. which tentacled towards Steenwijk. Small fortified positions were built and manned as a precaution against sudden sallies by the defenders.

The bombardment, from well sited cannon, began and continued. Verdugo attempted to thrust a relieving force through and managed to reinforce the garrison with a few dozen troops, the rest being killed or driven off by the besiegers. Some sudden sallies and counter-attacks by the defenders impacted and damaged the Dutch siege lines. However, the bombardment continued relentlessly, and specialist Dutch troops managed to mine the outer defences at 3 different points. After a 24-hour break in the fighting, the bombardment resumed with the Dutch forces still holding most of the positions in the town's fortifications they had taken with the previous assaults. The Spanish garrison realised that the situation was now untenable and surrendered on 5 July 1592.

Steenwijk had cost Maurits heavily in terms of casualties, with over 600 of his troops lost. However, this strongly fortified town had been well worth taking. Any Spanish threat to Friesland was nullified, and access to the Zuider Zee was under Dutch control.

Maurits next turned his attention to Coevorden in the east. Coevorden was a fortified town encased by 5 strong bastions with a garrison of 1,900, the majority of them being experienced veteran Spanish troops. By late June 1592, the Dutch forces had reached within striking distance of the town. William Lodewijk took charge of the siege itself, whilst Maurits hived off a force and positioned it in another location that could give advance warning about and engage with and block any relieving forces. As with the taking of other towns, siege work and trenches were undertaken, and Coevorden was soon cut off and effectively isolated by the besiegers. Preliminary attacks by the Dutch forces gained and held positions in the suburbs. Maurits and his forces rejoined the siege in mid-August, and the siege lines were further advanced and tightened. Then the weather changed, and there was a series of heavy and prolonged downpours, hampering further advances of the siege lines. The

Spanish were encouraged by this and were also aware that the lack of food and fresh water was severely debilitating the garrison. Accordingly, they launched a relief force of 5,000 troops from Grol. Maurits, on learning of the despatch of this Spanish relieving force, had fortified camps constructed at the rear of the besiegers and deployed units to man them. By mid-September the Spanish relieving forces had reached the first of these defences of the besiegers of Coervorden and launched concerted attacks upon them in attempts to break through to the besieged town. Their efforts almost gained one of the fortified camps and pushed back the defenders from another, but they were eventually repulsed and stood off. Maurits did not pursue; he was content to let the would-be relief forces stay in good order nearby provided they did not attack. The Dutch artillery, sited in their carefully dug emplacements, continued the relentless bombardment against the town. The besieged garrison, seeing the relief force effectively halted and realizing that relief was unlikely and by now desperately hungry and thirsty, surrendered. As with the other successful taking of the towns, all surrendering Spanish troops were allowed to march out and depart.

Maurits and William Lodewijk then turned south and made for Geertruidenberg. This town, just north of Breda (the scene of the starting point of the Dutch breakout) had been captured by the Spanish in 1589 and was situated in a favourable position on the southern limits of the Dutch territory. It was strategically valuable for whichever side held it. By late April siege works and trenches had been advanced towards the town, the digging and construction being done by specialist troops. Artillery was sited at various strongpoints. Also, to reinforce the blockade of the town, the besiegers floated dozens of small ships armed with cannon on the waterways near the town. The ships formed a continuous line and were held together in line by chains. An advance position of the defenders had been taken by a preliminary assault in the first week in April, and with the siege works complete, the besiegers settled down to a long blockade. However, a month later in May, a relief column of just under 9,000 troops including cavalry units appeared within 10 miles of the town. The relieving force attacked some positions but were daunted by the strength and depth of the entrenchments; the Dutch forces, including contingents of English troops, counter-attacked, and the relief columns retreated in good order and stood to. They were not pursued, the Dutch being content to let them remain in position provided they did not attack further. The steady relentless bombardment of the town continued, including those cannons mounted on the blockading ships. After some days of sustained bombardment and seeing that no further relief was likely, the garrison negotiated for terms of surrender, which they were granted. They were allowed to march out and keep their arms and standards, provided they agreed to remain non-combatants for the duration of the war. Geertruidenberg surrendered in June 1593 after a siege of 4 months.

In the north in 1593, Spanish forces made a counter-attack in an attempt to retake Coevorden but failed and were forced to withdraw. This spurred Maurits to push further to the north and approach Groningen. As we have seen Delfzijl, which was the main transit port of Groningen, had already been captured and was under Dutch control. Now it was the turn of Groningen itself to be besieged. By May 1594 the Dutch and their English units approached Groningen. However, before they arrived, the Spanish by swift action managed to deploy reinforcements into Groningen and brought up the numbers of the garrison to just under 1,000. Maurits carefully sited his artillery, positioning 36 siege cannons in 5 different locations around the town, all of the cannon having a clear field of fire. These siege cannon had been transported and moved to their positions on small boats along canals and waterways that had been cut and widened by specialist digging troops. These canals were guarded and then used to bring up more artillery ammunition and supplies for the army. At some stage during the siege, Maurits's forces were reduced due to the English contingent being withdrawn on direct orders from Queen Elizabeth. Maurits had also to divert some of the besieging forces to locations in the south to replace the English units departing from there. In late May the Spanish attempted to muster a relief column; however, this was hampered by disease and the near-constant problem of mutinies due to pay arrears. The siege—and the relentless artillery bombardment—continued. Mining and sapping of the defences had been carried out, and mines were exploded in early July under parts of Groningen's defences. This was followed by a frontal attack. The besieged garrison, realising that relief was unlikely and that their defences were severely breached, surrendered and by mid-July the garrison had been granted lenient surrender terms and marched out and departed. Groningen in the far north had fallen to the Dutch. Maurice's capture of Groningen was significant. It was part of the culmination of a victorious advance by the Dutch Army re-gaining valuable territory. It was the largest of the towns he captured. Its capture was the retaking of a town that had surrendered itself by betrayal to Parma in the early 1580s, and this had marked one of the nadir points of the Dutch Revolt.

Then in 1597 Maurits was to make another push in the eastern part of the Dutch Republic, capturing Rheinberg on the Rhine and exposing several Spanish fortresses. He then captured Grol and Enschede. He went on to cross the frontier and enter the territory of the Holy Roman Empire, taking the large fortress of Lingen. This short period of campaigning from after the capture of Groningen to the taking of Lingen resulted in another substantial chunk of eastward territory freed from Spanish control and added to the territory of the Dutch Republic.

Strategic cohesion in the army and administration had been enhanced with Maurits being appointed in 1590 and 1591 as stadhouder of

Gelderland, Overijssel, and Utrecht (and he was already stadhouder of Holland and of Zeeland) and with William Lodewijk being appointed stadhouder of Groningen and Drenthe (and he was already stadhouder of Friesland). And during these successful campaigns, at times he had acted against the advice and instructions of the States-General. As stadhouder of 5 provinces, as military leader and son of William of Orange, together with his fellow stadhouder and fellow military leader William Lodewijk, Maurits was his own person, subordinate to no one.

This period of the counteroffensive campaign of Maurits was a remarkable achievement. Maurits and William Lodewijk had marched, counter-marched, and manoeuvred back and forward in the north and east, breaking out of the Spanish-imposed constraints on Dutch territory and adding important gains to the amount of territory under the control of the Dutch Republic.

In fighting, they had concentrated on their strengths. This was utilising their armies' specialties of well sited fixed artillery bombardments and skilful construction of siege lines and entrenchments and by avoiding open pitched battles with the battle-hardened and experienced *tercio* veterans. (During the course of the Dutch Revolt between 1568 and 1589, there had been 8 pitched battles between Spanish troops and the Dutch rebels. In only one, the battle of Heligerlee, were the Dutch victorious.)

The sieges had been successful. In the sieges of Deventer, Zutphen, and Nijmegen, the use of heavy artillery barrages combined with skilful siege lines dug by the troops had resulted in a comparatively speedy surrender, before any Spanish relief forces could be assembled and deployed. In the sieges of Steenwijk, Coevorden, and Gertruidenberg, the Dutch forces defending the siege lines had successfully engaged with Spanish relief columns and had driven them off. In all the sieges, the siege lines and trenches had been skilfully made and advanced, with soldiers digging and constructing and taking time and care in doing so, as opposed to the normal practice of either paying or conscripting local civilians to perform this task quickly. On some occasions, the soldiers who were digging and constructing were paid a bonus. This was a forerunner of armies having a specialist pioneer corps of troops specialising in skilled labour. Also, the success of the sieges was due to the careful deployment and sighting of the artillery and of concentrated and sustained bombardments. Furthermore, the lenient terms given to the surrendering Spanish troops, an emulation of Parma's strategy in his own previous offensive, paid dividends in terms of reducing future enemy resistance. It prevented any desperate last-ditch resistance by defenders who knew there would be no mercy from the victorious besiegers. All told, Maurits and William Ludwig's counteroffensive had resulted in the taking of no less than 43 towns.

By 1597 the northern and eastern parts of the United Provinces were transformed with the Dutch entrenched and controlling the IJssel, Waal, and the Lower Rhine. Traffic, trade, and commerce with the German states of the Empire was opened. In an assessment of one historian:

> Maurits had not only securely padlocked the United Provinces, he had also gained control of the trade and navigation of the great rivers themselves.[5]

Several other significant aspects had become clear during the campaign of the 1590s. On the positive side, a significant precedent appeared to have been established in that the States of Friesland had been persuaded to allow their forces to be deployed outside the province.

However, the States-General's insisting on controlling military strategy had caused problems. They had taken control of military strategy after the failed attempt of the Governor Generalship of Leicester. But this had not prevented divided counsel in pursuit of the war, especially during this period in the 1590s. There had been 3 factions within the States-General, each advocating a different—and self-interested—strategy. Gelderland and Overijssel wanted an easterly thrust against Grol and Oldenzaal; Holland had wished an advance southward to take Geertruidenberg; Friesland wanted a north-easterly attack on Steenwijk, thus removing a threat to its border. Oldenbarneveldt made strenuous efforts to reconcile the factions and eventually managed to persuade the States-General to accept a compromise. By this William Lodewijk would deploy with part of the army and push northwards, whilst Maurits would take the other part of the army and deploy in the south. After some months, they would then join forces and advance into northern Brabant. This was a skilfully effected compromise, but it was due to a political imperative and was not necessarily the best military course of action.

In fact, Maurits had completely ignored the arrangement and ignored the directions for him to move south. Instead he had joined William Lodewijk's forces, which were besieging Steenwijk. He did this not because he sided with the Overijssel faction but because he judged this the most effective military course of action. Steenwijk had strong fortifications and was manned by experienced Spanish troops. However, as we have seen, Maurits and William Lodewijk took Steenwijk within two and half months, mainly due to the sheer ferocity of their sustained artillery bombardment. Then Maurits and William Lodewijk pressed on and besieged Coevorden. The States of Holland had complained and protested, but Maurits and William Ludwig pressed on and finished the siege of Coevorden. Its capture ensured that the province of Drenthe was completely free from Spanish control. Only when Maurits and William Ludwig were satisfied that they had militarily accomplished all that they had aimed for in the north-east did they agree to move the armies south, to the next target of Gertruidenberg on the southern border of the Spanish Netherlands.

However, provincial rivalries still reared their heads to disrupt the pursuit of the survival war. When rebels inside Groningen rose against the Spanish garrison, the assembly there voted to join and subscribe to the Union of Utrecht and appealed to the States-General for its States of Ommelands to gain formal admission to the States-General. Within the States-General, this proposal was blocked by Friesland, which wanted to "acquire" the territory of the Ommelands for its own. However, despite this setback, another province was in the making as part of a slow but sure process towards an emerging Dutch nation state. Just before Goningen was finally captured, the States-General voted and admitted the Ommelands (of which Groningen was part) to the States-General as a province with voting power. There were now 7 provinces in the States-General that had voting powers. After Coevorden had been liberated Drenthe made representation to the States-General to be recognised as a province. The representatives from Holland in the States-General were against this, arguing that there was danger of admitting and recognizing too many provinces too quickly. The real reason for their opposition was their fear that Holland's voting power would be further reduced by the creation of another voting province in the States-General. To this end, the representatives from Holland made a different proposal, that of merging Drenthe with Groningen and creating a large province that could counterbalance the troublesome Friesland. However, Groningen itself refused to be part of this. The result of the debates was that Drenthe had its status as a province confirmed, with its own stadhouder (William Lodewijk), and it raised its own taxes but was not admitted to the States-General and therefore had no voting rights.

The United Provinces were united in their rooted aversion to Spanish sovereignty and Spanish rule and in their commitment to being a component of the Dutch Republic. A national identity in the form of the Dutch Republic indeed had been forged, but the rights, sovereignty, and looking after interests of the individual province formed part of the ethos and of this nation that had been created. There were several differences and disputes over territories and jurisdictions between the provinces. Oldenbarneveldt, leading representatives of the States of Holland in the States-General, was the key to ministering to the quarrelling provinces and resolving their perceived grievances. The States of Holland were jealous and possessive of their role as leading province. They owed this to their comparative economic wealth, which had been and remained the financial mainstay of the Revolt. Oldenbarneveldt led Holland and led the States-General. Therefore Maurits and William Lodewijk may well have been the military *supremos* controlling the armies, but politically they needed the States of Holland[6] and were dependent upon Oldenbarneveldt. The partnership of Maurits and Oldenbarneveldt stood and worked well in the 1590s.

In the international and diplomatic arena, Oldenbarneveldt gave valuable service, showing both skill and wisdom. In 1597, whilst Maurits and William Lodewijk were completing their military reforms and their successful campaign, Oldenbarneveldt was monitoring the wider situation. He was keeping himself closely informed about the potential Franco-Spanish peace. Such a rapprochement would enable Spain to refocus and concentrate upon a single objective, the reconquest of the United Provinces. Oldenbarneveldt took the initiative and led a deputation from the States-General on a visit to the French Court. During the visit and the negotiations, he and his fellow delegates deliberately avoided any mention, acknowledgement, comment, or indeed any word or action that could be interpreted as interference in the ongoing negotiations between the French king and the differing religious denominations and parties, which were to eventually result in the compromise settlement of the Edict of Nantes. Oldenbarneveldt and his fellow delegates' scrupulous avoidance of these issues and their concentrating in their discussions on the international situation paid off. In April 1598, Henri IV of France undertook to provide financial assistance and subsidies to the Dutch.

Since Spain had—much to Parma's extreme reluctance—turned from total war to quell the Dutch Revolt and had become entangled in a second front by intervening in France, the Dutch had made large and significant gains in terms of military victory and territory. This had been due to Maurits whose strategic and tactical abilities had come to the fore. Parma had been an excellent soldier and commander, yet Maurits and the Dutch forces had prevailed.

Meanwhile in 1596, Philip II had decided to intervene and settle the issue of divided command in the Netherlands and secure unity of policy in Brussels and to ensure that orders would be carried out. His first choice as governor general was his nephew, Ernest, who unfortunately died in 1596 shortly after his appointment. He then appointed another of his nephews, Archduke Albert. Albert was the fifth son of the Holy Roman Emperor Maximilien II. Brought up and educated in Spain at the court of Philip II, Albert's life to date had been one of sincere, responsible, and dedicated service to the Spanish Hapsburgs. He was the viceroy of Portugal when that country was joined and united with Spain in 1583. He was part of the organising command of the 1588 Spanish Armada (the organisation and supply of which, it could be argued despite its ultimate failure, were themselves achievements). He had been the commander of the forces that had repulsed the English attack on Lisbon in 1589. Summoned to Madrid on 1593 to assist at the various Councils in governing Spain, Albert was then appointed Spanish governor general of the Netherlands in 1596. His first task was to stabilise and retrieve the deteriorating situation.

The situation facing the Spanish Netherlands was a difficult one. The United Provinces looked to reconquer them, the Spanish troops there were constantly short of funds, the Spanish armies were expected to fight on two fronts, and the provinces of the Spanish Netherlands were touchy regarding their rights and privileges, yet they still expected Spain to protect them. However, Archduke Albert was to prove a wise choice as governor general, and he was to make herculean efforts to bring about a situation more favourable to Spain. The situation was eased for Albert and his co-regent Isabella in 1598 when Spain and France made peace by the Treaty of Vervins. Henri of Navarre had finally triumphed in the so-called Wars of the Three Henris and had gained the throne of France. Spain undertook to cease intervention in French internal affairs. Now Spain was no longer fighting on two fronts.

One of Albert and Isabella's first major actions was to offer peace negotiations to the Dutch. The terms offered to the Dutch were extremely generous. Spain would accept most of the political and religious changes that had occurred and would recognise Maurits as stadhouder of Holland, Zeeland, Utrecht, Overijssel, and Gelderland and by implication recognise William Lodewijk as stadhouder of Friesland. Further terms were inserted by the Spanish first minister in Madrid, the Duke of Lerma. These further terms stipulated that the overall sovereignty of Albert and Isabella as Spanish governors of the whole of the Netherlands would be recognised, and some few concessions would be made regarding the practice of Catholicism. The sovereignty demand was for nominal *de jure* sovereignty and was a face-saving clause for Spain as a form of due acknowledgement to her as an imperial power. Some negotiations started between the two sides and went slowly throughout 1598–1599.

However, Dutch politicians had other ideas.

Notes

1. Israel, J *The Dutch Republic: Its Greatness, Rise, and Fall* 1477–1806 p 242
2. Parker, G *The Grand Strategy of Philip II* p 287
3. Parker, G *The Dutch Revolt* p 230
4. Israel, J *The Dutch Republic—Its Rise, Greatness, and Fall* 1477–1806 p 245
5. Wilson, CH *Queen Elizabeth and the Revolt of the Netherlands* p 116
6. Kossman, EH chapter XII "The Low Countries" in *The New Cambridge Modern History—The Decline of Spain and the XXX Years War 1609–1659* p 363

6 Politicians Meddling, Flanders "Invaded"

In 1589 the States-General, led by Oldenbarneveldt, formulated the strategy of striking south. This was not just to be a limited strike south, as with the taking of Breda at the start of the victorious breakout, but a complete invasion of the entire province of Flanders. This was a tempting strategy and, to Dutch eyes, apparently feasible, given the past half decade. Parma's armies in the 1580s had swept all before them in their reconquest of the southern provinces, and now that the tide of victories had turned, could not Dutch forces, buoyed up by success, do the same in reverse, at least as far as liberating Flanders? For Parma, at the height of his success, had been halted by royal orders to launch his forces in the opposite direction against France and, exhausted by fighting on two fronts, was now dead. The armies he had commanded in the Netherlands were afflicted by divided commanders with the newly appointed regent of the Spanish Netherlands Archduke Albert only in the early stages of uniting them. There were always the problems of shortage of funds and the threat of mutinies. On the Dutch side, the Dutch Republic was secure; Maurits and Willem Lodewijk had gained and controlled whole swathes of territory; with the exception of Groningen, all the reconquered territory was securely fortified and garrisoned; Oldenbarneveldt, leading the States-General, had a firm grasp of the international situation. In this, Oldenbarneveldt was confident that by a Dutch strike south, England would remain involved in the struggle as allies and that the population of Flanders would rise in support against the Spanish.

All told, it appeared that the time and circumstances were ripe for a deep thrusting invasion to reconquer Flanders—and soon, before Albert restored stability on the Spanish side.

But the projected Flanders invasion was not so feasible or tempting as it may have appeared to the Dutch. Groningen seriously needed refortifying and proper garrisoning if it were to avoid being a vulnerable point exploitable in the future by the Spanish forces. Various factions in Friesland were causing deep divisions within the province over privileges and taxation.[1] Perhaps time was needed for consolidation instead of an immediate forward policy into Flanders. Willem Lodewijk deemed the invasion of Flanders totally unfeasible, calling it "crazy and foolish"; Maurits was at best doubting and had increasing reservations about the strategy. He had no faith in Oldenbarneveldt's confident prediction that the population of Flanders would rise in support of the Dutch.[2] Both he and Willem Lodewijk resented the constant interference by civilian politicians like Oldenbarneveldt into military matters and campaigning. In the 1590s in the campaigns, the working relationship between Oldenbarneveldt and Maurits had been in harmony. When Maurits took the town of Breda, Oldenbarneveldt worked hard and ensured that the war-weary inhabitants of Breda were provided with victuals and supplies from the States of Holland for the next 18 months.[3] Such an example was that of the military under Maurits being supported by the civilian politician.

However, the decision to invade Flanders in 1600 was that of politicians taking over and deciding military strategy. They insisted that the invasion proceed. Maurits was empowered with an army of over 14,000 infantry and 2,300 cavalry, and the invasion was be to under the careful oversight of the States-General. Such was the intense scrutiny of the military campaigns by the politicians that Oldenbarneveldt and the States-General, at the start of the invasion of Flanders, moved *en masse* from The Hague and took up residence in Ostend in order to have oversight. The Dutch troops deployed and crossed the Scheldt at north-east Flanders and marched, passing Kaprijke, then Bruges, reaching Nieuwport on 1 July. The army units had issued proclamations and propaganda as they advanced, encouraging the population to regard them, the Dutch troops, as their liberators from the Hapsburg yoke and as their friends. There was no sympathetic uprising by the population against the Spaniards; if there was any reaction by the peasantry to the Dutch "liberators", it was that of passive resistance.[4] The Archduke Albert and his co-ruler Isabella had governed wisely, and their policies were already having conciliatory effects in the southern provinces, and any possible affinity with the Dutch had been nullified by frequent raids and pillaging by pirates based in Zeeland.

Maurits began the siege of Nieuwport. It had a strong garrison, but the Spanish forces in the region were considerably weakened by an ongoing mutiny by Spanish units—inevitably—over arrears of pay. The Dutch, as per their strategic assessment, anticipated that this mutiny would prevent any relief force from raising the siege and advanced confidently. However, the mutinous Spanish units at Diest, under their own elected officers, temporarily put aside their grievances and rallied, having been appealed to by the Archduke Albert and Isabella. The Archduchess Isabella had personally visited the area and had made a direct appeal to the mutineers, stating that rather than see the troops unpaid, she would sell all her jewelry to raise the funds. The mutineers responded,[5] and from Diest 1,400 infantry and 600 cavalry had been brought back to the colours. (Perhaps this serves as an interesting contrast to the 1570s of Alva and as an indicator of the effective legacy of Parma's enlightened leadership.)

The Archduke Albert was able to deploy a large force that marched on 31 June, and Spanish troops made towards the main body of Maurits's troops. Maurits became aware of the advancing Spanish troops only late the following day, by which time the Spanish had effectively defeated and swept aside an advance guard of Maurits's forces at Leffinge. Albert was able to place his forces between Maurits and Ostende, effectively severing Maurits's lines of communications and supply. Maurice saw the danger and resolved to fight his way back to Ostende. From Leffinge, Albert's forces moved along the beach, until Maurits's army was cut off between the sea and an estuary of the river Yser. With the incoming tides, both sides moved inland from the sea front but were still hampered by the sandy terrain. The Spanish forces, including the former mutinous units, all deployed with perfect discipline, attacked on a wide front, and sustained the attack.

The majority of Maurits's forces were Dutch troops, but there were also contingents of English, Welsh, Swiss, and others from various states of the Empire; they fought as fiercely as the Spanish *tercios* opposing them.[6] The discipline and reforms inaugurated in the Dutch armies by Maurits and Willem Lodewijk now paid off, and the Dutch forces stood firm, where necessary retreating in good order. The small contingent of Dutch artillery kept up a steady supporting fire against the Spanish attacks. After holding the Spanish attacks for hours, Maurits, with a superb sense of timing, deployed his cavalry forces, sending them into battle and outflanking the Spanish attacking forces. This, combined with the consistent and accurate fire from his small unit of artillery, turned the battle and caused the Spanish to retreat in some disarray. They were not broken, but they broke off the attack, allowing Maurits and the Dutch Army to retreat back into Ostend. The battle was a victory for the Dutch forces, and a vindication of the reforms of Maurits and Willem Lodewijk—but Archduke Albert and the Spanish had relieved Nieuwport. But Maurits was happy to retire and eventually get back to The Hague.[7]

The unsuccessful invasion of Flanders had 3 important results. After Nieuwport, Maurits never again fought an open pitched battle. The Spanish had caught the Dutch by surprise, and the danger of being hemmed in and overwhelmed had been averted by the Dutch troops standing firm, responding with well coordinated volley fire, and the units counterattacking with precision. This was all due to the Dutch military reforms implemented by Maurits and Willem Lodewijk. However, the Spanish forces were still as formidable as ever, and Maurits was determined to husband Dutch fighting manpower. Manoeuvring and sieges and fortified positions were to be the strategic way forward, and this strategy was continued by Maurits's successor Frederick Henry, who became known as the "taker of cities".

Secondly, the failure of the invasion made quite clear that any reunification of the loyal Spanish provinces and those forming the Dutch Republic, those of the Union of Arras[8] and those of the Union of Utrecht, was now long past and impossible. By the time of the turn of the Sixteenth Century, the southern provinces were firmly under Spanish control. The French ambassador to The Hague spoke of:

the gripping bit in which they are held.[9]

There may have been a tight grip, but it was partly a benevolent one, appreciated by the population, thanks to the wise and conciliatory policies of the Archduke Albert and Isabella.

The third result was that relations between Oldenbarneveldt and Maurits were irrevocably damaged. As we have seen, both Maurits and Willem Lodewijk, the military experts, had been doubtful about the invasion of Flanders. After the debacle, Maurits and Willem Lodewijk had a meeting with Oldenbarneveldt that was extremely acrimonious. Both Maurits and Willem Lodewijk made very clear to Oldenbarneveldt[10] that in military matters both strategic and operational, the sole decision was to be taken by Maurits in consultation with Willem Lodewijk, without any other interference or meddling. Maurice, after the 1600 debacle at Nieuwport, would brook no interference from the States-General, especially from Oldenbarneveldt, whom he informed in no uncertain terms that he, Maurice, was the individual who decides the strategy and wages the war.[11]

Even after Nieuwport, where it was only thanks to the discipline of the Dutch troops and the tactical skill of Maurits's leadership that disaster was avoided, Maurits was still pleaded to by the States-General and Oldenbarneveldt to again invade Flanders. However, Maurits had had enough of this unwarranted and uninformed interference in military matters and turned east. The Dutch forces took Rheinburg; then in 1601 he besieged s'Hertogenbosch. However, the siege only started in November 1601, and during the harsh winter, the ground was so frozen solid that it made trench and siege works impossible. He gave up in early 1602 and turned northeast, marched on, and took Meurs and then Grave.

The Spanish too were galvanised into mounting a counteroffensive. They attacked in the south and laid siege to Ostend. But they were hampered yet again by mutinies. During the next 5 years, two large-scale mutinies occurred in the Spanish armies, one between 1600 and 1602 at Weest. This was followed by another, more damaging mutiny occurring between 1602 and 1604 at Hoogstraten. The mutineers organised themselves, held the town, and even set up a self-styled Republic of Hoogstraten whilst negotiating with the Spanish commanders for their pay. Payments of the claimed arrears—as was usual in cases of mutinies during this period—were forthcoming, and the mutineers, as experienced and valuable soldiers, were reconciled, although some subsequently joined the Dutch forces. But it had cost the Spanish war effort a debilitating sum of 400,000 florins. The situation was stabilised by this dispensing of funds, and the situation was further restored to Spain with the advent of Spinola.

Ambrosio Spinola was the brother of the Genoese sailor Federigo Spinola who had been commissioned by Philip III of Spain to assemble and supply a fleet to attack Dutch shipping. Ambrosio was a wealthy banker and entrepreneur. In September 1603 he offered his services to Philip III. These services were that he, Spinola would finance troops to continue the siege of Ostend and to be principal banker to the Archduke Albert. In return, Spinola would be made overall commander of the Spanish forces in the Netherlands. The offer was gratefully accepted by Philip III, and Spinola proved himself an able commander, working well in cooperation with Archduke Albert.

He also reimposed stricter discipline. The Netherlands campaign had resulted in conditions of privation and hardship on many of the Spanish units, and, as we have seen, pay arrears became almost the norm, causing outbreaks of mutiny. These were settled, with back pay being paid in full. However, desertions also resulted due to shortages of food and provisions and, in many cases, sheer despair and lack of morale. Deserters were in theory and in law subject to the death penalty but in practice had been treated leniently. Considerable cost and expense had already been outlayed in transporting troops from Spain and other parts of the Empire to the Netherlands, and these were experienced and valuable troops; hence the leniency for recaptured deserters, who were generally restored to their units with a token punishment. However, Spinola realised the need for a new commander to make his disciplinary mark upon the troops. Accordingly, when a column of Italian troops drawn from Italy were *en route* to the Netherlands and deserted, Spinola organised a large force of troops that was deployed and that swept wide swathes of several kilometres behind the column. This force, working on a bonus rewards payment, netted a large number of deserters. Over 100 deserters were brought back and hanged. In the future, Spinola looked after his troops and was sympathetic and reasonable to their various complaints and grievances, but they knew he could not be taken for granted.

Unlike the previous Spanish commanders in the Netherlands, who were all of noble background and tended to order and delegate more, Spinola's background was that of commercial banking in Genoa. In this profession there was a need for constant direct oversight by senior officials and constant vigilance on changing situations. Consequently, Spinola was alert and vigilant in seeing that his orders, plans, and strategy were carried out.[12] He pushed on with the siege of Ostend, which finally fell.

The taking of Ostend by Spinola—finally—in September 1604 was an important gain. It heartened the population of Flanders, and indeed the other provinces loyal to Spain saw themselves as finally freed from the raids and pillaging of the Dutch. Also, the timing of its surrender was encouraging; Ostend had surrendered a month after the 1604 Treaty of London, signed between Spain and England, which ended hostilities between them. Philip III and his ministers were heartened, viewing the wider perspective that substantial damage could now be inflicted upon the Dutch, now that they were not fighting on two fronts.

However, Maurits and his forces had now taken Sluis, which fell in August 1604. Perhaps Maurits had lunged at Sluis to distract Spinola from besieging Ostend, in which case Spinola had diligently stuck to his purpose of gaining Ostend. Arguably, in terms of the two captured towns, Spinola had now possession of an Ostend in ruins, whilst Maurits, in taking Sluis, had gained for the Dutch a deep-water port[13] and had extended the south-west coastal port holdings. This was of strategic value and recognised in popular songs as a good recompense for the loss of Ostend and that it was taken with skill:

> How the noble Maurits
> With his soldiers brave
> Searched out the enemy.[14]

Spinola resolutely continued campaigning. He apparently had not given up on Sluis and gave the impression of starting a siege to retake the town. Then in July 1605 he broke off, moved quickly eastwards, and was far ahead of the Dutch forces, and for a period Maurits was unaware of the whereabouts of Spinola's forces. Spinola reappeared in the east in the first week in August before the town of Oldenzaal, which quickly surrendered. Just over a week later, Spinola took Lingen. The following year, in June 1606 Spinola advanced again, taking the towns of Grol and Bredevort, and then he recaptured Rheinburg. He then advanced and took Lochem, and in doing so threatened the strategic centres of Deventer and Zutphen, depending upon which direction he choose to follow, apparently having unopposed freedom to move and strike. The very interior of the Dutch Republic appeared vulnerable. Troops were redeployed from far-away garrisons and rushed to the IJssel area, reinforced by civic militia units from Amsterdam and Utrecht. Spinola did not advance any further, confident that his gains had consolidated Spain's position and shaken the Dutch Republic. Maurits was unwilling to risk Dutch forces in an ambitious counter-attack and made a limited counterstrike in November 1606 when he took Lochem but failed to retake Grol. However, he had partially filled the gap in the Dutch eastern defences.

Throughout 1605 and 1606, Maurice implemented the construction of defensive works. This was a long, solid earthwork, along the whole length of which were small forts, blockhouses, and redoubts. The line of these defensive works ran north to south, then east to west, from a small town on the Zuider Zee continuing south following the river IJssel to Arnhem, then south-west along the Lower Rhine, where it joined the rivers Lek, Linge, and Waal, to Schenkhausen, then turning west long the Waal to Tiel. The towns on the east-to-west line running along the rivers Lek, Linge, Waal, and Maas, towns such as Grave, Nijmegen, Gorinchem, Arnhem, Rhenen, and Wageningen, were fortified. These defensive works created in effect a 4-rank defence in depth against attacks from the south.[15]

After retrieving the situation in the "invasion" of Flanders, Maurits had held the Spanish counteroffensive under Spinola and had made gains of his own for the Dutch. Overall, honours were even, and both sides were approaching stalemate.

Notes

1. Israel, J *The Dutch Republic—Its Rise, Greatness, and Fall* p 258
2. Maland, D *Europe at War 1550–1650* p 29
3. Orders, J and van Haestens, H *The Triumphs of Nassau. A Description of all victories etc* p 131
4. Duerloo, L *Dynasty and Piety Archduke Albert and Hapsburg Political Culture in an Age of Religious Wars* p 119
5. Van Deursen, A *Maurits van Nassau* p 177
6. Duick, A *De slag bij Nieuwport, Journal van de tocht naar Vlaanden in 1600* (ed by Roeper and Uitterhoeve)
7. de la Pise, J *Tableau de l'Histoire de princes et principaute de l'Nassau* p 691
8. May 1579, consisting of Artois Flanders and Hainault
9. Buzenal, French ambassador to The Hague, cited in Geyl *The Revolt of the Netherlands* p 247
10. van Cruyningen, A *De Tachtjajarige Oorlog* p 105
11. van Cruyningen, A *De Tachtigjarige Oorlog* p 105
12. Van Deursen, A *Maurits van Nassau* p 194
13. Van Deursen, A *Maurits van Nassau* p 195
14. "Hoe Maurits des Edelyan Graf met allezijn soldaten brave De Vyand goet na poeren Inneming van Sluys" in Scheurleer, DDF *Onze Mannen ter Zee in dicht en bled Vol I 1572–1654* pp 29–30
15. Braudel, F in his monumental 3-volume work dealing with global economic history, mentions and maps the fortifications of 1605–1606 of Maurits, stating that it was "[t]urning the United Provinces into a fortress" Braudel *Civilisation and Capitalism 15–18 Century Vol III* p 202

7 The Twelve Years' Truce—And a Diplomatic Victory

Overall, after Maurits's success of the 1590s and the early 1600s, there was a period of balance. The period from 1599 to 1606 had been one of a series of campaigns and manoeuvres in which neither side gained or lost,[1] and both sides were increasingly concerned by their respective financial situations. Indeed, both sides had now reached stalemate. The Dutch under Maurits had held Spinola—just—but the Republic was psychologically less confident about continuing the struggle, and the financial cost of the military effort was increasing. On the Spanish side, Spinola realised that he had achieved all he could in countering Maurits's successful advances of the early 1600s. During the campaigns he had had to return to Madrid to ask Philip III for more funds to which Philip III replied that he was unable to provide them. Spinola then went to Genoa where he managed to raise 650,000 florins through a personal loan.[2] But the overall financial situation of Spain was still dire. Spain was increasingly aware that reconquest of the Dutch and the restoration of Spanish sovereignty were unfeasible. The situation overseas was also of concern to Spain. Throughout 1605 the VOC was expanding its activities, and in the Indies it took in succession the Spanish settlements of Amboni, Ternate, and Tidare. When news of these conquests reached Madrid, Philip III and his council realised that militarily there was no possibility of halting further VOC expansion; this brought home how much the Dutch naval warfare was damaging the economy of Spain.

On the Dutch side, whilst the overseas trade atavism of the Dutch Republic was successful, the internal finances of the Republic were under strain due to the conflict. In 1606 Oldenbarneveldt addressed a secret session of the States of Holland and starkly stated that the financial position of the Republic was untenable. The alternatives were to seek the protection of Henri IV of France or arrive at some form of rapprochement with Spain.

Informal talks between Spain and the Dutch began and lasted until the last month of 1606. The discreet communications were between the Archduke Albert on the Spanish side and Oldenbarneveldt on the Dutch, and then, in late 1606, Maurits and Willem Lodewijk became involved. The Spanish took a major initiative authorised by Philip III, stating that they would recognise the independence of the Dutch Republic. In exchange for this, they asked in return that the Dutch completely withdraw from the East Indies.

In fact, in starting the informal negotiations and in making this startling offer at the early stages it was Archduke Albert who quickly took the initiative. He sent a Brussels trader, Werner Cruwel, on a discreet mission to make contact with one of his, Cruwel's, relatives in The Hague. This relative was Corenelis van Aerssens, the greffier to the States-General. Cruwel arrived in The Hague, dined with Aerssens, and informed him that he had a message from Richardot, the president of the Archduke Albert's Council to Oldenbarneveldt. Cruwel then had a secret meeting with van Aerssens, Oldenbarneveldt, and Maurits where he made it known that the archduke was willing to concede full sovereignty and recognise the Dutch as independent. Cruwel also asked that permission be granted to Father Jan Neyen, head of the Franciscan Order in the Spanish Netherlands and who was also a friend of a relative of William of Orange, to open negotiations for a truce and that part of the terms of this truce would be that the Dutch cease advancing on the Indies. Cruwel was received courteously but with some suspicion. He was told that Neyen himself must come and present a formal document of his remit from the archduke and that such a document must stipulate in writing that the archduke would concede sovereignty. The following week, Cruwel returned from Brussels with a declaration from the archduke stating that he was authorised by the archduke to negotiate with the Dutch States-General who would be regarded as independent representatives and that the archduke gave up all rights and claims on the United Provinces.

This was more favourably received and negotiations continued, with Neyen officially accredited as the archduke's negotiator. During the course of these talks, Oldenbarneveldt gave assurances that the VOC would be restrained and that any plans and preparations to establish a new company, the Dutch West Indies Company, would cease. These negotiations were in secret, held at a location in Ryswick just outside The Hague. They were between Maurits and Oldenbarneveldt on the one side and Neyen on the other. Throughout March the archduke's official position on recognizing the independence was clarified and made more specific. A draft was drawn up by Oldenbarneveldt and given to Neyen, who took it back to Brussels. From this draft, the archduke drew up his document, which stated his recognition of the Dutch independence in accordance with the stipulation and wording of Oldenbarneveldt's draft. This was then presented officially to the States-General, which after debate and some convincing of the representatives of the States of Zeeland, finally accepted it and a ceasefire. In April 1607, a formal ceasefire between the two opposing armies was agreed and signed, Spinola as the operational commander signing for the Spanish. The ceasefire was signed by the operational commanders on 12 April but was officially dated 24 April, to go into effect on 4 May. Hostilities in the entire Netherlands ceased. The ceasefire was to be for a period of 8 months—provided the King of Spain gave ratification of the ceasefire within 3 months.

In late May 1607, an unexpected intervention occurred, causing concern to Archduke Albert. A French envoy arrived in The Hague on behalf of Henri IV of France to complain about the ceasefire being negotiated and signed without French knowledge and to pose the pointed question of what further action the Dutch were taking. The delegation also conveyed a projected offer from Henri IV. This was a possible offer of an increased French subsidy if the Dutch resumed the war against Spain forthwith. Oldenbarneveldt refused point-blank to break off peace negotiations. Henri IV's offer was a possibility and spoke of sums of monies far below what the Dutch would need to continue the war. Despite Neyen's anxiety over the French delegation being invited to a meeting of the States-General on 28 May, the Dutch, led firmly by Oldenbarneveldt, refused to permit any other course of action except the current one, that is, continuing negotiations with Spain. This particular difficulty that had loomed before Archduke Albert and his peace attempts had disappeared. But other difficulties were to come.

There were astonishment and anger in Madrid that the terms of the ceasefire, whilst formalising Spanish recognition of Dutch independence, made no mention of Dutch concessions in the Indies. Philip III had second thoughts and serious doubts about ratifying. This was smoothed over by Oldenbarneveldt who, during the signing, had given categorical assurances that in principle the evacuation of the Indies was fully agreed. Oldenbarneveldt's assurances were reported back by Spinola and Albert to assuage the doubts of Philip III and his advisors in Madrid who were scrutinizing the ceasefire agreement. These doubts were made worse by further disturbing news to Madrid in late April 1607. Whilst the two armies were implementing the Truce in the Low Countries, a Dutch fleet of 27 ships under Admiral Heemskerck had sailed into the Bay of Gibraltar and had taken on the large Spanish fleet there. Heemskerck was killed in the engagement, but over 20 Spanish ships were sunk, including 10 large galleons. Spain initially drew back, but then the realisation that the Bay of Gibralter victory showed that the extent of Dutch naval power made a peace settlement vital.

In July, Spinola sent an envoy to the States-General with documents containing the ratification of the ceasefire and further proposals. The envoy was Louis Verreycken, secretary of state for Archduke Albert. Maurits, ever suspicious, wanted to view the ratification before agreeing to any further negotiations, but he was overruled by a majority led by Oldenbarneveldt, who argued that the momentum of the peace process needed to continue.

Verreycken, accompanied by Werner Cruwel, discreetly entered The Hague and lodged at a quiet inn, meeting Maurits and some representatives from the States-General the following day. Verreycken delivered the document of ratification. However, it was in Spanish, and there was nowhere to be seen the vital clause regarding recognition of Dutch sovereignty. More discreet meetings followed at the inn with various members of the States-General; then Oldenbarneveldt visited them. Oldenbarneveldt advised that the document was unacceptable and pointed out the flaws. These were that it was in Spanish, not Latin the language of international treaties; it was signed "I the King" but with no titles and no seal of the King of Spain—that is, not acknowledging that the king of Spain was a direct party—and, above all, there was no clause clearly acknowledging recognition of Dutch independence and sovereignty. Verreycken wrote to the Archduke for further instructions, Albert and Spinola conferred, and in August Verreycken went before the States-General, again assuring them that the next document would comply with all their stipulations and also requesting the Dutch to recall their fleet from Spanish waters. This was agreed after some debate in the States-General, though it was emphasised that the recall was temporary, conditional upon the next document from Archduke Albert being acceptable. Verreycken returned to Brussels with the drafts and notes for the necessary amendments.

In October Verreycken, this time accompanied by Father Neyen, went to The Hague. They had both received accreditation by the States-General to come back to The Hague and appear before the States-General with a new, redrafted document. It had the same flaws in that it was in Spanish and signed merely "I the King" with no royal seal. Furthermore, while it contained the full acknowledgement of independence, it also contained a fresh clause stipulating that if and when the Truce was not concluded, then the ratification in this document would be of no effect, and the king retained all rights and the Dutch gained none. Anticipating and hearing out the States-General's wrathful response (Verreycken had come to know and recognise Dutch official feelings and reactions on certain points), Verreycken produced another document in Dutch and French and gave an explanation. However, the content of the new draft remained the same. In late October and early November, Oldenbarneveldt discreetly visited Neyen and Verreycken and patiently explained how the document with its offending clause(s) was unacceptable and gave help in redrafting. Neyen and Verreycken made further journeys back to Brussels to resolve the wording of the document, then back to The Hague in mid-November before the States-General, then back to Brussels for further redrafting.

In the meantime, the Dutch position had been somewhat weakened. They had requested James I of England to state his current stance should the Dutch resume the war with Spain. In September. King James sent a representative to The Hague to explain England's position to the Dutch. Also, the French representative in The Hague explained the French position, should war resume. Both England and France in effect would not support the Dutch if the peace talks were abandoned. They would be the allies of the Dutch in peace and in the peace talks, but if war resumed, the Dutch would be alone.

Neyen and Verreycken had gone back to Brussels yet again, then returned to The Hague, and on 29 November presented the amended ceasefire ratification to the States-General. The latter replied that they would consent to Archduke Albert's appointing representatives to eventually engage with the Dutch in full-scale peace talks and further that they would respond by 20 December. Encouraged, Verreycken and Neyen returned to Brussels, and they and the Archduke awaited further response. On 20 December, the States-General convened and considered and brought together the replies their representatives had received from the individual provincial States. There were reservations, but despite these, on 23 December they consented to sending a reply to the Archduke agreeing to full-scale peace negotiations and further that they would appoint the same number of representatives to the forthcoming formal peace talks and that the ceasefire would be extended. Full-scale peace talks between Spain and the Dutch, with the latter as equals, were achieved.

Formal negotiations started again in January 1608, with both sides sitting down opposite each other in the first week in February 1608. The Dutch had accepted and had accredited for safe travel to The Hague the official Spanish delegation consisting of Spinola, Neyen, Verreycken, Richardot, and de Mancidor, a secretary of state of Philip III. For the Dutch, Oldenbarneveldt, as representative of the States of Holland, was the principal negotiator. He led a Dutch delegation of negotiators, individuals representing the States of Gelderland, Zeeland, Utrecht, Friesland, Overijssel, and Groningen. The two teams of negotiators sat at one table, whilst also present at another table were commissioners from England, France, Denmark, and several German states from the Holy Roman Empire, observing and available to give guidance.

By mid-February 1608, the Spanish delegates had officially conceded and confirmed the principle of Dutch sovereignty and independence. From then on there was debate, discussion, and negotiations about the Spanish aims of the Dutch pulling back from the Indies trade and the possibility of toleration of the practice of Catholicism in the Dutch Republic

It did not take long before it became clear to the alarmed Spanish delegation that Oldenbarneveldt was rowing back on his previous verbal assurances that the Dutch would give up their conquests in and evacuate the Indies. Instead, Oldenbarneveldt conceded that indeed the creation the Dutch West Indies Company would be cancelled and nullified, but regarding the VOC, it was undertaken to restrain any further VOC expansion (but the present conquered territories would remain). Even these concessions brought Oldenbarneveldt into severe criticism from parts of the States-General. Spain was extremely agitated by this going back on what had been promised, and the negotiations were in jeopardy. However, calmer counsel amongst the Spanish prevailed, and the negotiations continued.

During the formal negotiations, in October 1608, the French representative in The Hague on instruction from Henri IV of France, sharply reminded Maurits that the French position regarding any Dutch renewal of hostilities remained unchanged, that is, France would not support the Dutch. Following this meeting, the French representative addressed the States-General where he suggested those representative(s) and State(s) opposing a Truce should go with the majority and accept a Truce, advising all the States to save and allocate funds for maintaining the troop garrisons that would be needed. The message to the Dutch could not have been clearer.

The Spanish delegation, authorised by the King of Spain, switched their negotiating emphasis. They put forward the demand for toleration of Catholics and permitting the practice of their religion within the United Provinces. This Oldenbarneveldt was unable to accept. Within the Dutch Republic, he was already fighting the criticism of some of the States and commercial interests against the proposed terms and even against the whole idea of making peace. He refused the Spanish toleration demand outright. Again the peace negotiations were in jeopardy, but again calm prevailed amongst the Spanish. Philip III and his advisers accepted the terms as they were; all hostilities in the Netherlands ceased—but not overseas; the sovereign independence of the Dutch Republic was recognised; all plans to set up the Dutch West Indies Company were cancelled indefinitely; the VOC attacks against Portuguese settlements in the East Indies were halted and further expansion curtailed.

By mid-November 1608, all the States except Zeeland were declaring for a Truce. The negotiating representative of Zeeland left the talks to go and work hard on persuading the States of Zeeland that further resistance and opposition to the Truce was futile.

The Truce was finally signed in April 1609 as the Treaty of Antwerp, at Antwerp. With the signing of the truce, there was much popular celebrating, and much expense paid to hold the celebrations. Perhaps these epitomised both the relief that the conflict had ceased and also a sense of national unity and independence. However, there was also stern disapproval amongst the Calvinist clergy and strict Calvinist sections of the population over the expense and the unrestrained (and non-sober) nature of the celebrations.

Also, Oldenbarneveldt and the Dutch negotiators had faced bitter opposition within the States-General. Zeeland remained vehemently against the Truce. Maurits remained suspicious of Spain and was conscious that in the event of war being renewed on the expiry of the Truce, he would be of advanced years and the army may have deteriorated. He still placed reliance upon and was vigilant about the state of the armed forces.[3] Friesland and Groningen had doubts but were also war weary, and they joined with Overijssel and Utrecht in voting for the peace. Amsterdam, with its large maritime-orientated commercial interests, was bitterly opposed to the peace, especially the aborting of the West Indies Company. Long after the Truce was signed, some representatives continued to pour scorn on the Truce, pointing to the wording of the Truce stating that Spain recognised the United Provinces "as if" they were a sovereign state and sourly stating that, since by its nature a truce was temporary, its recognition of the Dutch Republic as an independent state was only a recognition that independence was temporary. However, Amsterdam was the exception amongst the delegates of the States of Holland. The rest of the delegates of the States of Holland agreed with Oldenbarneveldt's arguments that peace was necessary, given the financial situation. Also maritime activity outside Europe—in fact, piracy against Spanish vessels—was still permissible within the terms of the Treaty.

Article 1 of the Treaty of Antwerp of 1609 specifically described the United Provinces as being accepted by Philip III as "free and sovereign states, provinces and lands" to which neither he nor his successor holds or will hold any claims. As the Amsterdam delegates in the states of Holland pointed out, there was some ambiguous language in that Spain acknowledged the Dutch Republic "as if" it were a sovereign state. It was understood by Spain that Dutch independence was to be ceded only as long as the Truce lasted. Symbolically, Archduke Albert continued to use the titles of all the provinces of the Low Countries and to keep the coats of arms of all the provinces in his archducal insignia ad robes.

However, the implications and results were clear; Spain had *de facto* ceded Dutch independence.

Significantly, negotiations had been conducted directly between Philip III and the Dutch.

This was the work of Oldenbarneveldt. He had shrewdly insisted upon the negotiations being conducted directly between the Dutch and the king. On at least two occasions during the process of the ceasefire ratification, he had made sure the ratification document was sent back for alterations to ensure that it was the king of Spain so undertaking, realising by the implications that this would afford the Dutch some form of nation status. In the preparations for the formal peace negotiations, Oldenbarneveldt insisted that the peace negotiations should be directly between the Dutch and the king of Spain. And Philip III had indeed participated at the negotiations through his personal representative rather than the negotiations being conducted between the Dutch and the Archduke alone. At first Philip III had refused, correctly stating that the sovereign's open and direct negotiation with rebels would afford the latter status. However, the crisis of Spanish finances and the Dutch naval victory off Gibralter had brought home the need of a truce. In January 1608, Philip III sent his personal representative de Mancidor to officially join the negotiations as part of the Spanish delegation and when he, de Mancidor, spoke, he spoke officially for the king.[4]

Indeed, the whole process had been one of Oldenbarneveldt's major achievements. The groundwork was done during the preliminaries in the ceasefire arrangements, where Oldenbarneveldt had been vigilant in the wording of the documents, holding discreet meetings with the Archduke's representatives, and working hard, patiently, and constantly explaining and redrafting. All the time he kept the Dutch opponents of any talks at bay, whilst being constantly helpful to the Archduke's representatives—all for gaining the benefit of Spanish full recognition of Dutch sovereignty and independence.

Maurits had remained watchful and wary. He had learned much from the negotiations and had ceased his opposition to the peace talks and Truce. He remained suspicious and mistrustful of Spain and envisaged the Truce as Spain's way of gaining time to recover and eventually restart hostilities with the object of regaining the northern provinces. Whilst some historians hold that Spain had abandoned the objective of total reconquest, one historian has held that the peace was only part of Spain's grand strategy to lull opponents—including the Dutch—into a sense of false security whilst they gained time to economically recover.[5] However, be that as it may, for the time being in 1609, it was a tremendous achievement and a diplomatic victory for the Dutch.

One historian, in a large and neoclassic work on the Dutch Revolt, is unequivocal about the Dutch achievement. Effusively he describes the Truce as:

> an event hitherto unknown in history. When before had a sovereign state acknowledged the independence of his rebellious subjects and signed a treaty with them as equals?[6]

Another historian states:

> After 40 years of bitter struggle the north Netherlands had at last won de *facto* independence and religious freedom,

whilst Spain

> had obtained nothing from the talks (except an end to hostilities in the Low Countries. Everything Philip III's negotiators were instructed to insist on had to be abandoned.[7]

Yet another historian states that the main result was:

> the enhancement of the Republic's international status. . . . Spain grudgingly acknowledged the Republic de *facto* as if it were a sovereign state.[8]

Another historian, sympathetic to the Spanish and Hapsburg side and giving an account from the viewpoint of Archduke Albert, states:

> Even without the formal recognition by the Hapsburg foes, the United Provinces had effectively been accepted as a member of the European community of states,[9]

Another historian points to the ambiguous wording acceptable to both sides, the result of which was the acknowledgement by Spain of the independence of the Dutch Republic.[10] A specialist work entirely on the Twelve Years' Truce, concentrating on several legal issues, repeats Morley's point that Spain had accepted the Dutch Republic as an equal Treaty partner and signatory. In doing so, the specialist work states:

> Spain took a significant step towards recognition of the Republic,

and the Treaty was:

> a crucial step in the birth of the Republic as a sovereign state.[11]

A Dutch historian, specializing in early modern Dutch history, states:

> Spain had not yet formally recognised the Republic as an independent state but its agreement to the truce made it appear to have done so. . . . The Dutch Republic had become a fact.[12]

However, a positive aspect for Spain is noted by another historian,[13] in considering the wider strategic view of Europe. He states that, with the Truce, over a period of the decade 1598–1609, Spain had successfully disengaged from 3 wars in Europe with France, with England, and with the Dutch Republic, and this was an achievement for Spanish diplomacy, which effectively broke the hostile Triple Alliance. (He does add the caveat that Philip III was still implacably hostile to the heretical Dutch and had to present the peace in the best possible light.)[14] This positive view is corroborated by another historian, a specialist in early modern diplomatic history. He points to the Spanish diplomatic service, which at this period, the late Sixteenth and early Seventeenth Centuries, was one of the most advanced and forward-looking organisations of the European powers, with highly skilled ambassadors in the key European capitals.[15] He further points out that during this very period when the Spanish economy was declining, her international trade was threatened, and her military strength was receding, her diplomacy was rectifying and steadying the overall decline:

> It was the chance for diplomacy to regain the initiative, and reassert the domination which arms had lost since the defeat of the Invincible Armada.[16]

The successful peacemaking by Spain and the dismantling of the hostile Triple Alliance reflected this skill of Spanish diplomacy.

As soon as the news of the Twelve Years' Truce spread, other powers' recognition of the Dutch Republic as an independent country followed. The same year as the Truce was signed, France and England officially designated the representatives of the Dutch Republic in their respective countries as ambassadors. The Dutch established diplomatic relations with the Ottoman Turks, following official communiques sent from the Sultan's court with an official invitation that the Dutch send a fully accredited resident ambassador to the Ottoman Empire. Full diplomatic relations were established in 1610 with the Republic of Venice. Between 1612 and 1618, the Dutch consular service became officially recognised and expanded. Dutch consuls were fully accredited and could officially act for Dutch merchants and seamen in Baltic ports and in other ports including Livorno, Cyprus, Genoa, and Zante.

The Twelve Years' Truce undoubtedly benefitted the Dutch Republic in terms of gaining independence and allowing further economic expansion. The gains far outweighed the potential adverse effects of not continuing the war, as well as allowing the loyal southern provinces, the Spanish Netherlands, to recover and reconstruct under the wise and farsighted rule of Albert and Isabella. The Truce was followed by significant developments and events within the Dutch Republic, to which we now turn in the next chapter.

Notes

1. Geyl, P *History of the Dutch Speaking Peoples 1555–1648* p 249. Parker in his *The Dutch Revolt* p 231 places the Dutch counterstroke as slowing down and "less fortunate" as early as after the capture of Groningen in 1594
2. Malan, D *Europe at War 1600–1650* p 34
3. van de Hoevel, L "Deductie en Declaratie ende beschvringe van den staat conditie en gelegendigheit de vrijheit Oisterwick" in *Bijdragen en Mededeelingen van der historisch Genootschap* reel 40 1919 pp 111–162
4. Maland, D *Europe at War 1600–1650* p 37
5. Allen, P *Philip III and the Pax Hispanica 1598–1621—The Failure of Grand Strategy*, in chapters 9 and 10 "Warrior Diplomacy" and "The Search for Advantage", gives a full and comprehensive account and chronicle of the complex negotiations and an equally full interpretation of how all this was part of the grand strategy of hoodwinking Spain's opponents until such time as Spain would recover and would be in a position to resume the offensive and regain her dominance
6. Motely, J *History of the Dutch Republic Vol 4* p 378
7. Parker, G *The Dutch Revolt* p 240. Parker, G *Europe in Crisis 1598–1648* p 135
8. Israel, J *The Dutch Republic—Its Rise, Greatness, and Fall 1477–1806* p 405
9. Duerloo, L *Dynasty and Piety—Archduke Albert and Hapsburg Political Culture in an Age of Religious Wars* p 214
10. Groeneveld, S *Het Twaalfjarig Bestand 1609–1621 De jongelens-jaren van de Republiek de Verenigde Nederlanden* pp 59–60

11. Lesaffer, R (ed) *The XII Year Truce* Introduction and pp 187–188
12. Prak, M *The Dutch Republic in the Seventeenth Century* p 24
13. Mattingly, G *Renaissance Diplomacy*, Part IV Early Modern Diplomacy
14. Wilson, PH *The XXX Years War* p 164
15. Zuniga and then de Guevara in Vienna, embassy of Spain to Austrian Hapsburgs; marquis de Bedmar, embassy of Spain to the Venetian Republic, Gondomar, embassy of Spain to the Court of St James, London England
16. Mattingly, G *Renaissance Diplomacy* pp 243–244

8 Internal Strife Within the Republic . . .

Maurits was a realist with regard to the situation at the turn of the Seventeenth Century, and he fully appreciated that the situation had changed since the 1570s. He had always been and was still devoted to the interests of his dynasty and his people, but his people were those of the United Provinces, the crucial word being "united".

The Cleves-Julich Crisis—A Foreign Affairs Portent

One year after the Twelve Years' Truce was signed, the Dutch were involved in the European powers' strategic deployments. The events known as the Cleves-Julich crisis of 1610 were a forerunner of the escalating conflict that became the Thirty Years' War. The territories formed part of the Westphalian Circle (an administrative region) of the Holy Roman Empire and were situated at the northern end of the so-called Spanish Road, near the south-eastern border of the Dutch Republic. They consisted of the Duchy of Cleves, the Duchy of Berg, the Duchy of Julich, and the smaller counties of Ravensburg and Ravenstein, a collective area of 1,200 kilometres. They were of mixed religions, both Catholic and Protestant. They had been the subject of a disputed inheritance by several claimants following the death of Duke John William. The strongest of these were the Protestant elector of Brandenburg and the Catholic duke of Pfalz-Neuberg. These two claimants formed an alliance, as the self-styled "Possessors" to fend off all other claimants. Adjudications and judgements from the Emperor were ambiguous and failed to impose any settlement. Other princes and nobles of the Empire became involved. These were aligned to both the Catholic League and the Protestant Union alliances, who saw opportunities in claim and counterclaim. The principal claimant, setting himself against the two Possessors, was the Archduke Leopold of the imperial royal family and a relative of the Holy Roman Emperor. The issue escalated into a disputed succession between Archduke Leopold and the Possessors.

With the escalation of the dispute, the situation became vulnerable to foreign intervention. France sent a small contingent of troops from

Metz, advancing down the Meuse. Maurits, watching carefully, deployed 14,000 infantry and 8,000 cavalry, moving them closer to Cleves. Philip III authorised Archduke Albert of the Spanish Netherlands to support the Archduke Leopold and engage in either event of French or Dutch troops starting hostilities. In The Hague, Oldenbarneveldt had no wish to violate the Truce with Spain and emphasised that any Dutch troop deployments were of a precautionary nature. Maurits was in discreet contact with Archduke Albert in Brussels, ensuring that a level of calm remained.

The Protestant Union of German princes mobilised 5,000 troops in support of the Possessors. The Archduke Leopold appealed to the German princes of the Catholic League, but its principal member, Maximilian of Bavaria, firmly made sure that the Catholic League did not officially become involved, although the Archduke Leopold did manage to raise a small *ad hoc* contingent of troops. Throughout May, troops of the Protestant League and those under Leopold manoeuvred and deployed, but by July the superior numbers of the troops supporting the Possessors, including those of Maurits and the French forces, ensured that Julich was wrested from Leopold. Leopold gave up, and the Possessors were left in joint possession of the territories. However, any final settlement was in abeyance. The Dutch left a small detachment in Julich and in another garrison nearby on the Wesel.

The events of the Cleves-Julich crisis were a forerunner[1] and highlighted the alignments and alliances of the future Thirty Years' War. Whilst Oldenbarneveldt ensured calm within the political dimension, Maurits had been alert to the military situation, which had yet again emphasised the strategic importance of the eastern frontier of the Dutch Republic. But internal convulsions were to completely preoccupy the Republic.

Theological Controversy Escalating into Political Conflict With Oldenbarneveldt

In the early years of the Twelve Years' Truce, an academic debate over theology escalated, and the issue eventually impacted and partially divided the Republic itself. In fact the origins predated the Twelve Years' Truce. The Union of Utrecht guaranteed religious toleration with the Republic, although the Dutch Reformed Church was the only religion that was practised publicly, though other religious faiths, including Catholicism, were generally tolerated. The Dutch Reformed Church, with its Calvinistic bedrock of faith, included no more than 10% of the population of the Republic,[2] but they were an intense, vocal, and strident section of society.

In the early 1600s, a professor of theology, Jacob Arminius, researched and reflected on Calvinist doctrine. As a result of his studies, he formulated a theory that amended Calvinism. His theory very respectfully remonstrated with parts of the doctrine. Calvinism, as laid down by its ice-cold fanatical founder Jean Calvin, held the doctrine of Predestination, whereby there are those individuals who would achieve salvation and those individuals who would not, and all was preordained by God. During his or her life, the individual could do nothing to alter or change this predestined fate. Jacob Arminius amended and softened this somewhat harsh doctrine by suggesting that whilst God remained omnipotent and all-powerful, there could be, perhaps, an offer or a possibility of salvation to the individual on certain conditions. To the faithful who could accept the offer and live by those conditions (of a blameless God-fearing life), there was a possibility of salvation; to those who did not, there was certain damnation. Arminius's theory made Calvinism less harsh and rigid and offered hope. However, the injection into Calvinism of any form whereby the individual could exercise free will and decision, however limited and however much he or she would be pursuing a possibility, was a complete anathema to devout Calvinists. Those adopting Arminius's theory became known as the Remonstrants.

Arminius and the Remonstrants were opposed by a fellow academic and purist Calvinist theologian, Francis Gomar. Gomar was an academic and a cleric who has been described by one eminent religious historian as an individual of inflexible mind and a veritable talent for setting theological decrees in their most repellent form.[3]

The controversy was an academic debate amongst university academics and theorists, but there were wider implications. Calvinism was practiced by only a small proportion of the population of the Republic. Nonetheless, the faith enjoyed a wide empathy with many in the Republic as this was the faith that had been one of the important drivers of the Revolt in the darkest hours of 1570. The debates had taken place at Leiden University, a highly charged symbol of the Revolt; the raising of the siege of Leiden by William of Orange and Admiral Boisot was a crucial stage in the survival of the Revolt. William offered the citizens of Leiden the nation's gratitude for their holding out, giving them the choice of freedom of taxation for a number of years or the founding and financing of a university. The citizens unanimously opted for a university. Now, a generation later, the bedrock faith of the Revolt was being questioned in an institution of learning that owed its existence to the survival of this Revolt.

A public debate took place between the two professors, followed by each side producing written manifestos, and by 1611 the whole issue had become public. Over the next 5 years, both sides produced written tracts and hundreds of pamphlets on the subject, widening public awareness of the dispute and escalating the controversy. The two sides, Remonstrants and Counter-Remonstrants, found supporters in the various political factions of the Republic. The Counter-Remonstrants were supported by those who viewed any altering or interfering with the national faith as akin to being pro-Spanish. Many of these were exiles from the southern provinces of the Netherlands with fears and bitter memories of Spanish

Catholic persecution. The Remonstrants had their supporters in those factions who were against Spain and who held that the Twelve Years' Truce was a mistake. These included the commercial interests in Holland and Zeeland who had profited by the naval war against Spanish trade.

By this time the academic Arminius, who had started the whole controversy, had fallen seriously ill. His place and role as the intellectual leader of the Remonstrants had been taken by Johannes Uyttenbogaert. Uyttenbogaert was an academic and also official court preacher to Maurits. When he had written his Remonstrant treatise in 1609, he pointedly dedicated it to the States of Holland. Oldenbarneveldt had initially refrained from entering the controversy, but eventually he chose his side, opting for the Remonstrants. This was due not to any fervent religious feeling but to his constant favouring of moderate ideology and his respect for the right to dissent. By the middle of the second decade of the Seventeenth Century, the controversy had imposed itself on and permeated the political affairs of the Republic to the highest level. In 1615 a Counter-Remonstrant group was formed within the States-General, consisting of delegates from Groningen, Friesland, and Zeeland. There was an attempt within the States-General to pass a law enacting a compromise doctrine, but this failed. Feelings on both sides were too intense for compromise, with certain States, including Holland and Utrecht, declaring for the Remonstrants.

By 1617, division and disorder reigned in many parts of the Republic. Within Holland, Remonstrant opinion and practice were in the majority. Uyttenbogaert was a member of The Hague council, and Counter-Remonstrant preachers were forbidden within The Hague. Those who wished to worship according to the Counter-Remonstrant doctrine went to discreet and obscure locations to hold services, and soon they formed their own church councils. This was part of a significant trend to a new church forming, a schismatic church from the national religion. In Gouda, a predominantly Remonstrant town, a group of Counter-Remonstrants in early 1617 presented a petition to the stadhouder of Holland—Maurits—requesting permission to form their own congregation and council, in effect to form their own separate church. They sent this petition directly to Maurits without obtaining permission or making reference to the Gouda town council, an omission that caused a furore. In Hoorn the town council was divided over the religious controversy, and all the Counter-Remonstrant preachers were expelled from the town. In Rotterdam an attempt by Counter-Remonstrants to set up a separate congregation and practice at its own church was forcefully repressed. There were disturbances in Brielle and in Amsterdam. In Amsterdam, Counter-Remonstrant mobs attacked Remonstrant services. The State of Utrecht was strongly Remonstrant, as was the city of Utrecht. Yet the nearby township of Vianen was Counter-Remonstrant, and Utrecht citizens who had been prevented or forbidden to hold Counter-Remonstrant services moved out every Sunday to Vianen where they worshipped their own services. A *de facto* schism in the national religion was occurring, and it was disrupting constitutional powers locally and nationally.

As we have seen, Oldenbarneveldt had opted for the Remonstrant side, and he and the States of Holland made efforts to control the situation. In doing so, he and the States of Holland would ensure that they maintained overall control of the Republic. Maurits had watched events with increasing unease, but he had delayed taking sides. However, in July 1617, he publicly aligned himself to one side, those of the Counter-Remonstrants. He stopped attending services in the royal chapel in the Binnenhof (the Parliament building where the delegates from the States met as the States-General). These services were officiated by Johannes Uyttenbogaert. Maurits then attended a Counter-Remonstrant service at a church in The Hague, the Kloosterkerk, a church that was located directly opposite The Hague residence of Oldenbarneveldt.[4]

Maurits himself was not fanatically religious and, like Oldenbarneveldt, had no real preference for either side in the theological dispute, but he had deep respect for Calvinism. Jan van Nassau's family, who had taken him in as a vulnerable young man, were devout orthodox Calvinists, and his cousin and close companion of arms, Willem Lodewijk, was a devout Calvinist. Just as Oldenbarneveldt in the early stages of the dispute had opted for the Remonstrants in a spirit of some form of religious toleration, so perhaps now Maurits was concerned that Counter-Remonstrants were in many locations being hounded and prevented from practicing the form of Calvinism they believed in. He was concerned at the increasingly divisive effect the dispute was having throughout the Republic. Also, he resented Oldenbarneveldt and the States of Holland's domination of the Republic, and he felt the necessity of drastically reducing Oldenbarneveldt's dominance, although perhaps not anticipating how drastic the outcome would be for Oldenbarneveldt, the devoted elder statesman who had given so much to the Republic. Furthermore, Maurits' position to engage in the struggle had strengthened in 1617, as he had in that year become Prince of Orange-Nassau.[5] He acted now as a prince in his own right, not merely as a Dutch office holder, albeit an important one.

Maurits, in finally siding with the Counter-Remonstrants and in doing so opposing Oldenbarneveldt, could not be sure of the final outcome. When he—finally—chose his side and attended a service in the Counter-Remonstrant church in The Hague in July 1617, he prudently and discreetly sent his father's widow Louise de Coligny and his half-brother Frederick Henry to stay with Johannes Uyttenbogaert, the principal theological leader of the Remonstrants.[6] In this way, the dynasty would be protected, irrespective of the final outcome of his taking on Oldenbarneveldt and the militant Remonstrants.

Maurits's choosing the opposing side caused uneasiness to Oldenbarneveldt. It may have all just been an academic dispute, but over a decade it had escalated into the political arena. Certain fundamental constitutional practices were being compromised, including the time-honoured tradition that the States of Holland controlled the direction of the Dutch Republic. The province of Holland indeed was mainly for the Remonstrants, the side chosen by Oldenbarneveldt, but it was by no means totally united. The significant towns of Amsterdam, Dordrecht, Enkhuizen, and Edam (two of them headquarters of Admiralties) were Counter-Remonstrant. It seemed to the States of Holland and Oldenbarneveldt that the situation was concerning and could slip out of control.

In August 1617, the States of Holland took a decisive—and irrevocable— step. Overruling the opposition from the delegates from Amsterdam, Dordrecht, and the other Counter-Remonstrant towns, under Olden- barneveldt's leadership they passed a resolution, known as the Sharp Resolution, empowering all towns in Holland to raise and pay for troops or *waargelders* to keep order, and all such troops were to swear sole alle- giance to the town raising them. Further, all regular Dutch Army troops paid for by the contribution of the States of Holland owed first allegiance to the States of Holland. Then Oldenbarneveldt took a further irrevoca- ble step. He sent two delegates to the province of Utrecht with instruc- tions to all army officers based within that province. The two delegates were officially from and empowered by the States of Holland, but the instructions were in writing and could be and were subsequently used in evidence. These instructions clearly stipulated that the army officers had the overriding and first allegiance and loyalty to the province that paid them (i.e. the province of Utrecht) and that loyalty and allegiance took precedence over that of any instructions or orders of the States-General and or the stadhouder (i.e. Maurits). When the instructions became known, the Counter-Remonstrants within the States of Utrecht and on the council of Utrecht protested, hastily made assurances to the officers and the rank and file of the army there that their pay was guaranteed, and made the whole issue of the instructions public.

It is one thing to recruit freelance troops; it is quite another to ensure the quality of the soldiering of the intake—and to ensure payment. In some towns the incoming *waargelders* came from other parts of the country and had little empathy for or understanding of the communities whom they were supposed to be serving. Some behaved like mercenaries, "req- uisitioning" food, supplies, and services and alienating the townsfolk. In other towns, arrangements for payment were flawed or delayed, causing mutual mistrust and further "requisitioning". To Maurits, steeped in gen- eralship and in the skills of leading professional soldiers, such situations must have been both repellant and spurs to his concern and anger at the treasonable outrage of subverting the loyalty of the regular troops and dividing the nation.

Maurits acted quickly. He was summoned to the States-General by del- egates from the States of Holland to give his advice and views. Maurits had little time for the avaricious merchants of Amsterdam, but he did realise their value as potential allies in opposing Oldenbarneveldt. He had little thought either way for both the Remonstrant and the Counter-Remonstrant sides. However, in his address to the States-General, he played upon his oath of loyalty to the States-General that he made upon assuming office in 1586. From this he quoted and referred to the passages whereby he and all the States or provinces bound themselves in unity and for the defence of the reformed religion. In this address, he played upon the sacrosanct nature of the unity of all provinces in contrast to the present disunion, which was exacerbated by Oldenbarneveldt and the States of Holland, and upon the need for the absolute defence of Calvinism as it was laid down then. It made a good impression on the States-General. No doubt they were also impressed by the serried ranks of disciplined troops of the national army that he commanded and was so obviously willing to deploy.

In July 1617 he marched with troops and occupied Utrecht and took control. The *waargelders* in the city were disbanded, allowing themselves to be disarmed quite passively. Prudently, Maurits guaranteed and saw to it that these *waargelders* were paid what was owed to them.[7] He then proceeded cautiously, gathering support. In October 1617 he travelled to Brielle, reformed its garrison, making sure of its loyalty to himself and to the Republic. He then quietly travelled to Nijmegen, and, exercising his powers as stadhouder of Gelderland, he formally dismissed and ousted the Remonstrant councillors and replaced them with Counter-Remonstrant individuals. Then he attended the States of Gelderland, laid out the reasons for his action, and persuaded the States to support a forthcoming resolution in the States-General calling for the disbandment of the *waargelders*. Then he attended the States of Overijssel, gave a similar address, and persuaded them also to support the forthcoming States-General resolution. Significantly, his speeches to both the States asserted that, whilst much sovereignty did indeed lie in the power of the individual provinces, the individual province did not have total sovereignty.[8]

In raising forces answerable only to the individual province, Oldenbarneveldt had been genuine in his attempt to quell increasing public disorders. He had taken the side of and decided for the Remonstrants only from a personally tolerant disposition, not from any deep-seated religious convictions. In coming down on one side and making this decision, he hoped that the matter would be ended. Holland's troops would settle the disorders. However, what to Oldenbarneveldt was a solution was to Maurits a retrograde step directly against his and Willem Lodewijk's creation, a national army, and as such this step was the cause of further divisions among the provinces. In his genuine attempt to restore tranquility, Oldenbarneveldt was to suffer the dire consequences of his action.

For Maurits, the Resolution of the States of Holland was a point of no return. The States of Holland could claim to base the Resolution upon a major constitutional principle of the Republic, that is, the inviolability of the authority of the States or provinces, and Oldenbarneveldt himself felt he was defending the system to which his entire life had been devoted.[9] However, the very Resolution that Oldenbarneveldt supported for defending his life's work was itself an attack on the life's work of Maurits. The resolution authorizing *waargelders* answerable to only the towns was, at best, the hiring of local mercenaries. This and the part regarding the allegiance of Dutch regular forces paid for by the States of Holland touched upon the Dutch Army. This was—to date—the life's work of Maurits and Willem Lodewijk, which he and Willem Lodewijk (and also Oldenbarneveldt himself) had forged and created into a national armed force, deployable throughout the Republic and existing for the protection of the whole Republic. The troops were answerable to and owed allegiance to him alone as stadhouder and commander in chief. The Sharp Resolution was totally contumacious. In the religious dispute, Maurits had chosen one side over the other. Now in the political dimension, he had to destroy the other side.

Accordingly, in August 1618, Maurits directed, through the States-General, an official decree that all *waargelder* units were to be disbanded. During the debates on this within the States-General, the delegates from the States of Utrecht and the States of Holland vigorously opposed, arguing that this was a violation of the sovereignty of the individual provinces. This argument was refuted and rejected by the other provinces who cited the terms of the treaty inaugurating the Union of Utrecht, which laid down that defence and the army, navy, and military command were all subject to the authority of the States-General and the stadhouder(s). Holland and Utrecht were outvoted by the other provinces. The *waargelders* were to be disbanded. They were disbanded, and no town or municipality demurred or refused to comply.

Oldenbarneveldt, sincere and confused, was still anxious to control the situation. However, on 19 August 1618, in The Hague, whilst *en route* to a scheduled meeting at the States of Holland, two individuals approached him with a summons to attend an urgent meeting with Prince Maurits. Lured away, he went to the urgent meeting where he was detained by government officials and placed under arrest.[10] The same day in Utrecht, the leader of the Remonstrant councillors, Gille van de Ledenburg, was also detained and placed under house arrest. There was no reaction in Utrecht, but in The Hague the States of Holland vigorously protested against this violation of their principal office holder. Their protests were ignored. The day before the arrest of Oldenbarneveldt, the States-General had passed a secret resolution giving Maurits and certain appointed commissioners authority to investigate the role and activities of the provinces of Holland and Utrecht relating to the disturbances over the entire religious controversy, along with the authority to take any necessary action in the interests of the security of the Republic.

Maurits meanwhile continued to enforce his authority and to eradicate political Remonstrantism. In October 1618 he sent troops into Leiden and purged the town council. 22 of the regents were dismissed and replaced with individuals who were deemed more suitable. In doing so Maurits had the loud support of the general population of Leiden. Then troops marched into Haarlem, whose town council was purged with 15 regents dismissed and replaced. Four days later, the Rotterdam town council underwent a similar purge with 15 of the regents being dismissed and replaced. In 1619, there was serious rioting in Alkmaar and Hoorn. In March 1619 Maurits had to send regular troops into those towns to quell the riots and purge the town militias, and regular troops were stationed there for some months afterwards.

Oldenbarneveldt was being held and questioned. He was an elderly statesman, experienced, dedicated, well meaning, and his actions were out of genuine concern for the well-being of the Republic. But he was not benign towards his questioners. His answers were lacking in conciliation and at times abrasive, and to the questioners he appeared arrogant. The indictment was treason, and after a short trial and lengthy deliberations by the judges in May 1619 he was found guilty and, to his astonishment, sentenced to death. Maurice did not wish the ultimate sentence and, upon receiving a letter from Oldenbarneveldt in his death cell, assumed that it was a plea for clemency which he would willingly grant. However, Oldenbarneveldt had written only a lengthy vindication of his conduct, and there was no request or plea. The following day, the elderly statesman was executed near the parliament building in The Hague.

It was tragic end for such a dedicated statesman. However, unlike the period of the 1580s and 1590s when the fortunes of the Revolt were fluctuating, Oldenbarneveldt in the peacetime period of the Twelve Years' Truce was not indispensable.[11] Oldenbarneveldt's successful struggle with Leicester owed much to his having the support of a unified States of Holland as well as the support of Maurits and Willem Lodewijk. However, in the religious controversy and in the struggle against Maurits, significant parts of the province of Holland were ranged against him. Also, the support of the province of Holland for Oldenbarneveldt during his struggle with Leicester was partly due to Leicester's attempts at imposing a trade embargo by the Dutch Republic against Spain and the loyal provinces of the Spanish Netherlands; yet during the Twelve Years' Truce period, Oldenbarneveldt had imposed a similar trade embargo.

The Arminian religious disputes had been serious and divisive, but contrary to contemporary fears amongst respectable citizens, it did not lead to civil war, and it did not threaten the Republic's survival. Nor did the Sharp Resolution and the *waargelder* crisis of 1617–1618 so threaten, although Oldenbarneveldt's stance constituted a serious danger to Maurits. Slow and cautious and apparently reluctant to act as Maurits had been, the events of 1617–1618 with the implications of the Sharp

Resolution of the States of Holland necessitated his decisive action to break the power of the States of Holland and Oldenbarneveldt. The crisis and its potential to cause divided loyalties in some parts of the Dutch armed forces had been serious, but thanks to Maurits's decisive actions, it was prevented from becoming existential in terms of the survival of the Republic. Economic growth and development continued. Maurits had successfully quelled the controversy, although towards the end of his rule he had to allocate troops to Amsterdam—units of the army he could ill afford to divert from the defence of the country—when Remonstrant town councillors gained power during disturbances caused by economic conditions. Also during the beginning of the rule of Maurits's successor, Frederick Henry, an outbreak of political Arminianism occurred in several areas, including Rotterdam, and it took all his skill and adroitness to deal with and defuse the situation.[12] The whole Arminian crisis did adversely impact the Republic particularly in one important aspect. During the period 1617–1619, it distracted Maurits, the government, and the Republic from giving due attention to foreign affairs.

The crisis within the Holy Roman Empire and the Bohemian Revolt occurred, resulting in the mobilisation of the forces of the Catholic League in Germany and the drawing together in alliance of the Spanish and the Austrian Hapsburgs for armed intervention in Bohemia, and in turn Protestant Europe looked to the Dutch Republic for support. All this was to have repercussions threatening the eastern frontier of the Republic. Perhaps in more tranquil domestic circumstances and had Oldenbarneveldt been in power, favourable diplomatic manoeuvres would have been carried out, ensuring that the Republic was in a more favourable strategic position. But Oldenbarneveldt was gone, Maurits the stadhouder and Prince of Nassau was in control, and he had just emerged from an internal power struggle caused by a divisive religious issue that had festered in the Republic for over a decade. Now the Republic faced threats abroad. However, this is to anticipate. In the following chapter, let us remain with the internal affairs of the Republic under Maurits and consider the important area of economic development.

Notes

1. Wilson, PH in *The XXX Years War* denies that the crisis was in any way a "dress rehearsal" for the XXX Years War, which started less than a decade later but does pinpoint the military lessons learned—which the main protagonists in the future struggle did not heed
2. Prak, M *The Dutch Republic in the Seventeenth Century* p 28
3. Chadwick, O *The Reformation* p 220
4. van Sande, J *De waekende leeuw der Nederlanden-Historie vertoonende 't begin oorlogen ende beroeten tot de vrede 1648*
5. The son of William of Orange inherited his father's title after William was assassinated in 1584. The son was for a time imprisoned in Spain, then released and was brought to Brussels. He became part of the Court of the

Archduke Albert, though closely watched. He died in 1618, and Maurits of Nassau became Prince of Orange-Nassau, a prince of the house of Orange. According to a distinguished historian of the Dutch Revolt, Professor Judith Pollman, Maurits delayed intervening in the Remonstrant versus Counter-Remonstrant disturbances, but his becoming a prince strengthened his position significantly, and his intervention—cautious at first—was all the more forceful and decisive

6. Prak, M *The Dutch Republic in the Seventeenth Century* p 34
7. van Vervou, F *Enige Aantikenningen van t'gepasseerde in der vergadering van Staten-General anno 1616 1617,1618,1619,1629* Leeuwarden 1874
8. Before 1617—and the Sharp Resolution—States of the provinces other than Holland had made requests to Maurits, as prince and as stadhouder, to intervene and restore order by force if necessary. Maurits declined such requests, pointing out that it was up to the theologians to resolve the issue and settle differences
9. Geyl, P in his *History of the Dutch Speaking Peoples 1555–1648* p 347 gives a vigorous defence of Oldenbarneveldt's stance as one of high principles and absolute sincerity. Elliott, JH in his wide sweeping *Europe Divided 1558–1598* p 396 cites Oldenbarneveldt, together with Walsingham, Cligny, and du Plessis-Mornay, as one-of-a-kind leaders in the society of that period who were prepared to dedicate their lives to a cause and who were "distinguished by a high seriousness of purpose and integrity"
10. Jan Franchen, cited in de Stipriaan, R (ed) *Oog getuigen van de Gouden Eeeuw*
11. Th historian van Deursen, A in his *Maurits van Nassau* argues that Maurits without the help and working relationship of Oldenbarneveldt was much diminished in his leadership of the Republic and in terms of his achievements
12. Israel, J *The Dutch Republic—Its Rise, Greatness, and Fall 1477–1806* pp 481, 489–491

9 . . . But the Economy Expands

Whilst Maurits can in no way lay claim to being a principal generator of the soaring development of the Dutch economy, nonetheless during his tenure of office(s) many important developments occurred.[1] One eminent Dutch historian, a specialist of the Seventeenth Century, directly links a principal cause of the economic rise of the Dutch Republic to the Dutch Republic being a nation state.[2] Therefore Maurits, by his ensuring the very survival of the Dutch Republic as a nation state, created the conditions whereby the meteoric economic rise throughout the Seventeenth Century could occur.

During Maurits's reign, the country made significant economic progress indeed, but the conflict did take its toll. The west of the country had proven resilient, Leiden's population having tripled between the early 1580s and the first decade of the Seventeenth Century, and the increase was due to skilled emigres from the Spanish Netherlands. This influx of skilled workers was to enhance the textile and manufacturing centres in the town; one historian has estimated that, due to this influx of skilled workers, Leiden became the largest cloth-making city in the world.[3] Amsterdam's population grew to over 70,000 by 1610, from 30,000 in the early 1580s. Holland and Zeeland continued to expand in productive trade. The east of the country did not recover so easily, however. The region around Lochem and Grol (Groenlo) had suffered from Spinola's early 1600s offensive, and the communities had been plagued by both sides requisitioning and imposing *ad hoc* taxes. By 1610, Deventer's population had halved, and the province of Twente had been reduced by a quarter.

Agriculture in parts of the Republic became commercialised. The province of Holland led the way in this, developing growing and production methods and marketing, with the social force behind this being the independent farmer who became a veritable independent capitalist farmer.[4] This commercialisation of agriculture was to some extent shared by Zeeland, which had long enjoyed being able to exploit its unique rich clay soil, although it became clearer during the Seventeenth Century that Zeeland, whilst having a degree of efficient commercialising agriculture, could not compete with Holland and so still retained much of its dependence on shipping and seaborne trade.[5]In both provinces, the dominant force was the freeholding independent farmer, not the landlord or the nobility. Later in the century, a contemporary writer was to observe of Dutch farmers:

> [I]t is not out of the way to meet a peasant here worth 100,000 livres or more.[6]

Agriculture made progress in differing ways in the western and eastern parts of the country. Commercial farming in the east of the country was less advanced due to the sandy soils. The province of Drenthe had a very small urban population, its two largest towns being Meppel with just over 1,100 inhabitants and Coevorden with 800 inhabitants (and the latter was this size only because it was garrison town). Consequently, there was little local urban demand and markets for farm produce. In Drenthe, provincial agriculture was self-supporting with the farmers eating most of what they grew and produced. However, cow raising in Drenthe flourished, and its produce was exported to Holland and abroad. Also, the type of wool from Drenthe-raised sheep was ideal for exporting to Leiden in Holland, where textile workers produced blankets. Dye plants were cultivated, the techniques having been introduced by Flemish refugees fleeing Parma's reconquest of the southern provinces in the 1580s. By 1600 they were so successful that woollens from England were imported undyed, to be dyed and processed by the Dutch, earning considerable revenue as dying and processing wool was twice as expensive as producing the cloth itself.[7] The Dutch were so successful that in 1601, James I of England prohibited any further export of undyed woollen cloth, insisting that the process be completed in England. It proved to be a failure as the Dutch were far more skilled and quicker in this activity, and English wool production continued to rely on Dutch dyeing. In the Veluwe area, tobacco was successfully cultivated and exported to Amsterdam, where dealers blended with tobacco imported from the Americas, producing a superior blend much in demand. To cultivate the tobacco, the Veluwe farmers imported sheep dung from Friesland, Groningen, and Holland and pigeon dung from Zeeland. Thus Dutch agriculture advanced in differing ways east and west in the country, but far from being an adverse division, provinces in both areas were to some extent linked in supplying and supporting each other's activities.

The increase in agricultural efficiency, the Dutch competitive free trade in textiles, and the rapid development of Dutch financial services paradoxically benefited the Spanish Netherlands to the south. The southern regions lost to the north skilled craftsmen, workers and individuals skilled in trade and finance. But they developed and financed industrial production techniques in textiles and other commodities, and developed mining. They eventually outstripped their northern neighbours in industrial production.[8]

In finance there were also significant developments in the early Seventeenth Century. In the late Sixteenth Century, the Amsterdam Bourse was established, and in 1592, the Bourse was expanded. In 1598, a Chamber of Insurance was established in Amsterdam. Insurance dated back to the mediaeval era and beyond. In the Thirteenth Century, Genoese financiers were drawing up marine insurance contracts, as part of their innovative competitiveness in their intense commercial struggle with the rival maritime power, the Republic of Venice.[9] However, Amsterdam and the Dutch implemented insurance on a larger and more efficient scale. Since 1585, Amsterdam was publishing weekly commodity prices, the first financial centre to operate a commodity price index. In 1614 a lending bank, a *huis van leenen*, was opened in Amsterdam, the Amsterdam Lending Bank. Its ethos was a continuation of the mediaeval lending banks, or *pieta*, that had spread over Italy in the Fifteenth Century. These did not lend start-up capital or give loans to small businesses. Much of their capital financing came from charitable donations, and their objective of such *pieta* was to enable poor people to take out small loans—sometimes 2 sometimes 3 ducats—at manageably low interest rates, enabling them to survive immediate extremes of poverty and at times starvation. At the time, the only other way of obtaining loans would have been through professional loan advancers, usurers, whose massive rates of interest bordered on loansharking. The Amsterdam Lending Bank was not financed by charity but issued interest-bearing bonds to investors; however, its principal aim was to facilitate loans to poorer individuals and also to provide some small amounts of capital to small businesses. Its careful management of issuing and handling loans made it a success; within two years, it had raised its capital to 1,200,000 florins. Its success was noted and was emulated by other countries. The Swedish National Bank opened a department devoted to small loans for the poor and small businesses, and some Swiss towns set up similar banks.

International exchange and credit transfer were advanced. In 1609, the *wisselbank*, or exchange bank—the Bank of Amsterdam—was founded. This type of bank with its function of money changing had its origins in the mediaeval era, and indeed the activities of the new Amsterdam bank were similar to those of the Venetian bank, Banco della Piazza de Rialto, which itself was partially modelled upon banks, or *taula*, which had been operating in Aragon as early as 1401.[10] Whilst it may have owed some of its origins to mediaeval times, the Amsterdam bank nonetheless was important for the smooth functioning of the modern Dutch money and capital markets. Large gold and silver coins, provided they were the correct weight, were accepted, and other coins were assessed according to their actual bullion content. The bank did not issue notes. Rather its remit was that of the central authority of receiving monetary deposits, transferring moneys, and acting as a clearing bank, based on current accounts, which were held in Dutch guilders. All bills of exchange with a value of over 600 guilders had to be paid through the bank, and all the principal merchants and trades held a current account. In volume, the Bank of Amsterdam was the biggest in Europe, and by the end of Maurits's reign, its number of accounts was greater than those combined held by the other two principal banks in Europe, the Nuremburg Bank and the Hamburg Bank. By the end of the Seventeenth Century, deposits had risen to 16 million florins.[11]

Other towns emulated Amsterdam. In 1616 a *wisselbank* was established in Middelburg in Zeeland and in 1621 in Delft. The latter lasted until 1635, when the investors moved to Rotterdam, which set up its own *wisselbank*. Within 5 years, the Rotterdam bank was cooperating with its Amsterdam counterpart in allowing bills of exchange drawn on Amsterdam to be cashed in Rotterdam.

The Dutch credit transfer and exchange system was able to function and expand because it was reliable. Significantly, 50% of the first deposits received were from individuals whose origin was in the southern provinces that had remained loyal to Spain. None of the depositors of the Bank of Amsterdam were permitted to be overdrawn, on penalty of severe fines. Also, the system was backed and firmly supported by the availability of cash funds. The province of Holland always had a favourable balance of payments and could supply funds if extreme circumstances required. However, there was in the early and mid-Seventeenth Century a constant inflow of large amounts of gold and silver bullion (much of the latter being re-exported to the southern provinces, to the profit of Dutch shipping) by currency traders and merchants in the Dutch overseas possessions, for whom the Amsterdam rates of exchange were favourable. This accumulation of ready capital was a sound basis for Dutch investors and lenders. The extent of this success was apparent in the later era when a contemporary writer observed:

> If ten or twelve Businessmen of Amsterdam first meet for a banking operation they can in a moment send circulating throughout Europe over two hundred million florins in paper money. There is no sovereign who could do as much.[12]

The same writer in a previous volume named the Dutch Republic as:

> the cashier of Europe.[13]

One of the mainstay economic strengths of the Dutch Republic was its maritime trade. An early Seventeenth-Century account of the period in the Netherlands stated simply:

> Holland and Zeeland are very rich in shipping.[14]

In the Seventeenth Century the Dutch pioneered the development whereby shipbuilding became an autonomous industry in its own right. Amsterdam was a market for building new ships, taking orders from Dutch and international merchants alike. The shipbuilding ethos has been summarised by an eminent economic historian as:

> modern dimensions inclining strongly toward standardised, repetative methods.[15]

By 1650 Dutch shipbuilding was between 40% and 50% cheaper than that carried out in England.[16]

It was also to become a flourishing market for the resale of second-hand vessels.[17]The mainstay of shipping was the Baltic. Since the Fifteenth Century, the Dutch had intruded into and then taken over from the Hanseatic League the herring fishing monopoly in the Baltic. They were facilitated in this by the use of a new type of fishing boat. This was a large fishing vessel with several decks, each containing a separate process, i.e. salters and coppers; by the time this equivalent of the factory ship reached port, the fish had been processed and barreled and were ready for export. By operating on the axis of the Baltic trade to the industries of Flanders, France, and the Empire, the Dutch were able to diversify and gain flourishing revenues in carrying and trading in naval stores, grain, and wood for shipbuilding. By the end of the 1560s, Amsterdam had replaced Antwerp as the principal grain distribution centre in northern Europe. By the same decade, the Dutch had cornered 60% of all trade in the Baltic.[18] In 1597, over 1,900 Dutch ships had entered the Baltic, trading and ferrying cargoes.[19]The entrepôt trade in commodities was greatly facilitated firstly by the Dutch ports, particularly Amsterdam's ability to turn commodities around and re-export them and secondly by the availability of large and numerous warehouses and storing facilities in Amsterdam.

The VOC

The commercial way to the Far East had been paved by several individual voyages of exploration. The actions of Cornelis Houtman were particularly noteworthy. Houtman in 1592 disguised himself and voyaged on board a Portuguese trading ship to the East Indies. When he arrived, his true identity—and nationality—were discovered, and the Portuguese authorities had him jailed. The merchants of Rotterdam combined and paid his ransom, and he was released. On his return to Rotterdam, the merchants equipped and furnished him with 4 ships in which he sailed from Rotterdam in 1595 to Bantam in the East Indies. He managed to return to Amsterdam with a cargo on April 1597. The profits were small, but the potential—and his enterprising bravery—were fully recognised. After that, Dutch East India companies engaged in a competitive free-for-all.

By the turn of the Seventeenth Century, several successful companies were striking out and trading in the Far East. The Amsterdam-based company van Verre had been founded in 1594, and its small fleet of 4 ships were armed with over 100 cannons supplied by the States of Holland. After some exploratory ventures in overseas trading to the East Indies, the company expanded, bringing the number of directors up to 18 and its capital raised to over 768,000 guilders in 1598. By 1599 its small fleet had returned from the Far East with full cargoes of expensive and high-demand commodities. The company made a 400% profit from this voyage. Also by this time, two companies with the objective of trading in the Far East, each with its own fleet, had been formed in Zeeland

With the differing companies seeking to trade in the East Indies, fierce competitive efforts developed among them. In a 4-year period 1598–1602, no less than 65 Dutch ships sailed in 14 different fleets. Mergers leading to a single corporate entity seemed the logical answer. Joining several different business companies into one was not insurmountable, and it was aided by the federal ethos and constitution of the Republic. This had facilitated the rise of the joint stock companies, which were encouraged, supported—and taxed by the state. They were federative in structure with differing divisions, or chambers, each keeping its own capital and carrying out its own business operations and enterprises but overall operating within the general guidelines and policy laid down by the central board of directors.

These companies were not entirely new. In the Sixteenth Century, the English Muscovy Company was established under similar terms, and other Mediterranean-based ventures that chartered shipping and cargoes were of a similar structural and financial configuration. One economic historian argues that joint stock companies can be dated back to earlier centuries.[20]

As early as 1598, the States-General suggested a form of amalgamation of some of the companies and a general increase of cooperation among them all. Oldenbarneveldt liaised and started negotiations with some of the companies to progress the amalgamations, but these were hampered by inter-provincial jealousy. During the Revolt, Holland and Zeeland had proven solid in support of each other in the struggle for and objective of independence. However, in matters of overseas trade, Zeeland was jealous of Holland's strong economic position and was wary of joining any company based in or any proposed any enterprise initiated by Holland. Negotiations were further complicated by the directors of the various Amsterdam companies involved in the mergers. They realised that their collective potential contributions to the capital of the new company would be more than half the total, therefore they wished to have more than half the seats on the new board of directors. Oldenbarneveldt pushed on in his negotiations, and at a crucial stage Maurits intervened and used his authority to push along the progress of the mergers. Both he and Oldenbarneveldt were spurred on by the recent establishment of an East India Company in England.[21]

The companies came together in a series of mergers. One of the provincial overseas companies, the van Verre Company, merged with two other companies in Amsterdam in 1598. Then two years later, these 3 merged companies united with the Brabant Company, also based in Amsterdam. One of the principal directors of the Brabant Company, Isaac le Maire, was originally a merchant in Antwerp in the late Sixteenth Century. When Parma's forces took the city in 1585, le Maire and his family availed themselves of Parma's offer of safe emigration within two years and moved to Amsterdam where he re-established his trading and became a director of the Brabant Company. The new company formed by the foursome merger of the Brabant Company, the former van Verre Company and its two new partner companies became the Verenigde Compagnie of Amsterdam.

Meanwhile, developments had occurred in Zeeland. Another post-1585 émigré from Antwerp, Moucheron, had established in Middelburg the Veere Company. In November 1600 the Veere Compagnie, after troubled negotiations, merged with another Middelburg trading company, Compagnie van Tenhaef, to form the Verenigde Zeeuwse Compagnie. However, Moucheron had opposed the merger and broke away, and with his assets he formed in 1601 the Compagnie de Moucheron. In the following year, the Verenigde Compagnie of Amsterdam unified with the Verenigde Zeeuwse Compagnie, together with other companies in Rotterdam and West Friesland. Eventually Moucheron and his Compagnie de Moucheron joined this "merger of mergers". By late 1602 the mergers were all completed, and Oldenbarneveldt's tireless efforts and facilitation and Maurits's stern urging and support had culminated in the Verenigde Ost-Indie Compagnie, the VOC.

In keeping with the nature of joint stock companies and the differing interests of the companies that had merged, the new VOC was a state-supported company but nonetheless a federate organisation divided into chambers.

The States-General granted the charter to the VOC. This gave the company a monopoly of all Dutch trade, exploration, and navigation within the large geographical area from east of the Cape of Good Hope to west of the Magellan Straits. Thus it was officially endowed and supported by the Republic through the States-General. However, it was given wide powers and scope of operations. The federal governing body, the board of directors, had the power to negotiate and conclude treaties of peace, to make treaties of alliances, and to build any fortresses, garrisons, and strongpoints it deemed necessary. The company carried out its own recruitment of military and civilian personnel including naval personnel. All recruits took an oath of loyalty to the States-General and to the VOC, emphasizing the dual nature of the VOC. The VOC set out and imposed a code of conduct and discipline for the VOC ships, and the captains and commanders enforced these. Discipline was enforced, but only offences of mutiny and murder carried the death penalty. Generally, floggings were avoided. Instead of these violent punishments, a wide range of fixed fines was imposed for lesser offences. This retrieved some pay expenses and ensured that valuable seamen were not damaged.

The company was subdivided into regional boards, or *kamers* (chambers). These were situated in the same locations and often in the same buildings or offices where the main merged companies were, in the towns of Amsterdam, Middelburg, Rotterdam, Deflt, Hoorn, and Enkhuizen. It was no accident that 5 of these were at the same location of the headquarters of the boards of the 5 Admiralties of the Dutch navy. Despite the bullish manoeuvres and posturings of the Amsterdam directors of the merged companies, the central board of directors of the VOC had fewer than half its members from the Amsterdam chamber. Amsterdam had 8 directors on the central board, the Zeeland (Middelburg) chamber 4, 1 from the Hoorn chamber, and 1 each from the Enkuizen chamber, the Rotterdam chamber, and Delft. The final director was delegated from each of the smaller chambers in turn. There were 17 directors in total, the body becoming famously known as the *Heeren XVII*.

From the start after its formation, the VOC was heavily armed, supported, and sponsored by the state and had as its avowed objective to establish itself in the dominant trading position in the Far East. However, in the early years, it was extremely reluctant to acquire or take possession of territories. Politicians and merchants alike, particularly those of or linked to the Amsterdam chamber, analysed the decline of Portuguese power. They concluded that the cause of this decline was that Portugal had wasted time, energy, money, and resources in acquiring territories. (Indeed the part of the charter of the VOC that authorised the company to make treaties and alliances had startled some shareholders of the new company into hastily selling their shares[22] as they were fearful that trade would be jeopardised by war and conquest.) The VOC according to their counsel, should strictly confine itself to trade and eschew regional politics and territorial atavism.[23] This became in the early years of the VOC the official policy of the *Heeren XVII*. Often this policy was ignored by the VOC agents *in situ*. Seven years later, one of the most successful of the VOC colonizers, Jan van Peiterzoon Coen who was to bring Java under VOC control, advised the *Heeren XVII*:

> Your Honours should know by experience that trade in Asia must be driven and maintained under the protection and favour of Your Honour's own weapons. [W]e cannot carry on trade without war and war without trade.[24]

Many of the territories across the known globe had been taken as a result of the Voyages of Discovery of the Fourteenth and Fifteenth Centuries.

So active were the Spanish and Portuguese explorers in finding and laying claim to territories that the Pope encouraged such loyal Catholic countries in their activities and in spreading the faith. In 1494, he mediated between the two Catholic powers in the conflicting claims. By the Treaty of Tordesillas in that year, an arbitrary imaginary north-south line was drawn down the Atlantic, and any territories discovered west of that line were to be under Spanish sovereignty and any territories discovered east of that line were to be under the sovereignty of Portugal. The papal cartographers, using rough-and-ready mapping methods, went slightly askew, and the north-south line dissected part of South America, designating modern Brazil as Portuguese. Another "exception" occurred, this time to the benefit of Spain when after Ferdinand Magellan's epic voyage from west to east, the Philippines in the Far East were claimed for Spain. However, overall the east-west global demarcation line laid down by Tordesillas held. The Treaty was sanctified by 4 papal bulls. Later popes reaffirmed the Treaty with further papal bulls.[25]

Whilst the traditional enemy of the Dutch was Spain, for the most part the main trading threat to and rivalry with the VOC was that of Portugal and her Far Eastern territories. The state-sponsored heavy arming of the VOC was initially for purely defensive purposes against the Portuguese, should they to attempt to prevent or disrupt trade. However, political alliances were soon made and force soon used. As early as 1607, instructions from Admiral Verhoeff, commander of VOC ships in the Moluccas, laid down:

> [T]he islands of Banda and the Moluccse form the principal target we aim at. We can give you no more positive orders than to draw your special attention to the islands where cloves, nutmegs and maces grow; and we instruct you to strive after winning these islands for the company, either by treaty or by force.[26]

Portugal bitterly complained that it was because they were part of the union of two crowns with Spain (since 1580) that their colonies and trade were being targeted by the Dutch in order to damage Spain.[27] This was not totally true, the VOC was orientated by its very charter towards the Far East, where the major trading presence was Portuguese, so inevitably there would be clashes and conflict. However, attacking the weaker country within the union of the two crowns would be damaging to the stronger power. Spain, the direct enemy of the Dutch, was certainly an incentive for Maurits and the Dutch state to give the VOC full support. In fact, the VOC attempts at harming Spanish interests in the region, the expeditions to the Philippines in 1610 and in1617, ended in failure.

However, their success in trade rivalry and acquiring by force Portuguese possessions was substantial. As early as 1600, they established themselves in Japan, and by 1609 a VOC was set up and operating in Hirado. The Portuguese traders and representatives repeatedly appealed to the Japanese authorities, even approaching as high as the emperor to expel the Dutch before the interlopers could gain a foothold, but in vain.[28] For the Dutch, Japanese trading was eventually to be valuable. Even when a civil war in Japan in 1613 interrupted trade, Dutch traders still managed to obtain copper and gold.[29] The Dutch finally gained an exclusive source of silver bullion, making them less dependent than the Spanish and English on the South American flow. Also, the Japanese tended to regard the Dutch favourably due to their maritime skills and shipbuilding and also due to the Dutch ethos of religious tolerance, contrasting favourably with the aggressive Catholic missionary efforts from Portugal and Spain in the mid- and late Sixteenth Century.

Farther south, in 1605 the Dutch took Ambona and the Moluccas islands in the Indonesian archipelago. Under the energetic Governor Steve van der Hagen, these and the island of Haroeke swore allegiance to both the stadhouder and to the States-General.[30] A decade later, they were engaging with naval forces and repelling incursions by foreign competitors in the Malacca area.[31] In 1619, Jan Pieterzoon Coen led a VOC force and seized the small port of Jakarta on the island of Java (ignoring the orders issued by the *Heeren XVII* stressing the absolute need for negotiation and peaceful policies towards the local rulers). This port, small though it was, was strategically vital as it lay at a point where trade routes leading to the Straits of Malacca where the trade winds converged. He followed this up by laying claim and backing up the claim with forces to the areas of Java, Cheribon on the east, and Bantam to the west. This included a new port that was to become Batavia and was to expand in population from 7,000 in 1624 to 70,000 by 1700[32] and that was to become the dominant European naval and commercial base in Asia. Then Coen advanced from Java to islands to the north and on to the territory stretching to the Indian Ocean to the south. Coen, in his two terms of office as VOC governor, laid the foundations by which, by the mid-1700s, the whole of Java was under VOC control with the local sultanates as client states. His forward-looking policy, although opposed by the *Heeren XVII* and some of the chambers of the VOC, later formed the basis of policy that was to result, by the 1640s, in gaining and holding territories in Ceylon and in Pernambuco in north-eastern Brazil.

The VOC was to expand. At its height in the following century, it was to have trading establishments, bases, and possessions on the tip of South Africa, on the Indian coast, in Ceylon, in China, in Formosa, and throughout the Indonesian archipelago. It gave to the Dutch Republic a flourishing trade and re-export revenues in spices, textiles, tea and coffee, tobacco, and silver bullion from Japan. Historians have focused, quite rightly, on the decline of the VOC in the Eighteenth Century, and its overall contribution to the economy has been questioned.[33] Also, the importance of the Dutch seagoing carrying trade to and from the Baltic should not be underestimated or overshadowed by the achievements of the VOC. However, the VOC gave employment to thousands and indirectly maintained the 30,000 sailors who manned the Dutch merchant fleet operating globally that drove the Dutch re-export trade of tea, coffee, tobacco, spices, and textiles. In doing so, the VOC, founded in the stadhoudership of, and partly as a result of pressure by, Maurits, significantly contributed to the general welfare of the Dutch Republic in the Seventeenth Century.[34]

The WIC

Some years after the foundation of the VOC, moves were being made to establish a state-backed company for Dutch trade and expansion westwards, i.e. against the Spanish possessions. Dutch private companies were already trading in the Americas, and they were anxious for state support. Amongst the merchants and directors of companies in Amsterdam and Zeeland, there was strong support for the formation of a joint stock company trading westward, in the same form as the VOC. One of the merchants, yet another emigre from Antwerp who fled following Parma's capture of the city in the 1580s, had established a reputation as an economist. He advocated a policy of breaking both the Spanish and Portuguese monopolies in their colonies and supporting and financing settlers and trading settlements in South America where the Spanish had not yet established themselves. He further advocated that the necessary strength of the Republic's commerce would be to establish colonies and to populate them by shipping out state-sponsored settlers from the Republic who would expand production of the colonies and thus provide its manufactures to a growing demand back in the Republic.[35]

By 1606 there was strong support for the formation of such a company, and throughout 1606, plans were presented before the States of Holland. However, Oldenbarneveldt, powerful as the leader of the States of Holland (and one of those dominating the States-General) stopped any further progress to this in 1607. The Dutch, led by Oldenbarneveldt and his team of negotiators, were in the middle of the Truce negotiations with Spain. To establish a company with official state support whose principal objective would be to break Spanish trade monopoly and whose remit would include conducting diplomacy and engaging in armed conflict would seriously jeopardise any peace settlement. And the Dutch at that time needed peace as much as the Spanish.

However, in 1621 with the Twelve Years' Truce expired (and Oldenbarneveldt's power broken), the Dutch West India Company (WIC) was formed. It was a joint stock company with a constitution and structure modelled on those of the VOC. It had 5 regional boards or chambers, located in Amsterdam, Middelburg, Rotterdam, the North Quarter of the province of Holland, and Groningen, emphasising the importance of the two provinces of Zeeland and Holland. The central board of directors consisted of 19 directors, known as the *Heeren XIX*.

Generally, the investors in the WIC were of a smaller scale than those investing in the VOC, and the influence of Amsterdam was less. The Zeeland investors were particularly prominent, and by 1648 one in 5 inhabitants of the towns of Middelburg, Vlissingen, and Veere were shareholders of the WIC. However, interest from Amsterdam financiers increased as time progressed, and Amsterdam investors bought up shares in the differing chambers so that, by 1670, over half the total capital of the WIC was owned in Amsterdam.

The formation of the WIC differed significantly from that of the VOC. The WIC was formed and financed by both commercial and ideological and chauvinistic motives. The VOC was formed for strictly commercial reasons, amalgamating different companies that would have otherwise been in unhealthy competition. The successful acquiring of the territories and engaging in local conflicts was due to the initiative of ruthless agents and officials *in situ* who successfully judged the situation and acted, sometimes contravening the official company remit.

The WIC, by contrast, was formed from the very start for commerce and conquest, as part of the offensive against Spain. The latter attracted investment from extreme Calvinists, generally staunch Counter-Remonstrants, who viewed the formation and activities of the WIC as the continuation of a just war. One historian emphasised the extreme Calvinist influence and ethos in the founding the WIC, stating that they were:

> bent on destruction of Spanish power.[36]

Part of this philosophy was that the Dutch, upon arriving in the Americas, would stir up and foment rebellion amongst the indigenous workers against their Portuguese and Spanish overlords.[37] Prevalent amongst investor thinking was a rather naïve belief that the indigenous Chilians and Brazilians would form and bond immediately with the Dutch and rise up in revolt, with an automatic empathy with the Dutch as fellow rebels against the Spanish Empire.

Even Maurits, level-headed and pragmatic, was seduced by this wishful thinking and actively supported the formation of the WIC and invested some of his own funds, placing them alongside those of other fervent supporters. In the early 1600s, he gave support and pushed for the formation of the VOC from a commonsensical instinct that the VOC would be a successful commercial enterprise that would inevitably benefit the Dutch Republic; in the early 1620s, he energetically supported the WIC as a commercial instrument of economic war and had a naïve assumption that the Dutch would speedily gain allies within the Portuguese and Spanish colonies and that, together, they would foment rebellion.

Initially the WIC was intended to target Spanish America with the silver treasures of Mexico and Peru. However, it increasingly found more productive and lucrative activities by concentrating on the sugar of Portuguese Brazil and on the gold, ivory, and slave trade of Portuguese West Africa. Contrary to the belief that by engaging in Brazil the Dutch would be joined by fellow kindred rebel spirits against the Portuguese, many Brazilians, if at all active, remained loyal to Portugal. Those who did support the Dutch were mainly the planter owners, and they did so out of a realisation that it was necessary to cooperate with the Dutch to maintain their positions in Brazil.[38] The Brazilian workers did indeed revolt, in 1654, but against the Dutch, and these rebels were assisted by Portuguese reinforcements sent from the Portuguese fort of Bahia.

The WIC was not nearly as successful commercially as its East Indies counterpart, and it declined throughout the Seventeenth Century. The main assets that kept it going so long were the West African holdings and the accompanying slave trade. By 1640 the WIC's debts had totalled 18 million florins, and by 1650, its share price had from 117 to 14 points. By the 1670s, it was no longer viable, and it all but ceased operations in 1674. However, as an entity engaged in Dutch economic warfare it was effective. In 1628 the Dutch privateer Piet Hein, commanding 30 ships, observed a Spanish bullion convoy off Cuba. He attacked and captured small vessels of the enemy convoy, but others escaped and made for the port of Havana. Hein pursued and attacked again to prevent them from landing their cargo. Over 70,000 bags of silver bullion, together with crates of sugar and dyestuffs, were captured. Hein returned to the Netherlands to a rapturous welcome and received a reward of 6,000 florins, with a 17-month wage bonus for each crew member from the WIC (which he begrudged, claiming he and his crew should have obtained much more). The total value of the haul was between 11 and 17 million florins. This was a vital addition to the Dutch war economy at a particularly crucial time in the struggle. For by this time, the Twelve Years' Truce had expired, and the Dutch Republic was again at war, this time embroiled in a pan-European war that was to last 30 years.

Notes

1. Israel, J in *The Dutch Republic Its Rise Greatness and Fall 1477–1806* places the start of much of the Dutch economic rise to the late 1580s and 1590s p 307
2. Professor Maarten Prak, University of Utrecht
3. Wilson, C *Queen Elizabeth and the Revolt of the Netherlands* p 117
4. Price, JL *Holland and the Dutch Republic in the Seventeenth Century* p 223
5. Price, JL *Holland and the Dutch Republic in the Seventeenth Century* p 223
6. Percival, J *Les Delcies de la Hollande* p 10
7. Wilson, C *England's Apprenticeship 1603–1763* p 71
8. Hobsbawm, EJ chapter regarding the general crisis of the Seventeenth Century in Aston, T (ed) *Crisis in Europe 1560–1660* p 42
9. Crowley, R *City of Fortune—How Venice Won and Lost a Naval Empire* p 139
10. Parker, G "The Emergence of Modern Finance in Europe" in Cipolla, M (ed) *The Fontana Economic History of Europe Vol II* p 549
11. Wallerstein, I *The Modern World System II* p 58

12. Accarios de Serionne, J *Les Interests de nations del'Europe developpe relativement au commerce Vol II* p 201, cited in Braudel, F *Civilisation and Capitalism 15th to 18th Century Vol III the Perspective of the World* p 245
13. In Vol I of Accarios de Serionne, J *Les Interests de nations del'Europe developpe relativement au commerce 1776* p 222
14. Orders, J and van Haestens, H *The Triumphs of Nassau. A Description of all victories etc* p 16
15. Wilson, CH "Transport as a Factor in the History of Economic Development" p 329
16. Wallerstein, I *The Modern World System* II p 55
17. Braudel, F *Civilisation and Capitalism Vol II—The Wheels of Commerce* p 366
18. Wallerstein, I *The Modern World System* p 52
19. Nordmann, C *Grandeur et Liberte de la Suede 1660–1672* p 45
20. Braudel, F in the second volume of his monumental *Civilisation and Capitalism 15 to 18 Century—The Wheels of Commerce* pp 439–440 argues that the definition of joint stock companies as those whose shares were not only transferable but available and negotiable on the open market as too narrow. Loosening this definition, he is able to cite joint stock enterprises in France and in Genoa in the Fifteenth Century
21. De Klerk, ES *History of the Netherlands East Indies Vol I* p 202
22. Boxer, CR *The Dutch Seaborne Empire 1600–1800* p 26
23. Parry, JH *The Age of Reconnaissance* p 249
24. Colenbrander, HT *Jan Pietereszoon Coen* p 34 cited in Boxer, CR *The Dutch Seaborne Empire* p 107
25. *Ea Quae* issued by Julius II in 1506, and *Praecelsi Devotionis* issued by Leo X in 1514
26. de Klerk, ES *History of the Netherlands East India Vol I* p 21
27. Boxer, CR *The Portuguese Seaborne Empire 1415–1825* p 108
28. De Vivero, R *An Account of Japan 1609* pp 102–103, 149–150
29. Colebrander, HT *Jan Pieterz Coen. Bescheiden Omtrent zijn Bedrief in Indie Vol I* p 128
30. Heeres, MJE *Corpus Diplomaticus Nederland-Indicum 1596–1650* Docs XV and XVi pp 32–35
31. Colebrander, HT *Jan PieterzCoen. Bescheiden Omtrent zijn Bedrief in Indie Vol I* p 171
32. Israel, J *The Dutch Republic—Its Rise, Greatness, and Fall 1477–1806* p 323
33. Professor Brugmans, in "De Oost India Compagnie in de velvaart in de Republiek" in *Tijdschrift for Geschiedenis Vol 61 1948* emphasises the increase volume of shipping and the diminishing returns of the VOC in the later era
34. Boxer, CR *The Dutch Seaborne Empire 1600–1800* p 316
35. Boxer, CR *The Dutch in Brazil* p 2
36. Plumb, JH in Introduction in Boxer, CR *The Dutch Seaborne Empire 1600–1800* p xxii
37. This mindset is extensively covered in Schmidt, B *Innocence Abroad—The Dutch Imagination and the New World 1570–1670*
38. Wilson, PH *XXX Years War* pp 372, 648

10 1621, Renewal of War Looms—And Playing for Time

Within the Dutch Republic certain economic interests had been damaged by the Twelve Years' Truce. The Dutch textile industry had lost ground in competition with its Flemish competitors. Also, investors had heavily committed financial outlay in militarised ventures and in the domestic armaments and logistics industry within the Republic.[1] Whilst the VOC had successfully been established, the Dutch West India Company had been prevented from being established during the years of Oldenbarneveldt's dominance years, due to Oldenbarneveldt's being anxious to establish peace.[2] The provinces of Holland and Zealand—both with great financial influence within the Republic—strongly opposed Oldenbarneveld's policy and indeed any long-term peace policy, as they expected great gains from attacking Spanish and Portuguese possessions in the Americas.

Maurice himself, on balance, had favoured continuing the war, for a combination of reasons. Namely his own self-interest in maintaining his dominant position and for the dynastic continuity of the House of Nassau and also a genuine conviction that war was necessary to preserve the union of the state, particularly after the trauma of the struggle with Oldenbarneveldt and the Counter-Remonstrants. However, during 1620 a complex diplomatic game leading up to the official renunciation of the Truce was played out.

On the Spanish side, Archduke Albert, long-headed and prudent, wished the Truce to continue.[3] He genuinely believed that peace would benefit all concerned. Philip II disagreed and made it clear to Albert that he was of the opposite view. Albert persisted, advocating a peace to allow the provinces that had remained loyal, the Spanish Netherlands, to consolidate economically.

In 1619 and in 1620, the situation changed, apparently to Spain's advantage. The Thirty Years' War had started with the rebellion in Bohemia against Hapsburg rule and with Frederick V, the elector of Palatine and grandson of William of Orange, accepting the crown of Bohemia, offered to him by the rebel regime. In October 1619, he left Heidelberg, in his electorate of the Rhenish Palatinate, and made for Bohemia.

Emperor Ferdinand and the Catholic League of German princes and states mobilised their forces. Soon these forces, together with the leaders of the Catholic League, Bavaria, and the Spanish Hapsburgs, were able to deploy no less than 6 armies against Frederick and the Bohemian rebels. Frederick had many of the Protestant Union, which had given open support to the rebellion. However, Protestant unity did not match that of the Catholic League[4] in the Holy Roman Empire, and the Bohemians found themselves with few active allies. In November 1619, at the Battle of the White Mountain, the imperial-Bavarian forces routed Frederick's Bohemians. They entered Prague, and Emperor Ferdinand was able to exact revenge, reward his allies, and reorganise the Empire. Frederick fled and found sanctuary in the Dutch Republic. Maurice granted him sanctuary, accommodation (for a time it was in the former official residence of Oldenbarneveldt in The Hague), and a small subsidy.

Maurits had given support to Frederick V in his bid for the Bohemian crown, as he, Frederick, was William of Orange's grandson and a Protestant elector, and the rebellion against the Hapsburg Empire during 1619 and 1620 would to some extent distract Spain. However, with the defeat of Frederick and the Bohemian rebels, it was over. The Dutch Republic itself was now under threat. Giving personal sanctuary to the fleeing elector and his wife was one thing, but:

> the States-General would take no chances. . . . [T]hey could not afford to be the paymaster of the Protestant cause.[5]

As part of their preparations against Frederick and his Protestant allies, the imperial–Catholic League–Spanish Hapsburg coalition had 18,000 Spanish troops standing to in Flanders, whilst a further 19,000 Spanish troops under Spinola left Brussels in August 1619, marched to Cologne, then east through Trier. They then overran the Rhenish Palatinate. After the Battle of the White Mountain, Bavarian troops had occupied the Upper Palatinate whilst the Protestant Union troops had remained in some parts of the Rhenish Palatinate. The Protestant Union forces came to an agreement with Spinola by the Treaty of Mainz in April 1620, whereby they were allowed to evacuate all their forces. Spinola with his large forces was now in total control of the Rhenish Palatinate. Then, in late 1620, Spanish troops from Milan captured the southern part of the Valtelline and in the subsequent fighting between Protestant Union forces and Hapsburg forces, the rest of the Valtelline was captured by early 1621.

The Protestant allies of the Dutch had suffered multiple defeats at the hands of the imperial–Catholic League–Spanish forces. The so-called Spanish Road was clear and under the control of Spain, open once again for troop movements to the north and eventually to the Netherlands. Spinola, with his substantial forces, was positioned in a vital part of this route. The situation had indeed changed in Spain's favour.

The Archduke Albert was still cautious, peaceable, and wished to maintain the Truce. A large number of Spanish troops, over 9,000, were still tied down in Bohemia, having been sent by the Spanish Road by Philip III in early 1619 as part of the mutual assistance agreed between the Spanish and Austrian Hapsburgs against the Protestant rebellion. Wishing for the continuity of the peace gained by the Truce, the archduke proposed a solution, offering terms similar to those of the 1499 Swiss-Austrian peace agreement. By this agreement, the Swiss were recognised as sovereign and independent but in permanent alliance with Austria. He was supported in this policy by several ministers and councillors at the Court in Madrid, who were conscious of the state of the imperial Spanish economy and the healing benefits that continuing the peace of the Truce would bring.

However, the king himself, Philip III, was determined to end the Truce and recommence hostilities. He also saw the possibility and opportunity of Spain agreeing to continue the Truce in exchange for Dutch acknowledgement of overall Spanish sovereignty—a radical change in the terms agreed by Spain resulting in the finalised Truce in 1609. With the strategic European situation changed, he felt Spain could dramatically increase its terms for any continuation of the Truce. This possibility and opportunity coincided with a change in ministers in Madrid. The Duke of Lerma's ministry had fallen in 1618. Lerma's policy of peace had been nothing more than *laissez-faire* in foreign policy, or even "an absence of foreign policy".[6]

During Lerma's ministry, whilst there was peace in the Netherlands, abroad in Italy, in South America, and in the Rhineland, Spanish holdings and interests had appeared constantly threatened by the Dutch, the English, and the Protestant League in Germany; even the situation in the Netherlands may have been jeopardised during certain periods when the Spanish Road had been closed by French incursions and military thrusts.

Baltasar de Zuniga previously had given distinguished service abroad. Over the preceding two years, he had coalesced a following around him at Court. He was arguing with increasing vigour for a more robust foreign policy, especially against the Dutch. His arguments were based upon what became known in a later era of international foreign policy as the "domino theory". This stated that, to prevent the total collapse of power and influence in a region, the prompt and final suppression of the first rebellious adversary is essential. If the Dutch—or the power of the province of Holland—were not halted in their forward policy of international trade aggression (also including, as well as colonial expansion and intrusion against Spanish colonies, outright piracy against Spanish shipping), then in a horrifying cycle Spain would lose the Indies, then the Spanish Netherlands, then the northern Italian duchies, and then the territorial integrity of Spain itself would be threatened.

This was a dramatic and cataclysmic line of argument, contrasting with the previous tired and apparently listless foreign policy, and it coincided exactly with Philip III's hostility towards the Dutch Republic. Lerma was dismissed, retiring, and dying on his estates in Valencia 7 years later. He was eventually replaced by his son Cristobal Duke of Ucedo.

Philip III died in March 1621, a month before the Twelve Years' Truce was due to expire. His successor Philip IV was conscientious, extremely aware of Spain's destiny. He was pious to the same extreme, if somewhat erratic. He would spend periods of time in brothels and then, in fits of remorse, engage in long periods of prayer and confessional, trying to avert what he perceived as divine retribution by periodically clearing the Madrid streets of prostitutes (who gave it some days for a calmer royal mood, then returned). Like his father, he was religiously intense and more obstinate.[7] In a policy of renewing the war with the Dutch Republic, he was of one mind with his late father. However, during his reign (1621–1665), the serious economic decline of Spain set in and intensified,[8] yet this was the very period when he set Spain on a foreign policy of aggression. Within a year, ministerial power in Madrid had passed from Lerma's son the duke of Ucedo to Zuniga; then in 1622 it was to pass from Zuniga to his nephew Gaspar de Guzma, Duke of Olivares. Olivares, a dedicated and hard-working first minister. Olivares worked assiduously, often 14 hours a day, and was eternally convinced of the righteousness of his own judgement. Unlike Lerma or his French counterpart Richelieu, Olivares was unostentatious and laboured long and hard but discreetly, preferring to work through the mechanism of existing councils and government ministries rather than create his own obedient department. Like his late uncle, Olivares was committed to renewing the war with the Dutch Republic, not merely on a local, i.e. Netherlands basis, but on a global scale to check Dutch incursions into Spanish territories and to halt the damage to Spanish trade in the Americas. Olivares adopted a policy whereby Spain held back from hostilities on the basis that they could increase their terms for continuing the peace.

In the negotiations with the Dutch up to the actual ending of the Truce, Spain did increase their terms and reiterated the terms it had adopted at the start of the pre-Truce negotiation, namely recognition of overall Spanish sovereignty by the Dutch (this was to be a nominal but nonetheless overall sovereignty of Spain), religious toleration for the Catholic minorities in the Dutch Republic, and the opening of the massive river Scheldt, freeing up trade with Antwerp.

Throughout the contacts and negotiations and even after the Truce was ended and war resumed, Olivares kept referring to the terms and reduced the demand from 3 to 2, namely, recognition by the Dutch to nominal sovereignty of Spain and toleration for the Catholic minorities. Arguably the most important issue remained the economic issue, that of freeing up the Scheldt so that trade from and to Antwerp—and from and to the Spanish Netherlands—could flow more freely. Indeed this issue was one facet of the wider economic issue, the impact of Dutch atavistic incursions into Spanish overseas possessions. From the Spanish viewpoint as of 1621, renewal of the war with the Dutch Republic was not one of expansion or of reconquering the lost northern provinces of the Spanish Netherlands but of economic survival.[9]

Let us return to the 1619–1621 situation and consider the Dutch position, especially that of Maurits. Maurits wished for a renewal of the war. Internally, in the Dutch Republic, Maurits was secure, having won the religious and constitutional struggle with Oldenbarneveldt and having stilled the remnants of opposition. Maurits's instinctive feeling was for renewal of the war, but the events of the Thirty Years' War had overtaken Dutch strategic planning, which had been in some disorder and internally preoccupied for half a decade due to the internal political and religious struggles. The Republic had been distracted from foreign affairs during a crucial period.[10]Therefore some time was needed. Accordingly, Maurits did not wish a renewal of the war immediately. He deliberately delayed during the vital two years 1619 to 1621 the establishment of the West India Company[11] so that its formation—and obvious remit—would not alarm Spain and lead Spain to conclude that hostilities were inevitable. Any negotiations. Also he was anxious not to appear the aggressor. Accordingly, he facilitated the dissemination of false information. This false information was to the effect that Dutch internal dissension and division—which, as will be seen later in the chapter, did indeed exist and were occurring—were greater than reported and that the Dutch Republic was hopelessly divided. In spreading this false information, the Dutch were aided by deliberate rumours from both France and England,[12] rumours that also exaggerated Dutch political divisions and appeared to corroborate the intelligence coming from the Dutch Republic. This was the reason why Olivares had mistakenly escalated the Spanish negotiating demands to include recognition of overall Spanish sovereignty and toleration of the Catholic minorities; also, in doing so, he and Spain were willing to put off hostilities, mistakenly thinking that they were in a strong negotiating position.

Archduke Albert continued to advocate and pursue a renewal of the Truce. He took some encouragement from the fact that Maurits's fellow stadhouder, cousin and comrade in arms, Willem Lodewijk had died in 1620. Whilst Albert had no doubt that Maurits, as a leader and military man could hold his own and that Willem Lodewijk's death would not affect these abilities, Willem Lodewijk had been an ardent Calvinist, and so, according to Albert's thinking, Maurits would no longer have either the advice or influence of such a prominent and close Calvinist relative.

In February 1621, Albert informed Madrid that France was offering their diplomatic services to intervene and mediate and also that his ministers in Brussels had received an emissary direct from Stadhouder Prince Maurits of Nassau. The emissary was a Catholic noblewoman, Bethode, Madame de T'Serclaes who knew Maurits and was also an acquaintance of General Count Tilly. Tilly commanded the forces of the Catholic League, which had defeated the Protestant forces of the elector Frederick V during the latter's recent unsuccessful rebellion in pursuit of the throne of Bohemia. Madame T'Serclaes had a residence in The Hague, and two of her daughters had married into nobility in the Spanish Netherlands. So with her family connections, she could travel back and forth between The Hague in the Dutch Republic and Brussels in the Spanish Netherlands discreetly and without difficulty.

Maurits had deliberately created a totally false possibility in the message. The emissary's message to Albert was to the effect that, if Brussels (i.e. the Archduke) were to send an emissary (i.e. Madame de T'Serclaes) to The Hague (i.e. Maurits) and propose that the States-General recognise the overall sovereignty of the Spanish king, then Maurits would ensure this recognition in return for permanent peace and future favours and concessions from the Spanish king. Archduke Albert conveyed all details of this proposed opportunity in a despatch to Madrid.

Here the Archduke Albert was himself engaging in some disingenuousness, though from the highest motives of maintaining peace. Whilst the false message itself was entirely the work of Maurits, initiating the contact between Madame de T'Serclaes and Maurits, as well as the subsequent shuttle diplomacy, was started by Archduke Albert himself. Once Albert had informed Madrid of the contacts—without specifying that he himself had initiated them—Madrid encouraged him to continue, although Philip III did caution Albert to be on his guard[13] against possible Dutch duplicity. However, Philip III and his advisers were confident that they could gain better terms in the renewal of the Truce. But France also was engaging in duplicity. Whilst coming forward at one stage and offering to mediate, Paris had also sent instructions to its ambassador in The Hague to strongly encourage the Dutch to end the Truce.

Having made sure that Spain was willing to hold off from immediately ending the Truce and to increase its terms for doing so, Maurits next set a diplomatic trap that would ensure that, on the Dutch side, any divisions amongst the provinces about the renewal of hostilities would be circumvented. In early 1621, Maurits gave full encouragement to these potential negotiations with the inherent terms as they stood, and Albert assured Madrid in March 1621 that Maurits was fully agreed to his ensuring that the States-General would accept Spanish overall sovereignty. Albert's assurances to Madrid were accepted, and Zuniga, by now having taken power from Lerma, authorised Albert to fully pursue and advance the negotiations. Spurred on by another message from Madame T'Serclaes that Maurits was urging haste, Albert sent Peckius, chancellor of the Spanish Netherlands, province of Brabant, from Brussels to The Hague.

Peckius was the son of a distinguished jurist and a distinguished jurist in his own right. His father was a university professor, and one of his pupils was the diplomat Richardot, who, as we have seen, was part of

Parma's ministerial advisory team and who was anxious for a moderate and agreed settlement to the whole Netherlands issue and who, as a diplomat, had attempted to mediate between Parma and the Dutch in the latter's proposed peace. Throughout his career, Richardot kept in touch with Professor Peckius and was of the same mind of moderation and diplomacy as the professor's son, Chancellor Peckius. As a lawyer, Peckius (the son of the professor) had conducted pleading in his early career before the Mechelen Grand Court. This court was based in Mechelen which had been the capital of the entire empire of Charles V and as such was the Supreme Court of all the 17 provinces of the Netherlands possessions of Charles V. Only members of the imperial court and of the Order of the Golden Fleece could be tried for offences in that court. It had been the court of final appeal of the whole judicial system of the Netherlands under Charles V. To plead and conduct cases in that court, a lawyer had to be of heightened calibre and distinction. Archduke Albert recognised his abilities and eventually made him chancellor of the province of Brabant and used him for diplomatic missions. He was sent in 1620 to mediate between the Emperor Ferdinand II and the Bohemian rebels in attempt to bring about a peaceful solution—a near-impossible task, but that he was sent at all was testimony to his abilities.

He was sent by Archduke Albert to The Hague on a delicate, discreet mission, an attempt to prevent Spanish-Dutch hostilities and an eventual renewal of the Twelve Years' Truce. To Peckius, his mission concerned a highly contentious issue, but the mission itself was reasonably easy and straightforward: state Spain's terms of renewing peaceful relations with the Dutch Republic in return for Dutch acknowledgement and recognition of the overall sovereignty of Spain, terms that he sincerely thought would be accepted by the Dutch in their eagerness to have peace and terms that Prince Maurits had guaranteed would be accepted and implemented. In this Peckius was mistaken, having been briefed by Archduke Albert, who himself had been hoodwinked by Maurits.

It became known in most if not all of the 7 provinces of the Dutch Republic that Peckius was en route from Brussels to The Hague, and it was assumed—either in anger or in hope—that this would be a stage in the process leading to an extension of the Twelve Years' Truce. The provinces through which Peckius had to travel to reach The Hague were Zeeland and Holland, both of which were opposed to renewing the Truce. This opposition by the two provinces was due to commercial reasons as war would bring old-time trade opportunities. Also these two stalwart provinces which had maintained the struggle in the darkest hours of the Revolt still nurtured hostility to Spain. This hostility was constantly being inflamed by Calvinist preachers who were denouncing the Truce in the two provinces. In Rotterdam, there were civil disorders as an unpleasantly surprised Peckius passed though. In Delft, there were attempts by gangs of youths to stone the barge that was transporting him by canal, and within the town of Delft, there were hostile demonstrations against his visit. Peckius kept calm and patient. When he finally reached The Hague, he was escorted and shown into the States-General, where he made his address as scheduled. As per his remit, Peckius cited the Low Countries as the 'common fatherland' and appealed for Dutch submission to overall Spanish sovereignty in return for a renewal of the Truce and lasting peace between the Dutch Republic and Spain. The reaction of the States-General was more silent than that of the populaces of Holland and Zeeland, but it was no less hostile. A silence concealing barely suppressed anger greeted his speech, which all the provinces in the States-General found completely unacceptable during the subsequent debate.[14] The representatives from Holland and Zeeland wished to expel Peckius immediately from Dutch territory, but more moderate counsels prevailed giving due consideration to Peckius's diplomatic status. It was decided that Peckius should be given a reply from the States-General and that he would have a further audience in secret with Maurits to further discuss the Spanish proposals, subject to Maurits's agreeing to this further meeting. Two days later, the States-General issued their reply to Peckius, which was that the sovereignty of the United Provinces was beyond discussion or dispute and that war was preferable to surrendering this sovereignty.

Maurits consented, and this ensured that he had absolute control, not only on whether any negotiations went further, but he that maintained control of the information flow and decided what would be divulged to the States-General. At the secret meeting between Peckius and Maurits, the former gave full details of the king of Spain's proposals and committed Spain to an extension of the Truce under the existing terms. (This would have enabled the Dutch to continue the *de facto* actions outside Europe against Spain's overseas possessions.) Maurits, for his part, was conciliatory, apologizing to Peckius for the disturbances at Delft and reassuring him that he, Maurits, had the situation in hand and that all would be well. He withheld details from the States-General of what was discussed at the secret meeting to avoid debate and possibly causing division between the provinces; he wished to leave the States-General as they were, i.e. furious and united against the arrogant demands of Spain.

Peckius experienced further hostile demonstrations in Rotterdam and Dordrecht as he travelled through the Dutch Republic on his way back to Brussels. However, he held sincerely to the meeting he had had with Maurits and to the overall positive signals that he had received. He reported favourably to Archduke Albert, who in turn reported to Madrid that if Spain agreed to renewal of the Truce on the present terms, then Maurits would be agreeable to Spain's demand, and so would the States-General, with the dissent of Holland and possibly that of Zeeland. Maurits's deceiving of Spain was continuing to be successful.

There was hostile speculation in contemporary reports regarding Maurits's intentions. After Peckius's departure from the Dutch Republic, the contemporary press and broadsheets railed against what was perceived as Maurits's hesitation, warning of the dangers in delaying the renewal of hostilities. They warned that any delay would mean Maurits would be too old to be an effective military leader and that the battle-hardened and experienced Dutch armies would stagnate and the maritime trade of Zeeland would continue to decline under the moribund peace of the Truce.[15] Later in the century, a Dutch contemporary historian, Aitzema, held the firm opinion that Maurits manipulated the Peckius diplomatic mission and was determined on war before he became too old to function as a military leader and while the Dutch Army still had experienced serving officers.[16]

Maurits continued to maintain discreet contacts after Peckius had returned and reported. He was in no special hurry to make the final break and take the final irrevocable step to war. Archduke Albert ordered the secretary of finances of the Spanish Netherlands, and Maurits ordered the treasurer of the States-General to meet each other (the two officials were cousins). The treasurer of the States-General conveyed sentiments and messages from Maurits to the effect that he, Maurits, wished not only to renew the Truce but also to explore the possibility of opening the river Scheldt and that the VOC would be restrained against any further attacks upon Spanish overseas possessions in the Far East. This was followed by a mission by Madame de T'Serclaes, who brought to Brussels the profuse apologies of Maurits for the hostile reception given to Peter Peckius in the provinces of Holland and Zeeland. Madame de T'Serclaes also repeated Maurits's willingness to renew the Truce with a hint that he could ensure further alterations to its terms that would be more favourable to Spain. Whilst these discreet meetings of the two cousin high officials in The Hague and Madame T'Serclaes in Brussels were going on, Archduke Albert continued to send messages of reassurance to Madrid, advocating to avoid war. Madrid was impressed by the activity and positive traffic, which appeared to be leading to some sort of eventual recognition of Spanish sovereignty. Albert, by this time in declining health, was authorised to continue the discreet negotiations, and he was to use whatever intermediaries and go-betweens whom he deemed appropriate to obtain a suitably adapted Truce—i.e. one incorporating recognition of Spanish sovereignty.[17]

However, Maurits suddenly veered in his position. He sent message in June that he, Maurits, would agree to make efforts on the Dutch side, only if both the king and the Archduke committed themselves in advance to the terms of the 1609 Truce. If such an advance commitment was forthcoming from the Spanish side, then it would be up to Maurits as to how far he could—and indeed would—go in modifying the Truce whose default position was that of 1609. Taking this apparently sudden turn by Maurits with remarkable patience, equanimity all the more remarkable due to his failing health, Archduke Albert continued to plead with

Madrid for a continuation of the Truce, repeating his warnings of the dire economic consequences of renewing the war. However, the king of Spain was resolved on conflict. In July 1621 Archduke Albert died, so any further conciliatory or halting influences were no longer present. Archduchess Isabella was declared regent of the king of Spain in the Netherlands, emphasizing a return to direct rule from Madrid. The Truce was at an end; Philip IV and Spain chose war.

Maurice had achieved a twofold objective. By the false information that had been disseminated, Archduke Albert only too willingly believed and Madrid came around to believing that restoration of Spanish sovereignty was a feasible demand to make and acceptable by the Dutch. By pursuing this demand, Spain appeared to be the intense aggressor, forcing war. Secondly, Maurits's prolongation of the negotiations by his discreet contacts had stalled Spain successfully, and by sowing confusion amongst Spain and the Spanish Netherlands—for Archduke Albert, it had all been a trap[18]—Maurits had bought valuable time for the Dutch Republic.

Notes

1. Israel, J *The Dutch Republic—Its Rise, Greatness, and Fall 1477–1806* pp 410–415
2. Price, JL *Culture and Society in the Dutch Republic During the 17th Century* pp 3–4
3. Van Cruyningen, A *De Tachtijaarige Oorlog* p 127
4. Wilson, PH *The XXX Years War* p 285
5. Parker, G *The XXX Years War* p 63
6. Kamen, H *Spain 1469–1714—A Society in Conflict* p 206
7. Ashley, M *The Golden Century* p 84
8. William, EN *The Ancien Regime in Europe—Government and Society in Major European States 1648–1789* p 77
9. Kamen, H *Spain 1469–1714* p 207
10. Parker, G *The Dutch Revolt* p 263
11. Israel, J *The Dutch Republic—Its Rise, Greatness, and Fall 1477–1806* p 472
12. Parker, G *Europe in Crisis 1598–1648* pp 172–173
13. Polisensky, J *Tragic Triangle—The Netherlands, Spain and Bohemia* p 241
14. States-General Secret Proceedings 11/Number .01.02/4562 Depot 502C/27.04.01
15. *Gazette van Antwerpen* April 1621 nos 220 and 222, and *Den Compaignon* April 1621, cited in Israel, J *The Dutch Republic and the Hispanic World 1601–1661* pp 79–82
16. Cited in Israel, J *The Dutch Republic and the Hispanic World 1601–1661* p 79
17. King's instructions to Archduke Albert April 1621, ARB SEG 185/fo.37, cited in Israel, J *The Dutch Republic and the Hispanic World 1601–1661* p 84
18. Duerloo, L *Dynasty and Piety Archduke Albert and Hapsburg Political Culture in an Age of Religious Wars* p 508. Israel, J *The Dutch Republic and the Hispanic World* p 76

11 War Again—And the Dark Hour Before the Dawn

When the Truce officially expired in April 1621, conflict did not resume immediately. Maurits renewed his secret messages to Brussels, stating that he and the Dutch were ready for some sort of settlement, provided Spain did not insist on concessions. After several months of these contacts, he then sent another message to the effect that, in return for a renewal of the Truce, consideration would be given to freeing the Scheldt for international (i.e. Spanish) trade and possibly some concessions in the Indies. Any messages and contacts sent and made after April emanated purely from Maurits; neither the States of Holland nor the States-General were aware of them and certainly not of the details. Rumours did circulate in political circles that Maurits was in discreet contact with Brussels, and there were misgivings in the States-General. But Maurits had gained further time by his diplomatic procrastination and averted actual hostilities for some months.

Even then, the Spanish renewed the war slowly. The government in Brussels under Isabella (Albert had died in July 1621) was anxious. Isabella herself pointed out that it was a momentous struggle and that troops of the Army of Flanders were dispersed as far as Hungary and Bohemia.[1]

However, Spain had started the economic blockade in May 1621 as part of renewing the war in which the Dutch Republic became increasingly under siege. The Spanish embargoes and trade blockades had a significant impact on the economy. Spain, pursuing a European campaign cooperating with the Austrian Hapsburgs and the Catholic League, expanded the army of Flanders to 60,000 men. These troops were deployed to encircle the Dutch Republic. The Dutch Republic increased the size of the regular army from 30,000 to 48,000[2] in order to fully man the defensive ring of forts and fortified works. Its navy between 1621 and 1624 was increased by over a third.[3] This was expensive but also fortuitous for it enabled abler commanders and admirals such as Piet Hein and, in the later years, Maarten van Tromp and Michael de Ruyter to emerge.

And indeed expenses were one cause of internal dissention within the Republic in the early 1620s. The Spanish embargo was taking effect on Dutch commerce, and at the same time increased taxation was necessary to expand the army and navy. Maurits and the States-General were part of the anti-Hapsburg strategy, a strategy designed to distract Spain and minimise the threat to the Netherlands. They had subsidised Protestant Elector Palatine Frederick V in his attempt to take the crown of Bohemia. When he and his armies were crushed by the imperial and Catholic League forces under Tilly, further Dutch subsidies were granted and redirected to the armies of Christian of Brunswick, who had taken up arms on behalf of the Protestant cause in the Empire. It was waging war by proxy and hopefully keeping imperial and Spanish troops occupied in the Empire, but it was expensive.

Also the internal politics of the Republic revealed fractures. Instances of violent political subversion occurred. In 1621, a conspiracy of 5 nobles in Gelderland was discovered, whereby they planned to betray the town of Tiel to the Spanish forces; the perpetrators were quickly tried and executed. In February 1623 a conspiracy to assassinate Maurits was discovered. The son of Oldenbarneveldt, William, together with his brother and landowner Renier, had conspired with a zealous Remonstrant preacher named Hendrik Slatius to have Maurits killed. They hired a group of sailors who would assemble on a given day when Maurits's official schedule would afford an opportunity of a mob attack and killing. Renier was responsible for financing the plot, ensuring payment of several hundred guilders to the sailors. However, the plan was discovered the day before the attack, Maurits was forewarned, and the perpetrators were arrested as they grouped together. William managed to escape the round-up and fled abroad, but Renier and others were arrested. Renier was found guilty of financing the assassination attempt and executed.

Religious differences also came violently to the fore. Maurits, in his victory over Oldenbarneveldt, had purged many town councils of Remonstrants and. in doing so deprived local government of many able individuals. His substitutes, whilst politically and religiously loyal, were generally inadequate. The overall leadership fell on his shoulders alone. Now elderly and sick, he felt the strain, and local leadership was lacking. In the early 1620s, Remonstrant demonstrations caused a reaction against Counter-Remonstrant councils in several towns in Holland. Even in Amsterdam, Adrian Pauw, Maurits's staunch political ally, held onto power in the council only with great difficulty. Increased direct taxation on commodities and foodstuffs was also causing discontent. More taxes were introduced in the province of Holland in the mid-1620s than at any other time between the 1590s and 1672.[4] Public disturbances became frequent, riots occurred in Hoorn, Delft, Haarlem, The Hague, and Amsterdam. Troops normally deployed in the towns in Holland were unavailable to nip the disturbances quickly, as they had been deployed to the front-line defensive ring. Maurits was unable to give due attention to these domestic disturbances, let alone intervene, as he too was urgently needed at the front.

The front was the widening in the Thirty Years' War, escalating throughout Europe, in which the Spanish commander Spinola focussed on the Dutch Republic. Unlike Spanish ministers and members of the various councils in Madrid who were reconciled to the impossibility of the successful reconquest of the Dutch, Spinola had never given up. Indeed, Spinola's zeal was welcomed and supported by Madrid, but as an attritional war that would harm a trade rival. If all went well with Spinola, the Dutch would be damaged (but not reconquered).

Throughout the Twelve Years' Truce, Spinola had thought and planned for victory over the Dutch, and for him this pivoted on controlling the Rhine and attacking the eastern frontier of the Republic. When Elector Palatine Frederick accepted the crown of Bohemia, effectively starting the Bohemian Revolt, Spinola started collecting and deploying units from Spain and Spanish Italy and intensified recruiting in Flanders. By participating in quelling the Bohemian Revolt and conquering the rebel Frederick's electorate, he would gain the territory of the Rhine Palatinate. He would gain this territory for Spain, and, more important, this barrier to the eastern frontier of the Dutch Republic would be removed and the way open. In the words of an eminent historian, in a trenchant summary of the strategic situation in the 1620s:

> [T]hrough control of Germany, and more especially the Rhine provinces, the King of Spain saw his way to the defeat of the Dutch.[5]

Accordingly in April 1620 while Maximilian of Bavaria, allied to the Emperor Ferdinand, crossed the Austrian frontier with over 25,000 troops of the Catholic League to confront the rebellion of Frederick in Bohemia, Spinola advanced with large Spanish forces from Brussels towards the Rhine. The Twelve Years' Truce was still in force, and Maurits, watchful and apprehensive, dared not violate it by any form of hindrance or intervention. Spinola headed south-east, crossed the Rhine at Koblenz, and continued towards Bohemia. But Bohemia was just a feint. Suddenly, in mid-August, he deployed, wheeled his troops about, and headed back towards the Rhine, straight for the Palatinate. Mainz was taken in August, and the following month Kreunach and Oppenheim were occupied. The rebel Elector Frederick had failed in his bid for the Bohemian crown and had lost his electorate, the Palatinate, which was now occupied by Spanish troops. They were now strategically in place when necessary (i.e. when the Twelve Years' Truce ended) to advance up the Rhine against the eastern side of the Dutch Republic.

As soon as the Twelve Years' Truce ended, Spinola left about 11,000 troops under General Cordova in the Rhenish Palatinate whilst he sent Count van den Bergh and 10,000 troops northwards towards Julich. Bergh took the small town of Julich from the Dutch garrison in July 1622. The elector of Brandenburg, having isolated possessions in the

Cleves-Julich area, sent 1,300 troops to assist the Dutch forces, but then in a volte-face made peace with Duke Wolfgang Wilhelm. Duke Wolfgang Wilhelm was the son and heir of the original 1609–1610 claimant Philp Ludwig of Pfalz-Neuberg, and he and the elector of Brandenburg settled on Brandenburg surrendering the small county of Ravenstein in exchange for accepting and recognizing the remaining territories as those of Brandenburg. Ravenstein itself was a small enclave actually within Dutch territory. By 1622, the small Dutch territory within the county of Ravensburg had also surrendered.

Spinola, by capturing Julich, effectively cut off the Dutch Republic's lines of communication with their Protestant allies of the Palatinate. The Dutch managed to repel Spinola's drive on Bergen op Zoom, inflicting heavy losses on the attacking forces. However, the pressure on the Dutch line in the east continued with the imperial forces, and the Catholic League advanced against the Protestant ruler Christian of Brunswick, who was forced to fall back against the Dutch frontier, making a stand near the border with the Dutch Republic. At Stadlohn, near Gelderland, his forces were utterly routed by those of the Catholic League.

From December 1622 and throughout 1623, Maurits sent secret messages indicating possible concessions which could be made to Spain. Some of King Philip's ministers, conscious of the spiraling financial costs of the struggle with the Dutch and wishing to give priority to the wider struggle within the Empire, were willing to consider the proposals. However Olivares in Madrid counselled that there was nothing of substance in these proposals and that Spain and the Spanish army needed to brush them aside and continue vigorously pursuing the war. Yet Maurits's secret messages and overtures continued to both Peckius in Brussels and to Spinola at the head of his armies, both of whom for a time took them seriously. Peckius gave them consideration. More important, Spinola paused and halted his advance. In making this choice, he missed an opportunity made available to him by the weather. Dry weather and little rain had dramatically reduced the level of the river IJssel along which part of the main eastern defensive line of the Dutch Republic was formed. Spinola could have crossed the IJssel and advanced, coinciding with the Catholic League's victory at Stadlohn, and inflicted further substantial pressure on the Republic. However, he paused, possibly chastened by the repulse at Bergen op Zoom and also judging that Maurits was seeking a new truce that would give concessions to Spain. When he came to realise that Maurits was merely playing for time, he resumed the offensive. But by his clandestine overtures and messages, Maurits had gained a further precious respite.

When Spinola finally realised the true motivation behind Maurits's overtures, he renewed the offensive, which he did ruthlessly, and the intense pressure on the Dutch Republic continued. He adopted a scorched earth policy around Grave and laid siege to the strategically vital town of Breda. Cleves and Gennep to the east were captured, and finally Breda was taken in June 1625. Maurits was still full of fight in spirit but had been ailing fast. He died in April 1625. Whilst he was gravely ill and clearly failing, a teacher in The Hague wrote in his diary of his eventual death:

> [T]he changes with which we are threatened. O dark day for Holland! May the Lord be merciful for his people and his church.[6]

A distinguished historian has summed up the situation at Maurits's death as:

> Maurits died . . . with the Republic's fortunes at a lower ebb than any time since 1590.[7]

For the Dutch Republic it was a dark hour. However, it was the darkest hour before the dawn. And inexorably, the dawn was to come due to several factors, at least some of which were thanks to the unceasing efforts of Maurits. That the defensive ring of fortified positions and fortresses around the south east and east, bending and cracking under enemy pressure, was in existence at all and had held so long was thanks to Maurits. It was his initiative to build the defensive line, and, thanks to his deployment of troops, made with care to eke out limited manpower to cover the lines, that it held. The successful spirited defence of Bergen op Zoom was due to Maurits.

Moreover, however dire the situation, there was an inherent realisation in Spain that the northern provinces of which the Dutch Republic consisted could not be reconquered, and perhaps the struggle was no longer worth the costs and effort. In 1598 a member of the Spanish Cortes spoke out, stating:

> [W]hy should we pay a tax on flour here in order to stop heresy there?

And in 1593 in the Cortes, another member called for an end to the war, dismissively stating:

> [I]f they want to be damned, let them.

In 1624, an official of the Council of the Indies wrote:

> Why should we have to pursue a harmful and ruinous war that has lasted sixty-five years? Christ never ordered conversions by force of gun, pike or musket.

One historian has explained Spanish opinion with regard to the attempted suppression of the Revolt that was reached by 1600—at the height of

Maurits's successful offensives against the Spanish—as that of informed Spanish opinion being almost entirely at variance with official policy.[8] By the second decade of the 1600s, official policy seemed to have realigned itself with informed opinion when Philip III's chief minister Baltasar de Zuniga, in 1619 counselled:

> We cannot by force of arms, reduce those provinces to their former obedience. Whoever looks at the matter carefully and without passion, must be impressed by the great armed strength of those provinces both by land and sea
> . . . [T]hat state is at the very height of its greatness, whilst ours is in disarray. To promise ourselves that we can conquer the Dutch is to seek the impossible.[9]

The policy of Zuniga in the second decade of the 1600s was to attempt to improve economic relations between the United Provinces and the Spanish Netherlands in order to improve the situation of the latter. His successor, Olivares, pursued a more hawkish policy, but he too never imagined that war with the Dutch would bring about the collapse or reconquest of the Dutch provinces.[10] The reconquest of the Dutch Republic was impossible, and the realisation by Madrid had been made as early as 1606.[11] The Dutch Republic was firmly and irrevocably established as an independent nation state.

Olivares himself realised the unfeasibility of the spiraling costs after the pressure on Spanish finances caused by the unsuccessful siege of Bergen op Zoom and then the successful offensive against Breda. In mid-1625, the Council of State in Madrid decided that the Army of Flanders would cease operations and would be placed on a defensive footing with a reduction in funding. Even with the capture of Breda, even Spinola was advising Madrid to engage in peace talks as:

> the experience of sixty years of war with the Dutch has shown how impossible it is to conquer the provinces by force.[12]

Whilst Spanish finances were causing the faltering of the Spanish offensive, Dutch finances, though also under severe pressure, received a small boost thanks to Maurits. In 1621 a delegation from the States-General had been sent to Paris. Since the fall of Oldenbarneveldt, French-Dutch relations had deteriorated, and this delegation was an attempt to renew the alliance and, of paramount importance, to obtain financial aid. It failed completely. However, in 1624 Maurits had personally sent a specially appointed embassy, led by a noble who was one of his loyal followers,[13] to Paris to approach Louis XIII. It succeeded. Louis XIII was uneasy about the success of the various Hapsburg forces in the Empire. The mission succeeded, and the Treaty of

Compiegne was signed in June 1624 and undertook a French subsidy to the Dutch of a million guilders every year for 3 years.

On the wider strategic front, whilst Christian of Brunswick's forces had been routed, a new Protestant power, Denmark, entered the fray in 1624 to confront the imperial forces and the Catholic League. In December 1625, Denmark, England, and the Dutch were to form an alliance, by The Hague Convention, in support of the exiled Frederick V, the defeated and exiled elector Palatine. Christian IV of Denmark invaded from the north and advanced. But in 1626 he was defeated at the Battle of Lutter, and for the next 3 years had to fight a rearguard action, eventually taking Denmark out of the conflict. However, the following year—and within a decade of the renewal of the Spanish-Dutch struggle—in 1630 imperial and Hapsburg forces were to be confronted by the whirlwind intervention of Sweden under Gustavus Adolphus. The following year in 1631, Sweden was supported by French diplomacy under Richelieu and subsidised in the secret Treaty of Barwalde.

Also in the late 1620s another factor of the Spanish failure to defeat the Dutch Revolt reappeared. This was the distraction of another front in conflict. In late 1627, news reached Spinola, busy and inexorably campaigning against the Dutch, that Olivares was starting a war on a new front in north-east Italy with offensives from Spanish Milan against Mantua, which was situated just south of the Venetian Republic. He departed for Madrid in December 1627 to plead for Spanish resources not to be divided and for reinforcements for the Army of Flanders. The new conflict centred on a struggle over the disputed inheritance over Mantua and its dependent territory of Monferrato. Monferrato itself had already been the subject of a territorial dispute between the Duke of Savoy and Spain. France also coveted parts of Mantua-Monferrato.

One of the claimants to the Duchy of Mantua was Duke Charles, holder of autonomous duchies in France, a fanatical Catholic, and pro-imperialist. Duke Charles acted quickly, marched his forces, and arrived in the Mantuan capital. He then appealed to the Emperor to recognise his title. Emperor Ferdinand II was reluctant to give such recognition, for fear of offending certain factions and families in Mantua who had supported him during the Bohemian Revolt and remained loyal; Richelieu and France held back from supporting Duke Charles who, though a French nobleman, appeared to be aligning himself with the Hapsburgs. The situation drifted, with neither Madrid, Paris, nor Vienna giving any guidance or orders. Cordova, the Spanish governor of Milan, took the initiative and signed an agreement with the Duke of Savoy, settling the Spain-Savoy dispute by partitioning Monferrato between Spain and Savoy. However, Duke Charles resisted the takeover, raising 13,000 mercenary troops from within Mantua and reinforcing these with a further 6,000 troops raised from his French duchies. Cordova, with his 1,000 troops, was obliged to urgently request more troops from Spain.

Richelieu then sent a large French force across the Alps to restore the situation in favour of France, though not necessarily to assist Duke Charles. The Duke of Savoy then made peace with France, gaining recognition of its possession of part of Monferrato in exchange for French possession of the strategically important fortress of Casale. This was too much for Olivares in Madrid, who had been caught by surprise at the rapid turn of events (despite Cordova's warnings). Refusing Spinola's representations for prioritizing and reinforcing the Army of Flanders in 1629, he sent Spinola to Milan to replace Cordova. Spinola was sent with a force of 18,000 troops with the strategic objective of joining forces with imperial troops to overthrow Duke Charles and overturn any French-imposed settlement.

In the meantime, in 1628 a Spanish treasure fleet collecting and transporting valuable cargo and silver bullion in the Caribbean was captured by the fleet of the Dutch admiral Piet Hein, and all of it was brought back to the Netherlands. The amounts gained were between 11 and 16 million florins, a massive boost to the Dutch war economy. And as if to emphasise Dutch survival, in 1629 Maurits's successor Frederick Henry captured the town that had long resisted Dutch attempts, s'Hertogenbosch.

All told, despite the darkest hour at Maurits's death, the survival of the Dutch Revolt and the Republic was assured. The dawn would come. Survival had been thanks to Maurits.

Notes

1. Maland, D *Europe at War 1600–1605* p 86
2. Ten Raa, T and de Baas, JC *Staatse Leger 1568–1795 Vol III* pp 292–293
3. Wilson, P *The Thirty Years War—Europe's Tragedy* p 435
4. Israel, J *The Dutch Republic—Its Rise, Greatness, and Fall 1477–1806* p 485
5. Wedgwood, CV *Richelieu and the French Monarchy* p 40
6. Beck, D 18 November *Spiegel van mijn leven Haagse Dagboek 1624*
7. Israel, J *The Dutch Republic—Its Rise, Greatness, and Fall 1477–1806* p 485
8. Kamen, H *Spain 1469–1714* p 138, and also the cited examples pp 138–139
9. Brightwell, P "The Spanish System and the XII Year Truce" cited in Limm, P *The Dutch Revolt* p 132
10. Parker, G *The Dutch Revolt* pp 264–265
11. Israel, J in *The Dutch Republic and the Hispanic World 1601–1661* p xiv is quite definitive that Spain fully recognised by as early as 1606 that reconquest was impossible:

    > [T]here can be no longer any doubt that the Spanish Crown had come to accept the principle of Dutch political and religious independence and there was *never subsequently* any Spanish ambition or plan for reconquering the break-away northern region [italics mine].

    Another eminent historian of this period, Parker, G in his *The Dutch Revolt* pp 264–265 writes of the period of the final years of the Twelve Years' Truce:

At no time did Zuniga . . . or Olivares imagine war with the Dutch was likely to bring about collapse of the Dutch Republic. . . . Spain made it clear her aim was not to force unconditional surrender of her adversaries but to improve relationships especially over economic relations between the powers and to secure better terms for the southern Netherlands.

Another historian, E.S. de Clerck, this time looking at the situation at the end of the Twelve Years' Truce and taking the viewpoint of the period of the growing Dutch commercial empire in a comprehensive 2-volume *History of the Netherlands East Indies* states directly of 1621, stated:

It was no longer a struggle for liberty, for the independence of the Republic was already an accomplished fact, although as yet not acknowledged by Spain [volume I pp 32–33].

12. Debates within the Council of State 1628, Archivo National Historico, Madrid HN Estado Libro 620, cited in Parker, G *The Dutch Revolt* p 265
13. Price, JL *Holland and the Dutch Republic in the Seventeenth Century* pp 123–124, 223–225 points out that historians have underestimated the political role of the nobility. Whilst the regents were indeed all powerful in provincial States and the States-General, and whilst during the period of Oldenbarneveldt's ascendancy they were totally eclipsed, and whilst in agriculture the independent freeman peasant was predominant, some of the nobility, dependent on the stadhouder, had a political role to play. The 1624 extraordinary embassy to Paris and its excellent timing and skilful pleading led by Van den Bouchorst may be such an example

12 Reasons Why the Dutch Revolt Survived

Geography has been cited as a major factor for success in many revolts, including that of the Dutch Revolt. Let us first consider geography—the so-called matrix of history—as a major factor in the gaining of independence of what are now two of the world's most powerful nations, and then let us turn to the Dutch Revolt.

The success of the 13 British North American colonies in achieving independence from Britain and becoming the United States was in a large part due to the vast distance between the possessing mother country and the colonies and the failure of the British Navy, the most powerful in the world at the time, to cover the various logistical and combat duties over such a wide geographic expanse. This was predictable, arguably even inevitable. The British politician Charles James had no military background or experience and was a tyro in international relations. Yet even he realised that this war had its particular problems of strategy and tactics, supply and logistics,[1] all due to distance. He stated in a parliamentary debate with uncanny foresight that the conquest of America:

> was in the nature of things absolutely impossible. . . . [T]here was a fundamental error in the proceedings, which would prevent our generals from acting with success.[2]

He finished by saying that quite simply the generals were too far apart in distance to aid one another. Less than a fortnight later after he made this speech, the rebel colonists had won the crucial victory of Saratoga, due to their exploiting and the British underestimating the distances involved in operating on the American continent. Saratoga was the turning point of the American War of Independence.

Turning to the other powerful nation, Russia, during the period 1919–1921, the revolutionary regime of the Russian Revolution fought for its survival against 3 differing armies of counter-revolutionaries. These counter-revolutionary movements and their forces were financed for a period by France, Britain and Japan. These countries also sent units of their own armed forces to reinforce the counter-revolutionary armies.

For the revolutionary communist regime in power in Russia, the conflict for survival was a near-run thing. The counter-revolutionary forces, at the zenith of their success, had reduced the territory controlled by Soviet Russia to just under a third. However, the communist regime survived due to several reasons, one crucial factor being that of geography. The Soviet Red Army, ably led by Trotsky, had significant advantages of manoeuvring on an internal axis, involving shorter distances. Trotsky and the Red Army commissars and commanders took full advantage of this, engaging and dealing with one set of counter-revolutionary forces, then turning to another, holding them, and repelling their invasion. By contrast, the counter-revolutionary forces were operating on 3 different fronts: south Ukraine, the territory around Archangel, and the eastern extremes of Kamchatka-Siberia. They were generally disconnected[3] and uncoordinated in their operations and advances.

Turning back to the Dutch Revolt, one historian, in a short history of the Dutch Republic, states that geography was a crucial factor in the success of the Dutch Revolt.[4] He points to Spanish attempts at the reconquest of the north, which advanced from the southern areas of Flanders and Brabant, having to surmount extreme difficulties of the barriers formed by the rivers and the terrain. This was also pointed out and summarised by an eminent Dutch historian in a series of essays on Dutch history describing the actions and campaigns of Maurits of Nassau in that:

> for the first time the rebels were able to take the offensive and . . . Maurits succeeded . . . in firmly . . . securing the river barrier to which the truncated Union owed its survival.[5]

He then points out that as part of the terms of the Twelve Years' Truce, the frontier of the Dutch Republic was based mainly on following the course of the great rivers.

And again, in another work specifically on the Dutch Revolt, the same historian emphasizes that:

> the geographical configuration of the country, in particular the strategic importance of the great rivers, was to be the determining factor.[6]

Another historian, in detailed analyses of the campaigns in the Low Countries, makes the qualification that the river barriers aiding the Dutch Revolt both to the south and to the east, however substantial, were not the decisive factors alone. The decisive factor was the erection by Maurits of a well placed line of forts and barriers following the line of the rivers; this made the essential difference.[7] Geographical factors were an important reason why the Dutch Revolt succeeded.

Let us turn to other reasons why the Dutch Revolt survived and consider "our" 4 factors, namely strong national identity, having adequate armed forces, exploiting the international dimension, and having adequate financial resources.

National Identity

Whilst the initial disturbances of the Dutch Revolt were of mixed causes impacting upon differing classes and levels of society—the upsetting of traditional privileges and customs of the various territories and jurisdictions, the reorganisation of the bishoprics, the intensification of the anti-heresy campaign, and the economic burdens of Alva's taxes—a national sentiment, a feeling, and patriotism arose amongst the Dutch with the common purpose of throwing off foreign Spanish rule at a comparatively early stage of the Eighty Years' War. Calvinism was a potent dynamic force that bound the provinces of Holland and Zeeland. William of Orange's constant and tireless in efforts to maintain religious toleration and to keep Holland, Zeeland, and the other provinces together ensured that, by the early 1570s, there was a national identity. The *Justification* was an embryonic national appeal, and as early as 1569 the *Wilhelminus* national song was becoming widespread.[8] The meeting at Dordrecht of the first States-General further embodied and legalised the national cause, and the Union of Utrecht in 1579 gave a defined territorial imperative. Throughout whole of the Eighty Years' War, complete unity between the provinces was certainly not assured, and a form of provincial sovereignty always had to be acknowledged. Provincial rivalry, particularly Holland against other provinces, and the jealous guarding of the provincial States' privilege, constantly bedeviled unity of purpose against the enemy. Even at the final settlement of the struggle in 1648 at the Treaty of Münster acknowledging full independence of the Dutch Republic, the States of Zeeland initially refused to ratify until finally brought round. Sir William Temple, English ambassador to the Netherlands in the late Seventeenth Century, was to remark that a more apt name for the United Provinces would be Disunited Provinces. One historian observes:

> [E]ven at the best of times they would have been described more accurately as Allied than as United.[9]

However, whilst divisions, often serious, did occur, these were divisions among provinces within a national entity and with a common national cause of wishing independence free from foreign rule. That national identity developed early in the Eighty Years' War[10] and was never lost.

Adequate Armed Forces

The Dutch Revolt was rarely short of numbers, but the quality and efficiency of its soldiery, though sufficient to confront the experienced and well trained Spanish troops, were a problem in the early stages. Thanks to the military reforms of Maurits and Willem Lodewijk, this was rectified. Combined with the strategy of preserving soldiers' lives by concentrating upon sieges, it was effective and ensured that this problem was remedied. Also, Maurits had the benefit of English contingents sent by Queen Elizabeth to fight alongside the Dutch forces. These English troops had several notable commanders, like Roger Williams, John Norris, and Francis Vere, the latter described by one historian writing of the English assistance to the Dutch Revolt as:

> the George Patton-crossed-with-Montgomery of Maurits' campaigns.[11]

Vere and his units distinguished themselves in several of the sieges, as shock troops being first to exploit breaches in the town's defences and on other occasions fighting off Spanish relieving forces. The English units, although at the time volatile and unpredictable, were overall valuable reinforcements and worked well in tandem with the Dutch with "businesslike if not cordial relations".[12] English participation assisting the Dutch Revolt was yet another distraction for the Spanish in that the international affairs worked against Spain (see the factor in the next section).

One distinguished historian has taken a long-term assessment of the Netherlands and points out that they never forgot the past in terms of being formed and maintaining their constitutional formation of a complexity of jurisdictions and local rights. As a result, a state system was never built that had the capacity of quick, secret, and decisive action (causing disunion). Yet, he continues, they were able to maintain a strong navy and a strong army.[13] That a strong army was created and that at times the Netherlands in their Revolt and during internal strife did engage in quick and decisive action was due to Maurits of Nassau. In doing so, Maurits ensured the survival of the Revolt and the Dutch Republic

The International Situation and Its Exploitation

The third factor, the international situation, was fully exploited by the Dutch. As early as 1578 William of Orange wrote secretly to Henri III of France,[14] urging him to intercede with Spain to ensure that the terms of the Pacification of Ghent were upheld. In 1598 Oldenbarneveldt's delegation, sent in haste but also careful and measured in negotiations and avoiding touching upon internal French matters, gained the vital subsidy from Henri IV of France. These funds ensured the continued financing of the struggle. The terms of the Twelve Years' Truce certainly exploited the international dimension in favour of the Dutch. The actual terms themselves, as we have seen, gave *de facto* recognition to an independent Dutch Republic as a sovereign state. Moreover, clause 4 of the Truce stipulated that the terms did not apply overseas, giving both protagonists full freedom to continue hostilities and a commercial war overseas, which the Dutch successfully carried out.

Maurits himself was at times cautious by nature, but he always realised when urgent action was needed, and this was shown in decisive and urgent action akin to that of Oldenbarneveldt in 1598, when his delegation to Louis XIII of France gained the subsidies of the Treaty of Compiègne in 1624. In the period following 1618, the crushing of the Bohemian Revolt and the start of the Thirty Years' War, Maurits realised the need to play for time. The crisis of the internal struggle for authority within the Dutch Republic between Maurits and Oldenbarneveldt throughout the second decade of the Seventeenth Century had distracted all parties and politicians of the Republic from international events during that crucial period.[15] Now those events were running against and threatening the Republic. Maurits recognised that war with Spain was likely, and indeed some contemporary opinion opined that Maurits himself was wishing the end of the Truce as another truce, once this second one expired, would mean that he would be too old as an effective military leader.[16] However, he and the Dutch Republic needed some time. Between late 1619 and 1621, he exploited the caution of the governor of the Spanish Netherlands, Archduke Albert, by his (Maurits's) mixed signals and secret correspondence and exploited the differences between Albert on the one hand and on the other the hawks in Madrid who were increasingly in favour of ending the truce. He played the well meaning Peckius in the latter's visit to The Hague. The result of these diplomatic manoeuvres was that he gained time for the Republic.

Also during this same period, Maurits exploited the international situation by pursuing a prudent strategic policy with regard to the start of the European-wide Thirty Years' War. This was in keeping with his playing for time. He—as William of Orange-Nassau's grandson—gave the elector Frederick V assistance, but he realised that Frederick could never be a substantial or credible ally. However, arguably, Maurits gave just enough assistance to Frederick and the Protestant Union to increase hostilities in central Europe, thus drawing away Spanish forces from the Netherlands. It meant keeping the affairs and conflicts of the Holy Roman Empire firmly at a distance. The Dutch Republic avoided any formal declaration of war relating to any of the imperial conflicts, and it was not until 1646 that an official diplomatic envoy from the Dutch Republic was accredited to the Empire.

Throughout the Dutch Revolt, the Dutch were greatly helped by the international situation in that Spain, whilst extremely powerful, was at crucial points in the Revolt distracted by other pressing priorities. Such distractions from quelling the Dutch Revolt were to occur again and again.

Also, the Turkish threat to Europe, particularly the Hapsburgs, was a long-term threat. The Turkish threat to the Austrian Hapsburgs from the south-west was not to be finally nullified until the 1680s, with the campaigns of Prince Eugen of Savoy driving back the Turks down the Balkans.[17] The Turkish expansion in the Mediterranean—as far along as modern Algeria and Tunisia in the reign of Charles V—was a recurring threat to Hapsburg Spain. When Pope Pius V ascended the papal throne in 1566, within 4 days of his accession, he granted a large papal subsidy to Spain,[18] a subsidy specifically to meet the expenses of the Spanish galley fleets. Phillip II, zealous in his faith and in his belief in Spain as the chief Catholic power, was nothing loath to receive the monies, but it committed him and Spain more strongly to combating the Turks in the Mediterranean.

In the early part of the Dutch Revolt in the late 1560s and 1570s Alva was of one mind with Philip II on the need for robust and repressive action in dealing with the Revolt. Yet other regional conflicts impacting upon Spain and its Empire preoccupied Philip II. On this occasion, it was the Turkish threat that rendered the troubles in the Netherlands a secondary priority. In May 1565 the Turkish forces besieged Malta, which was only relieved in September 1565 after a bloody and bitter siege by the Spanish fleets from Naples. In February 1570 Turkish envoys demanded the surrender of the territory of Cyprus from the Republic of Venice, and finally captured the whole of Cyprus in August 1571. Pope Pius founded an anti-Turkish coalition of threatened countries and states. In this coalition, Spain commanded the naval operations and made the largest financial contribution. Being too late to save Cyprus, the combined coalition fleet sailed from Messina in Sicily, passed Corfu, sought out the Turkish fleets, and in a one-day naval action was completely victorious over the Turkish fleet. Only 15 galleys of the original 300 Turkish ships managed to escape and make it back to the Sublime Porte. The commander of the coalition fleet was Don Juan of Austria. The Turkish threat was stilled—for the moment—but it had been a distraction for Philip during at least two vital years in the early 1570s of the Dutch Revolt.

Alva himself, while entrenched and fully preoccupied with the Dutch Revolt at the crucial points of the sieges of Alkmaar and Haarlem, warned in 1573 that:

> if some new problem, however small, were to rise, His Majesty's resources are so exhausted that he might not have the strength to resist.[19]

England was another commitment for imperial Spain.[20] This was partly for ideological reasons. Spain as the principal Catholic power had a mission, deeply felt by Philip II, to reconquer England for the true faith. Also in the late Sixteenth and early Seventeenth Centuries, the English fleets were harming the Spanish economy by their raids and attacks on Spanish convoys. The support for the various plots throughout Elizabeth's reign and then the so-called Enterprise of England of the ill-fated Armada all took resources and distracted strategic counsel and thinking away from the Netherlands Revolt. Nor did it end with the defeat of the Armada. In 1596 Philip II ordered the fitting out, supplying, and deployment of another armada to invade England. In this he invoked for the Duke of Medina Sidonia, the commander of the failed Armada of 1588 and the commander of this second armada, the same messianic concept of the spiritual mission of Spain to reconquer England for the true faith. Significantly in 1597 the High Seas fleet of Spain mutinied, every ship refusing the specific and categorical orders to sail against England. In 1599 a new armada was assembled and sailed for England but had to be diverted to the Azores to counter an Anglo-Dutch fleet deploying there. A final invasion fleet was assembled and set sail in 1601, this time for Ireland, where it landed a Spanish army in support of the rebellion of the earl of Tyrone against England. By 1603 the Tyrone and Spanish forces had been outmanoeuvred and outfought. The Spanish forces capitulated and were allowed to sail for home. For decades whilst attempting to deal with the Netherlands Revolt, Spain became embroiled and distracted with near-continuous warfare against England.

Finally, for Spain there was the near-constant preoccupation with France. Although both were Catholic countries, Spain and France were rival powers and France constantly feared the might of the Hapsburgs. From the French perspective, the combined Hapsburg territories of the Holy Roman Empire, Spain, Italy, and the Netherlands encircled and threatened France. From the Spanish perspective, French ambitions in Italy threatened the logistic flow of troops from Spain to Italy and then up the Spanish Road to the Netherlands. Also, France's close proximity to the Netherlands could enable clandestine interference. And the Netherlands at the start of Philip II's reign were one of the most valuable territories of the empire of Spain with their high productivity and contributions to the imperial budget. As we have seen, at a crucial period in the attempts at quelling the Dutch Revolt, just as Parma's counter-offensive was regaining the southern provinces and making inroads in the northern provinces, he was ordered to cease offensive in the Netherlands, stand to there, and turn his troops for an offensive to assist the Catholic League in France. That period 1589–1595 was fully exploited by the Dutch counter-offensive, Maurits and Willem Lodewijk's campaigns expanding the territory and ensuring the security of the Dutch Republic.

The Spanish Empire had vast resources but used them inefficiently in facing the different fronts in conflict. The Turkish threat was dealt with spasmodically, with no long-term plan, as stated by a historian whose work covered a period of 80 years of the Sixteenth Century:

> Philip had no strategy for the Mediterranean, only piecemeal responses to a thousand problems.[21]

To contemporaries, there was a lack of long-term coordinated strategy, and there was never any dealing in depth with any given threat. One Spanish diplomat wrote in despatches:

> We flit so rapidly from one area to another without making a major effort in one and then . . . I do not know why we eat so many snacks but never the real meal.[22]

This "flitting" from one front to the other was indeed to the advantage of and exploited by the Dutch.

The fourth factor was that of adequate finances. This is covered in detail in the following chapter.

Notes

1. Derry, JW *Charles James Fox*
2. Tuchamann, B chapter 4 'The British Lose America' in *The March of Folly* p 216
3. Pares, B *A History of Russia* p 542
4. Wilson, CW *The Dutch Republic* p 13
5. Geyl, P *History of the Low Countries—Episodes and Problems* p 14
6. Geyl, P *The Revolt of the Netherlands* p 179
7. Parker, G chapter on the characteristics of war in the Low Countries in *The Army of Flanders and the Spanish Road 1567–1659* p 17
8. Wedgwood, CV *William the Silent* p 116
9. Boxer, CR *The Dutch Seaborne Empire* p 15
10. Parker, G in his *The Dutch Revolt* argues that a distinct national identity and strong sentiment amongst all 17 provinces of the Netherlands had developed by the 1550s, with the adopted common emblem of the Dukes of Burgundy of a lion holding a sheaf of 17 arrows p 33; distinguished historian Judith Pollman, specialising in the Dutch Revolt, has put forward one interpretation of the Eighty Years' War as less of a revolt and more of a civil war with a nation of 17 provinces, Pollman, J "Internationalisering en der Nederlandse Opstand" in *Bijdragenenmededelingen betreffende de geschiedenis der Nederlander* p 124
11. Wilson, CW *Queen Elizabeth and the Revolt of the Netherlands* p 112
12. Wilson, CW *Queen Elizabeth and the Revolt of the Netherlands* p 113
13. Plumb, JH in his Introduction to Boxer, CR *The Dutch Seaborne Empire* p xxiii
14. Letter despatched from Antwerp 28 April 1578, Konenljike Bibliotheek, The Hague Special Collections KW121A1:1
15. Parker, G *The Dutch Revolt* p 263
16. *Den Compaignon*, cited by Israel, J *The Dutch Republic and the Hispanic World 1606–1661* p 79
17. Fraser, D *Frederick the Great* p 13
18. Braudel, F *The Mediterranean and the Mediterranean World in the Age of Philip II* p 1029
19. Kamen, H *Phillip II of Spain* p 308
20. Wilson, CH in the Conclusion of his *Elizabeth and the Revolt of the Netherlands* analyses differing interpretations of the English participation in and assisting of the Revolt. However, whatever the motives of Elizabeth and the interpretations of the extent and result of the English intervention, it is clear

that England was yet another hostile country preventing Spain from concentrating solely on quelling the Dutch Revolt

21. Crowley, R *Empires of the Sea—The Final Battle for the Mediterranean 1521–1580* p 204
22. Duke of Sessa, Spanish ambassador to Don Balthsar de Zunije, Spanish ambassador to Brussels 9 November 1602

13 The Sinews of War

The two protagonists, Spain and the Dutch, maintained their war efforts throughout the Dutch Revolt, but the finances of each at times were perilous. Spain managed to continue the war effort through international borrowing and drawing upon silver bullion imports, whilst the Dutch relied on various *ad hoc* means for finances and the wealth of the province of Holland. One distinguished historian ascribes the greatest single reason why the Dutch Revolt was able to continue and be ultimately successful to the economic strength of the provinces of Holland (and to a lesser extent Zeeland[1]).

For Spain, the fastest increase in the Spanish national debt corresponded to the greatest expenditure on the Army of Flanders. The army required more and more men and more and more monies. Between 1567 and 1574 alone, over 42,000 soldiers were deployed from Spain to the Netherlands.[2] Local recruiting of levies from Flanders who remained loyal to Spain was implemented throughout the entire Dutch Revolt, but, to deal with the Revolt, there was always a need for Spanish troops to be sent from Spain and the Spanish territories in Italy to the Netherlands. Alva's harsh rule had encompassed crushing the Revolt, the imposition of religious intolerance, making a standard judicial system of various provincial jurisdictions, establishing a relentless tribunal for hunting down and punishing rebels, and the imposition of taxes. The imposition of taxation for a brief time, a period of two years, made the Netherlands self-sufficient in terms of maintaining and paying for the Army of Flanders.

Alva's successor, Requesens, attempted more overall conciliatory policies including the approach to revenue raising. A regularised and more equitable system of contributions was attempted in those provinces that had remained loyal to Spain, based upon proportional amounts depending on the wealth of the province. Communities and villages paid a fixed amount in return for guaranteed immunity from further demands for contributions. Such paying communities received official, formalised documentation that they had paid. For a while this worked. Artois and Hainault, comparatively unscathed by the conflict, maintained their normal levels of taxation. Other areas of the Spanish Netherlands adhered to the Requesen's regime of the proportional quota and contributions system. However, as Parma engaged in reconquering Brabant and Flanders and thrusted evermore towards the United Provinces, the contributions became more important and were raised with increasing vigour, and the amounts demanded greatly increased. The States of Flanders and the States of Brabant formally agreed that, for purposes of funding Parma and the Army of Flanders, they would pay the regular fixed amounts. Yet still the funds raised were insufficient. As the Revolt kept flaring up, the situation became more complex, more troops were required, and increasingly Spain needed to provide the funds. Philip II had warned Alva, as he had warned Requesens, that Spain could not keep sending money indefinitely. But that was precisely what occurred over the decades.

Taxation in Spain was increased. Until the first decade of the Seventeenth Century, when an ill-fated attempt was made to impose a more equitable revenue gathering regime covering the whole of Spain and the Empire, the fiscal burden fell most heavily upon Castile. These taxes were repeatedly raised, and the burden on Castile increased. By the 1590s, as much as one-third of the average Castilian peasant's income was appropriated as tax.[3] Another excise tax on landowners was introduced towards the end of the Seventeenth Century, the *milliones*. This coincided with several years of declining harvests. Philip II and the Council of Finance and the Treasury were in extreme need of raising revenues to finance the Army of Flanders and the attempted reconquest of the United Provinces, but they had reached a point beyond which they could not impose new taxes or increase existing ones.

Inevitably Spain resorted to heavy borrowing. Borrowing large-scale funds was one thing, and banking houses were generally sympathetic to loans taken out on generous terms, but placing these funds in the Netherlands for use by the Army of Flanders was another. The amounts involved were large. In 1573, the amount made available by Spain was 3.4 million florins, and the following year, with the conflict intensifying and involving the long sieges of Haarlem and Leiden, the amount rose to 7 million florins. Physical transportation of such sums was cumbersome and dangerous. After being shipped across the Mediterranean from Valencia to the Spanish territory around Naples, it could then be sent overland by the Spanish Road via the Valtelline. However, the security of sections of this route during several periods was threatened by their falling under hostile control. Sea routes involved a long journey following the Spanish and French coasts, then passing through the English Channel; along the French coasts, the English Channel could be risky depending on the changing allegiances of France and England. In the late 1580s, the English effectively closed the Channel to all Hapsburg shipping. Transportation by either land or sea had potential hazards.

The solution lay in transferable credit, a sector whose financial instruments of various bills of exchange had increased exponentially since the mediaeval era. It was facilitated by the major banking houses of Europe, whose assets often dwarfed the royal revenues of the countries to whom they were lending. In 1318 the Italian banking house of the Bardi had a total capital of just over 875,000 florins, the contemporary equivalent of 130,000 sterling when the revenues of the English crown were worth only 30,000 sterling.[4] The researches of an eminent economic historian[5] revealed that credit played a major part in the total volume of mediaeval trade in Europe. One banking firm based in Lombardy had loans out to England valued at 1,100 sterling, as opposed to their total remaining capital of 1,400 sterling. Since then, credit and borrowing formed a major proportion of the revenue of city states and countries of Europe, particularly in times of war.

Money credit transfer was carried out not by physically transferring and transporting the bullion but by bills of exchange and promissory notes. This development of financial instruments was the start of paper currency. Bills of exchange, promissory notes, and other instruments between merchants and traders were agreed, redeemed, offset against other credit notes, resold—all carried out initially at trade fairs in the mediaeval era. Such fairs were held in a regular cycle, held at one town for periods of several weeks, then moving on to the next. The predominant fair towns were those of the French province of Champagne, in which Lagny-sur-Marne, Bar-sur-Aube, Provins, St. Ajou, and Troyes predominated, each one hosting a massive trade fair for a period of two months. In the words of one historian:

> [T]he originality of the Champagne fairs lay less in the superabundance of goods than in the money markets and the precocious workings of credit.[6]

Eventually the fairs of Champagne and other towns were ousted as the main centres of trade and credit exchange as various cities in Europe established themselves as financial centres and gained predominance. Then these cities, in turn, lost their *primus inter pares* position to another city, a period of over a century in which Bruges, Genoa, Venice, Lisbon, and Antwerp all enjoyed their heyday. This was a continuous process up to the mid-Eighteenth Century, with Amsterdam being the last city to hold sway.[7]

At the time of Philip II and the Dutch Revolt, Antwerp was the major financial city in Europe, where the banking house of Fugger carried out many of its financial operations. The Fuggers were based in Augsburg where the other large banking house, the Welsers, were also based. Together, these two banking giants had risen to be amongst the largest and most influential banking institutions in Europe. Arguably the Welsers were more adventurous and speculative, investing in the precious stone and jewel markets in the Far East and financing trading ventures in South America; but the Fuggers, more reliable, were steadier in their financial expansion.[8] By the end of the Sixteenth Century the Fuggers had ousted the Medici family bank from European predominance and had taken over many of its assets. The Fuggers had given help to Philip II's father, Charles of Hapsburg, during the imperial election, which resulted in Charles being elected as Emperor Charles V over the rival candidate Frances I of France. The help was that of providing "contributions" —or bribes—and inducements to various imperial electors and their entourages. The head of the Fugger bank, Jacob Fugger, afterwards asserted to Charles that he, Charles, would not have been elected without the help of the Fuggers. This was an exaggeration, but there was some truth in the frank statement. Charles's election campaign cost over 830,000 florins, some provided by the Welsers and by two Genoese banking houses; however, the Fuggers provided over 65% of the total.[9] The Fuggers continued to help Charles V in 1531 when Charles managed to ensure that his brother Ferdinand was elected king of the Romans, the customary second title of the Holy Roman Emperor; the Fuggers provided 36,000 florins for "contributions". In the early 1540s, Charles made preparations for war to quell the Protestant Schmalkaldic League; the Fuggers provided a substantial part of the 500,000 ducats advance loan.

Charles's loans were paid for by the credit instrument of the *asiento*. By this arrangement, the bank would agree to pay the monies through an agent bearing a bill of exchange to one of Charles's representatives abroad, and the monies would be drawn on presenting the bill of exchange at one of the banks in the locality. The bank would be reimbursed at the exchange in Antwerp or in Spain. Charles often promised prompt repayments but often deferred payment was the bank's preferred option, as the bank would add a "handling charge" to the sum owed—a form of additional interest. These handling charges varied, depending upon the political and military situation confronting the Emperor. On making peace with France in 1544, handling charges for the loan fell to 20%; in 1545, when the struggle with the Schmalkaldic League would last an inordinately long period, the handling charge was a massive 80%; after Charles's complete victory over the League at the Battle of Muhlburg in 1547, the handling charges fell to just 14%. Under the Emperor Charles V, the Fuggers had virtually become bankers to the Emperor. Also under Charles V, borrowing had become the only way to balance the Spanish budget. In transferring monies to various parts of the Empire, including the Netherlands, the banking and finance centre of Antwerp was key.[10]

Within a decade of his accession, Philip II was confronted by the early stages of the Dutch Revolt, which accordingly increased the national debt of Spain. The borrowing and credit transfer were effected by continuing the *asiento* system and bills of exchange. The king, through his financial officials, would make an arrangement with a merchant or financier or bank, whereby the lender would furnish a fixed sum to the Army of Flanders via the paymaster and his staff. The *asiento* was a short-term loan of one or two years at comparatively high rates of interest.

The merchant, financier, or a representative of the bank would be repaid or given the interest payments due in Spain by the Spanish Treasury at the fairs, usually at the giant fair at Medina del Campo. Significantly, now such fairs were named "Fairs of Exchange", and whilst dealing in some commodities and trading, they dealt mainly in currency changing, loan repayment, and loan transfer. They were held several times a year in Spain so, in theory, the merchant, financier, or bank did not have to wait indefinitely for the repayment of monies due. But as the amounts of monies borrowed mounted and spiraled, there was an increasing trend to draw up and agree *asientos*. The Spanish Treasury and Court raised revenues in Spain that were earmarked specifically for servicing the interest payments and eventually for repaying the original loan.

This trend was significant. The Spanish Crown turned to the sums raised from the *asiento* loans to supplement the inadequate sources of imperial revenues to fund the Army of Flanders. Now some of those same imperial revenues were being diverted for repayment of the very loans raised to supplement them.

Philip had little understanding of finances.[11] However, the exponential rising costs finally caused even Philip to realise action was needed. In early 1574 he sought the advice and counsel of Juan de Ovando, a priest and president of the Council of the Indies. In this function Ovando had made significant reforms and rationalised the bureaucracy responsible for running Spain's territories in the Americas. Ovando analysed and laid out in a stark and frank resume the perilous state of Spanish finances and what must be carried out. Philip procrastinated, preoccupied with religious issues in Spain and with events in the Netherlands and the Mediterranean. After a year, Ovando lost patience with Philip and forced his advice on him even more strongly, insisting upon bankruptcy as the only solution.

In 1575, to alleviate the spiraling debts on the *asientos*, Philip II issued a decree. This was known as the "Decree of Bankruptcy". It froze the capital of all loan contracts worth between 15 and 20 million ducats. All payments to bankers ceased. It was not a total abrogation or cancellation of the state debts; Spain would certainly need large-scale loans again and could ill afford to cut loose from the banking houses. The *asiento* loans and repayment schedules were suspended, payments and settlements to be resumed when Spain so chose and deemed it an appropriate time, that is, when financially viable. Bankers, merchants, financiers, and all creditors were given a choice. They could retain their holding and full rights of repayment of the *asientos* and await the resumption of settlements and repayments—unlikely, given the conflict and continued spiraling spending of the Spanish Treasury on the Army of Flanders—or take in exchange an income-bearing bond, or *juros*. *Asientos* were usually short-term loans bearing high interest rates and handling charges, whilst *juros* were long-term bonds with much lower interest returns. Bankers and other creditors accepted with an ill grace the changeover to *juros*, and in this way the huge Spanish floating debts were consolidated into long-term loan bonds at moderate interest rates.

Juros indeed imposed upon the Spanish Crown interest repayments, but these were comparatively low and the effective cancellation of the *asientos* increased the revenues that had been raised from extraordinary taxation hastily imposed for *asiento* repayments. With these revenues now remaining in the Treasury instead of going straight out for servicing *asientos*, they could be used as security to gain further loans from bankers to finance the war—and a cycle of high loans and compromise bankruptcy could begin again.

Charles V had made such "conversions" of *asiento*; Philip II carried this out through decrees to a greater extent and more frequently. Almost the first act of his reign was a decree of 1557 consolidating existing *asientos* into *juros* at the lower long-term interest rate of 5%.[12] The rising costs of the Army of Flanders made this Decree of 1575 necessary, and other Spanish monarchs and the Treasury were to use such decrees throughout the Dutch Revolt. Decrees were issued in 1596, in 1607, in 1627, and in 1647. Decrees of bankruptcy did leave bankers with low-interest-rate bonds, or *juros*, and, overall, the loss of significant sums in the cancelled *asiento* repayments. However, the effects of the decrees were often alleviated by a compromise agreement made with the major creditors one or two years later, such as an agreement known as the *medio general*. By this, the Spanish Crown agreed to repay or reimburse some of the lost *asiento* payments with grants of royal lands. In drawing up these *medio general*, the Spanish Crown was often able to insert into the agreement a further advance of monies or terms of another loan.

By the cycle of short-term *asientos* being converted into long-term *juros*, the Spanish war effort against the Dutch Revolt was able to continue, albeit in a somewhat financially ramshackle way. Nonetheless, the Decrees did take their toll. The first Decree of 1557 had an impact on the Fuggers, who effectively ceased to be bankers to Spain. After the 1557 bankruptcy, or conversion to *juros*, the Fuggers withdrew from any dealings in the *asiento* market and went into decline, along with several other prominent banking houses.[13] The Fuggers were supplanted as lenders in bankrolling the Spanish war against the Dutch Revolt by the Genoese banking and finance houses.[14] Crucially, the Decree of 1575 disrupted the Army of Flanders. Two years after the bankruptcy decree of that year was issued, a *medio general* was agreed with Spain's banking creditors. Until the *medio general* was agreed, Philip had deprived himself of any credit, and no bills of exchange could be issued or drawn upon. Don Juan was reported as saying:

> The Bankruptcy Decree has dealt such a great blow to the exchange that no-one in it has any credit. . . . I cannot find a single penny, nor can I see how the king could send money here.[15]

Spanish troops in the Netherlands were already suffering pay arrears. Three mutinies had occurred throughout 1573 and 1574 caused by discontent over arears of pay. The last mutiny in 1574 ensured that the Dutch victory in raising the siege of Leiden was complete and also that strongpoints around the city of Utrecht could be taken and occupied by Dutch forces. Then in 1575, a full-scale mutiny occurred, caused by non-payment of arrears[16] and the impossibility of any settlement due to the bankruptcy. With the September 1575 Decree of Bankruptcy passed, any possible credit or money transfers were curtailed, and army pay arrears kept accruing.

The Spanish government in the Netherlands hastily resorted to a compromise solution, agreeing to find and pay half the total of the pay arrears claimed by the mutineers in exchange for an agreement with the troops that their loyalty would be restored and that the other half of the arrears would be provided in free accommodation and the government's tacit, discreet approval of the troops engaging in stealing and plunder. Even the agreed payment of half the total of the agreed payment, 400,000 florins, had to be raised by loans from the merchants of Antwerp, who were anxious to preserve some degree of stability and order. This settlement was a temporary measure, not a solution to the eternal problem of the pay arrears of the Army of Flanders, whose Spanish veterans were superb soldiers and essential if the Dutch Revolt was to be quelled. A more permanent measure was negotiated by William of Orange, who had deployed his own troops in the north and around Ghent to maintain order. He, together with the Council of State in Brussels, agreed that the States cooperating with and through Brussels would raise their own troops and ensure order and that Spanish troops would be withdrawn from the Netherlands. Also, there would be some form of religious toleration. This negotiated settlement, as we have seen, was known as the "Pacification of Ghent".

Philip and Requesens, the governor of the Netherlands and the army commander, could only wait and hope that no further untoward happenings occurred. Their hopes were soon dashed by ongoing events.

If the mutinies were terrible, they had had far-reaching consequences when combined with other mutinies in 1576 caused by the Bankruptcy Decree. Spanish units, still due their pay arrears, attacked Aalst, just north of Brussels. Another group in November attacked Antwerp. At Antwerp, the Bourse ceased to function, and the murder of civilians and material damage were:

a disaster, nothing short of appalling.[17]

So irate were the Flemings with the disorders that soldiers from the States of Brabant, a southern province that had remained loyal, arrested the members of the Council of State in Brussels. The States of Brabant then met with representatives from the rebellious States of Holland and Zeeland, and these talks were expanded to other States, and terms were agreed with the mutineers. The States then refused to recognise Don Juan as governor-general until all Spanish troops were withdrawn and the Pacification of Ghent ratified.

Adequate finances had been totally lacking, causing the mutinies from 1574 to 1576. This halted the Spanish war effort in its tracks and abruptly ended Requesens's attempts at a compromise peace. Requesens was confronted by all provinces, those loyal to Spain and those in rebellion alike, demanding action and withdrawal of all Spanish troops from the Netherlands.

As well as the financial manipulation by the bankruptcy settlements with creditor bankers, Spain could and did use another resource in its struggle, that of the supply of silver bullion from its American possessions. Since the second decade of the Sixteenth Century, Spain had been receiving an increasing number of smaller amounts of gold bullion. Silver had been discovered in the Central and South American possessions of the Empire in the 1540s, and the mines were working at a regular production capacity by 1560. By the 1580s, the silver bullion entering Spain had become a veritable flood. Between 1581 and 1585, an average of nearly 2 million ducats, or 7.5 million pesos' worth, a year came to the Spanish crown alone.[18] Bullion imports into the port of Seville alone rose by over 40% between 1570 and 1590.[19] In 1590, Spain was receiving 7.5 million pesos' worth, and it remained at that yearly level until 1607.[20] The increase in wealth from the Americas, particularly the silver from Peru, was a welcome alleviation to Philip's cash problems. By 1592 Philip was expending over 12 million ducats every year, of which over a quarter was provided by the imported silver.[21] Payments to the Army of Flanders were all the more readily facilitated. However, he was still dependent upon the Genoese bankers for funds.[22]

The silver from the Americas had an additional advantage. The silver coin, or *reale*, had the silver content that made the individual value of this coin increase by at least 4% more outside Spain. This coincided with the demand by many Italian merchants for high-grade Spanish silver coins for trading purposes in the eastern Mediterranean area. Following the mutinies of 1574–1576, most units in the Army of Flanders insisted upon being paid in gold coin. Accordingly, the Genoese bankers who granted loans to Spain had the silver shipped to Italy, where they exchanged either the silver *reales* or their bills of exchange for gold at one of the major European fairs, that of Picenza, and then transported this by road to Flanders.

Officially it was strictly prohibited to export from Spain any silver arriving from the Americas. But the Genoese bankers and other lenders upon whose loans Spain depended easily obtained permission. During the period 1580–1626 Spain, through loans and *asientos*, spent just under 2.2 million kilos within Spain; during the same period, it spent a further 2.5 million kilos in the Netherlands.[23] Some bankers transported the silver, without changing it into gold direct, to Antwerp. This was needed to facilitate the encashment of bills of exchange coming from Spain by Antwerp, which was in decline as a European trade centre but still a functioning financial exchange centre.

As the bills of exchange proliferated—i.e. as Spain committed to larger and more frequent loans—the sheer amount of bullion arriving in Antwerp increased, but even then during some periods it failed to meet and cover the demand from the amounts being drawn upon. Genoese bankers transporting the bullion by road took considerable time to deliver it, and the passes of the Spanish Road were vulnerable to harsh adverse winter weather. Even lightweight document bills of exchange took over a fortnight to reach Antwerp. A paradoxical solution was found to be the availability of specie and coin in Antwerp—the Dutch themselves. The insurgent would-be nation state whose expanding navy wrought havoc in the Atlantic against Spanish convoys bearing supplies and monies also furnished funds to merchant shipowners who were willing and able to ship silver bullion down to Antwerp—for suitable carriage fees. Leicester's attempted trade embargo, whereby the United Provinces were prohibited from any commercial relations with either Spain or the loyal southern provinces, had been bitterly resented and discreetly circumvented. In fact, contraband trade between the Dutch insurgents and the Spaniards occurred in significant amounts in both directions throughout the period of the Dutch Revolt.[24] Thus the Dutch partially enabled the Spanish sinews of war to remain supple.

Let us now turn to the Dutch and consider their finances during the Revolt.

The prosperity of the province of Holland was undoubtedly a major economic factor in the financial sustaining of the Dutch Revolt. One eminent historian of the Netherlands places the province of Holland throughout the crucial period of the 1580s as contributing as much as two-thirds of the expenses of the Revolt.[25] After the split of 1579, the formation of the Union of Utrecht, and the years of endurance of the 1580s, the United Provinces came to a provincial quota agreement of each province for financing the Republic. Between 1586 and 1616, the province of Holland's contribution was never less than 55% of the total, and in the early part of this period it was as high as 64%. Together with the province of Zeeland (with whom Holland had formed a union in 1576, a union that continued in parallel to that of the Union of Utrecht), the combined contributions of Holland and Zeeland to the overall finances of the Republic were never less than 69%, and during the earlier part of this period, it stood as high as 80%.[26]

The individual provinces enjoyed a large degree of autonomy, and each raised taxes in its own way. The taxation regime in Holland, although initially heavy on the lower classes, was overall flexible, broad-based, and efficient. Indeed Holland provided over half the tax revenue of the Dutch Republic and was the only province to pay its quota to the general budget promptly and in full.[27] There was a standing ordinary tax in Holland, the property tax, and to this was added on occasions an extraordinary property tax. These were calculated as fairly as possible, Holland being divided into differing tax districts. Other revenues were raised by stamp duties and excise on certain commodities, excise that could be spread on differing items due to the large urban population. As the Republic evolved fiscally in the later Seventeenth Century, the burdens caused by the inevitable increases in taxation fell more upon the wealthier classes. The poorer classes were not hard-hit by excise duties, and anyone earning or having less than a thousand guilders was totally exempt from the extraordinary property taxes. Any loans raised by the States of Holland could be secured by the regularity of taxation revenues. Under the leadership of Holland, the increase in public debt of the Dutch Republic was well managed compared to other European countries, and the debt could be spread widely amongst savers,[28] the majority and most affluent of whom were based in Holland.

Holland's wealth—and that of the Republic—came from trade, and much of that from maritime trade. As early as the Fifteenth Century, ships from Holland's ports were competing with the wide and powerful Hanseatic League for carrying fish and salt. By 1555, Amsterdam had become one of the major redistribution ports in Europe for grain and corn, and by 1560 Dutch ships were responsible for almost 70% of bulk trade in the Baltic.[29] Amsterdam was a major entrepôt port for grain and shipbuilding materials and naval stores. The fleets, sailing from Holland and Zeeland, included many merchant vessels of the *fluyt* design, a strong ship of round sides with a large carrying load span but able to be sailed with a small crew. Also, running costs of the Dutch fleets were comparatively low. A French maritime report of a later century would point out several significant differences: the differing rates of pay, with French seamen being paid between 12 and 20 livres a month, whilst the Dutch seamen were paid between 10 or 12 a month; French seamen demanding 4 meals a day, whilst the Dutch adequately subsisted on two; and the food that had to be provided to the French crews including bread, wine, wheat meal biscuit, salt meat, cod, herring, eggs, butter, and peas, whilst the Dutch crews, though eating the same healthy size helpings, consumed beer, cheese, eggs, butter, and rye biscuit, with a little salt meat and dried herring.[30] Dutch crews were not underfed, but the British ambassador to The Hague did remark how frugal the rations were on board Dutch ships.[31]

Seaborne trading, in which Holland and Zeeland predominated, was further enhanced by the development of business and investment arrangements known as the *rederij*. By this, a group of individuals would combine in purchasing, owning, or hiring a ship and its cargo. It was a highly flexible form of business arrangement, with varying roles. Some *rederij* would consist of investors who were all land based; in other *rederij*, one of the investors would be the ship's captain and/or ship's master and/or other members of the crew, all contributing in differing proportions to the total capital outlay. These *rederij* made increased capital available to the enterprise(s) and facilitated extremely widespread investment in shipping and in trade. It bonded merchants and maritime workers.

In the province of Holland lay the jewel of Amsterdam. The fall of Antwerp to Parma's troops in 1585 as part of his reconquering drive in the southern provinces, occurring as it did a year after the assassination of William of Orange, marked a low point in the Dutch Revolt. However, a silver—or at least a commercial—lining appeared in this dark cloud over the Revolt. Part of Parma's terms to surrendering Antwerp were that practising Calvinists who would not renounce their faith were given two years to remove themselves, their capital, and their goods from Antwerp. This section of the Antwerp population included wealthy merchants, skilled and well versed in banking and financial bookkeeping. They left Antwerp for safe havens in Europe; many of them emigrated to Holland and Zeeland, settling their businesses, some in Middelburg but most in Amsterdam. So many established themselves in Amsterdam that one observed in 1594, less than a decade after the fall of Antwerp:

> Here is Antwerp itself changed in Amsterdam.[32]

The influx of capital, businesses enterprises, and business connections proved a significant stimulus to trade and investment, further benefitting the Dutch Republic.

Import-export entrepôt activities of Amsterdam boomed, with the innovative and skilful practices of storing and warehousing becoming a vital part of Dutch commercial strategy. The booming seaborne trade led to large investments by merchants into grain and timber from the Baltic, into wine, fruits, and salt from the south, and into fleets engaged in herring fishing and in fish exporting. All this in turn generated further wealth and stimulated the rise of the Dutch Republic to its commercial greatness. By the early Eighteenth Century, the English writer Daniel Defoe stated the Dutch were:

> the carryers of the world, the middle persons in trade and the Factors and Brokers of Europe.[33]

A trenchant summary of the position of Holland has been stated in a monumental span of European history:

> It would indeed have been disastrous for the Republic as a whole if Holland's power had been eliminated. For Holland was the mainstay of all Dutch activity.[34]

In short, the province of Holland and to a lesser extent that of Zeeland were the economic powerhouses of the nascent Dutch nation state, and to a large extent it was the finances of Holland that sustained the Revolt. In any struggle, economic or political, the support of Holland was vital. This lesson was recognised by William of Orange, learnt to his cost by Leicester, adhered to by Oldenbarneveldt until his last struggle and downfall, and fully realised by Maurits.

Another factor in the Dutch finances was their trading with the enemy. As we have seen, enterprising Dutch merchants and financiers in the late Sixteenth and early Seventeenth Centuries were happy to engage on behalf of the government of the Spanish Netherlands, in shipping and transporting bullion to the Antwerp banks and exchanges in order that bills of exchange could be drawn to pay the Army of Flanders. However, this was not the only form of trade that was embargoed—and circumvented—by both sides. Spain gradually realised that they could not do without the raw and finished materials, without grain, and without naval equipment and stores, all of which the Dutch fleets carried from the Baltic. Spain and Portugal increasingly found that any trade embargo against the Dutch was counterproductive and was more harmful to the Iberian economy than the economic damage it was intended to inflict against the insurgent Dutch. For their part, the Dutch, especially the States of Holland, found it expedient to allow illicit trade with Spain to continue. Between 1572 and the Peace of Münster in 1648, contraband trade and smuggling between the two sides were carried out to "unprecedented lengths", and in the post-1579 period after the two Unions of Utrecht and Arras, the same trade consuls represented both the United Provinces and the Spanish Netherlands in some European capital cities.[35]

The nascent Dutch nation state depended on the province of Holland and to a lesser extent that of Zeeland. These provinces in turn depended on the navy for economic strength. Yet, perhaps incredible to the modern reviewer, the structures and finances of the navy left much to be desired. It was governed by no less than 5 different Admiralties, each one based in a different location.[36]

In the early years of the Dutch Revolt, *ad hoc* funding methods were used. Louis van Nassau, leading the Dutch insurgent forces, was the victor against the Spanish government forces led by the pro-Spanish nobleman Aremberg (a rare victory in open battle by the Dutch insurgent forces in these early years). After the Battle of Heiligerlee the Dutch forces captured tonnes of enemy powder, cannon, and wagonloads of silver plate. The silver plate was used to pay the insurgent troops. (On the other side, plunder was also used by Alva in this period of the Revolt to supplement the Spanish war coffers in 1567 and 1568, when he sequestered the estates of the arrested members of the Golden Fleece. The confiscated household plate filled 16 coffers,[37] which he diligently added to the Treasury of the government of the Netherlands.) During these years, Dutch insurgent finances were all hand-to-mouth measures, and in this period William and his followers had precious little finances. By late 1569, William had retreated into the Strasbourg area of France and was disappointed at the lack of reinforcements from France. Accordingly, he went into hiding. By this time he had pledged his own finances to the Revolt and owed over 2 million florins to his creditors.[38] His brothers rallied round him when William's credit was exhausted and raised loans from their own estates; between 1568 and 1573, they raised over 500,000 florins.[39] It was spasmodic, *ad hoc*, but it all helped.

During the period of Alva's imposing the hated 3 sets of taxes and the rising resentment amongst the Dutch populace, a rebel nobleman, Dirk Sonoy, raised monies from his own estates. He and a companion physically courier the cash in several journeys between Dillenberg and Holland, placing it at the disposal of William of Orange. The merchants of Zevenbergen raised several private loans, which they too gave to William of Orange.[40] The so-called Gueux de Mer (Sea Beggars) in 1572 laid aside some of their piratical plunder for William of Orange's war chest; after the taking of Brielle and Vlissingen and then in quick succession Rotterdam, Schiedam, Gouda, and with the whole of Zeeland and Friesland declaring for the Revolt, supplies and foodstuffs became available for the insurgent forces, freeing up monies already accumulated to be spent on arms, equipment, and pay. In June 1572, William made a secret visit to Frankfurt where he raised more monies from loans from sympathetic bankers.

The following month, in July 1572, more official and substantial funds became available to William of Orange. A meeting was held by delegates from the rebel cities and provinces under the presidency of one of the leaders and close followers of William, Sainte Aldegonde. William, in his capacity of commander-in-chief of the insurgent army in the provinces of Holland, West Friesland, Zeeland, and Utrecht, was voted funds of 100,000 crowns for his immediate needs for the next 3 months, and the delegates undertook that further funds would be forthcoming.

William of Orange, according to a detailed account of the progress of the Dutch Revolt, was reported to have observed ironically of the voted funds:

> The tenth the twentieth and hundredth penny would not have cost them that sum.[41]

Two years later, after the successful relief of the siege of Leiden in October 1574, William took the initiative and requested the States of Holland that they give him a freer hand in the military campaign and more resources, including a further sum of 45,000 florins. The States offered 30,000, upon which William threatened to go into exile. Realism fell over the States of Holland, who granted William the full amount he had requested and made him sovereign over the States of Holland with a fixed regular budget.[42] (During the course of the next two years, the provinces of Holland and Zeeland would complete the process, resulting in a Union of the two provinces with William appointed as joint stadhouder.)

As bits of territory were captured and recaptured in some border areas, the dividing lines were inevitably blurred. Both sides, but more so the Dutch insurgents, engaged in *ad hoc* extortion raids, extorting payments from neighbouring villages located in enemy territory. In the 1590s, this practice was placed within a formalised system. The Council of State appointed 3 officials in the "border" or frontier towns of Ostend (until its recapture by the Spanish), Sluis (after its capture by the Dutch), and Bergen op Zoom. One official was the Collector, who "assessed" nearby villages in enemy territory and issued "requests" to the villages to come to a certain location and make a payment. Failure to do so would be punished by punitive retaliatory raids by the nearby Dutch garrison. The second official was the Collector of Confiscations, who had the remit of collecting imposed dues on any ecclesiastical domains in every territory. The third official was the Auditor, answerable directly to the Council of State, who inspected the differing accounts of the Collector and the Collector of Confiscations. The Auditor oversaw, accounted for, and was responsible for the custody of the total amounts of monies collected. It was all grist to the financial mill of the Dutch Revolt.

As the Dutch Revolt continued, foreign subsidies were added to the Dutch financial resources. As early as 1570, William was writing to John van Nassau that the people of the Low Countries were:

[s]trong and robust who can count on help from every part of the world.[43]

However, this was mostly optimistic morale boosting. Often in revolts and rebellions, the insurgents need to firmly convince foreign countries that there is the extreme likelihood of the ultimate success of the insurgency. Such convincing can take years of discreet approaches, meetings, and talks, combined with successful actions and hard evidence that the insurgency is gaining the upper hand before foreign countries will commit to "help" in terms of financial support.

However, as the Dutch Revolt continued, subsidies from foreign countries did arrive as a result of the changing dynamic of diplomacy and foreign alliances. The alliance with England of the mid-1580s resulted in the controversial and brief governor generalship of the Earl of Leicester; it also brought reinforcements of 4,000 English troops and a subsidy of money. Parma's crucial distraction of his having to intervene in the French civil wars of the 1590s and the success of Maurits's campaigns reduced the financial pressure on the Dutch to some extent. Moreover, in 1598 Oldenbarneveldt and his delegation (which included the brilliant young scholar Hugo Grotius) engaged in urgent negotiations with Henri IV of France. The result was an agreement made with Henri IV in

April 1598 whereby he would grant a subsidy of a million ecus over the next 4 years. This helped to sustain the Dutch war effort.

However, by late 1606, Oldenbarneveldt, as we have seen, informed the States-General that the overall financial position of the Dutch Republic was nearly untenable and that a stark choice had to be made. The options for the Dutch Republic were to make peace with Spain or to place itself under the protection of Henri IV of France. In fact, peace was eventually made with Spain in 1609, resulting in the historic Twelve Years' Truce. Spain was severely suffering economically. The VOC conquests in the East Indies, starting in 1605, were to Spanish ministers and councillors the first sign or straw in the economic wind of dire consequences to Spain and its Empire if some sort of settlement was not accomplished. On the other side, Oldenbarneveldt's admission of the States-General in 1606 was significant as a sign that foreign subsidies had run out and that the Dutch were struggling to fund the continuing struggle.

Indeed, before the Twelve Years' Truce ended, foreign subsidies to the Dutch Republic had run out, and the political dynamism in Europe had escalated. The first stage of the Thirty Years' War, the Bohemian Revolt, had occurred, and the war was widening. The Dutch had given financial help to the Bohemian rebels under Frederick V, the elector Palatine and briefly the rebel king of the Bohemian throne. Finances in the amount of 250,000 gulden were raised for the Bohemians in 1620. A Prague merchant of Dutch origin, Abraham Sixt, acted as the financial facilitator. Sixt personally couriered 50,000 gulden to Bohemia; the remaining 200,000 were drawn on a bill of exchange at Nuremburg.[44]

The rebellion was crushed, and Frederick was in exile, having gained sanctuary in The Hague (where he and his exiled queen were lodged for a time in the former official residence of Oldenbarneveldt). The Dutch Republic and other Protestant countries were facing the forces of imperial Spain, Hapsburg Austria, and the Catholic League, and the Dutch urgently needed war funds. The situation in 1624 was crucial for the Dutch Republic but was retrieved by Maurits. With the same urgency that Oldenbarneveldt had started negotiations with Henri IV of France in 1598, Maurits despatched an extraordinary embassy to Paris, headed by the experienced politician van de Bouchorst. Although a Catholic power, France under Cardinal Richelieu had been concerned at the ease at which the Bohemian Revolt had been crushed by the Hapsburgs, concern that turned to anxiety at the subsequent troop movements, deployments, and territorial occupations by Tilly's Catholic League and the occupation by Spinola's Spanish troops in the southern and western territories of the Empire. The Edict of Restitution had been decreed by the Emperor, restoring Protestant church holdings and benefices in the captured territories to their former Catholic holders. However gratifying ideologically this was to Catholic France, it was a further ominous sign of the growing power of the Hapsburgs, the traditional dynastic enemy of France. Accordingly, by the Treaty of Compiegne in 1624, Louis XIII agreed to provide a subsidy to the Dutch Republic of 1.2 million livres for 1624, 1 million livres for 1625, and 1 million livres for 1626. This was in return for Dutch naval help in assisting the French siege of the Protestant Huguenot–held port of La Rochelle. (In fact, a substantial part of the Dutch fleet, manned by ardent Calvinists, refused to fight on the same side as a Cardinal against fellow Protestant Huguenots.[45] Fortunately, Richelieu managed to force the surrender of La Rochelle with the forces he had, and the Dutch continued to receive the subsidies.) Even an eminent historian, critical of Maurits, acknowledges this as an achievement, and one that boded well for the future.[46] Financial pressure was staved off and the Dutch Republic had gained financial support in the renewed struggle.

Gaining the subsidies of the Treaty of Compiegne was just as well for the Dutch Republic, for in 1624 the Spanish started intense economic warfare.

One scheme of Spain that ultimately failed was a massive construction work to divert river trade going into the Dutch Republic by constructing a canal cutting into the Rhine in Spanish-controlled territory just south of Wesel and running directly to Venlo on the Maas. Authorised by the then Spanish Regent of the Spanish Netherlands, Isabella Eugenia, and named by Spanish troops working on it as the Fosse Eugeniana. The canal was planned in the period of the final months of Maurits's life, and work started a short time after Maurits's death in 1625. Building went on apace for over 8 months in 1626–1627, but finally the project was halted. This was partially due to spasmodic Dutch attacks and partly due to inclement weather, but the main reason for halting and then abandoning the project was a lack of funds. Nonetheless, it was a sign of how determined Spain was to inflict economic war on the Dutch Republic.

More successful in terms of damage inflicted upon the Dutch economy was Spain's economic blockade. Spain had made previous attempts to impose various trade embargoes and blockades, the effects of which on the Dutch Republic had been alleviated. However, this particular action, according to an eminent Dutch historian, significantly impacted and truly hit and harmed the Dutch economy.[47] Spain carried it out by a licensing system. The ultimate objective of this would be for Spain to monopolise European trade or, failing that, to curtail and severely damage Dutch trade. By these licenses Denmark and the Hanseatic League were given "favoured nation" trading status. Commissioners of Commerce were appointed in ports including Seville, San Lucar, Lisbon, and Oporto. They were also appointed in the Azores and Canaries, in anticipation that the Dutch would try to trade there for products closed off to them in the Iberian Peninsula. A special department of state was created, the Almirantazgo de los paises septentrionales, or Admiralty of the North, at Seville with its own agents and enforcers, and an *almirantazgo* was established near Dunkirk, acting closely with that at Seville. The Court of Seville was given jurisdiction over all agents, who ensured that ship-ping cargo consignments coming into and leaving Spanish ports were checked and certified as having no Dutch connection. (As we have seen, the trade connection was already illegal, but this system of smuggling had previously been passing off the goods as being of German, or impe-rial, origin.[48]) Prosecution of offenders was undertaken by the Court of Castille. Interstices and ways round the prohibited trade persisted, but Dutch merchants were put to considerable trouble—and extra expense—to continue. Some Dutch merchants relocated to London to continue trading with Spain, which caused a trade loss to the Dutch Republic, whilst others commissioned foreign ships at higher fees. The amount of Dutch shipping carrying goods from the Baltic to Spain fell dramatically. In 1623 Spain more rigorously enforced the system in Galicia with stand-ardised boarding and inspection procedures. In Catalonia and Aragon in the previous year, whilst being mindful of local and provincial privi-leges, viceroys of Catalonia and Aragon implemented measures for more stringent checks on foreign ships entering the ports of eastern Spain, and also on consignment entering the provinces from the north over the border with France. These measures particularly affected the Dutch salt-carrying activity from the deposits of La Mata and Ibiza to Italy. Salt was an essential and valued commodity as a nutrient, seasoning, and preservative, and curtailing the Dutch carrying trade in this commodity cost the Dutch dearly. In 1623 the Archduchess Isabella of the Spanish Netherlands prohibited the entry of any English cloth that was being re-exported from the Dutch Republic to the Spanish Netherlands. This resulted in an increase of English cloth exports directly to the Spanish Netherlands. The system of embargoes was applied to the Spanish pos-sessions in Naples in 1621, and then to Sicily, Sardinia, and the duchy of Milan. Grain supplies were particularly affected. There was a bad harvest in Italy that year, but the Dutch were prevented from carrying supplies and trading. Even the Genoese, despite their previous loans and their bringing strenuous diplomatic pressure on Madrid, were refused consent to engage with Dutch trade for potential supplies.[49]

Overall, contraband trading between the Dutch and Spain continued but Olivares's system and Spain's embargoes made it more difficult and considerably less profitable. The system significantly impacted upon the Dutch economy at a time, in the 1620s, when both the military and the diplomatic situations were precarious[50] One historian, in a detailed study, has summarised: "Together, the total package of Spanish mercantalist measures in the 1620s and 1630s represents one of the most fundamental and decisive factors shaping the development of the world economy in the XVII century".[51]

Both Spain and the Dutch throughout the Revolt were faced with debilitating expenses for waging the war. Two sets of figures are telling. Between 1566 and 1654, Spain sent 218 million ducats for expenditure in the Netherlands and in the same period received 121 million ducats from the imperial territories in South America. For the Dutch the army expenditure alone[52] had, by 1592, cost 3.2 million florins; by 1607 it had cost 8.8 million florins. Both had staved off financial ruin—Spain with constant borrowing and the bullion wealth from the Americas, the Dutch with the reliable wealth of Holland. Throughout the Revolt, the sinews of war were constantly strained and overstretched. Economically, it was hard pounding—or rather hard ducats and hard florins—and a near run thing, but Spain broke first.

Notes

1. Boxer, CR *The Dutch Seaborne Empire 1600–1800*
2. Limm, P *The Dutch Revolt 1559–1648* p 96
3. Limm, P *The Dutch Revolt 1559–1648* p 96
4. Bernal, J "Trade and Finance in the Middle Ages" in Cipolla, M (ed) *Fontana Economic History of Europe Vol* p 311
5. Postan, M "Credit in Mediaeval Trade" in Carus-Wilson, E (ed) *Essays in Economic History Vol I*, cited in Bernal, J "Trade and Finance in the Middle Ages" in Cipolla, M (ed) *Fontana Economic History of Europe Vol I* p 324
6. Braudel, F *Civilisation and Capitalism 15 to 18 Centuries Volume III—Perspectives of the World* p 112
7. Braudel, F in his *Civilisation and Capitalism 15 to 18 Centuries Volume III—Perspectives of the World* traces and gives a detailed analysis of the rise and decline of each city. He places this process in the overall context of a global financial order in which these differing cities operated and interacted economically in an area stretching from the Low Countries to the Mediterranean. He views the sequence of events of the rise and fall of each city as a north-south macro struggle within this area
8. Braudel, F *Civilisation and Capitalism 15 to18 Centuries Volume II—The Wheels of Commerce* p 191
9. Polnitz, G *Die Fugger*, cited in Rady, M *The Emperor Charles V* p 16. Brandi, K *The Emperor Charles V* p 106
10. Bindoff, ST chapter on "Antwerp" in *New Cambridge Modern History Vol II—The Reformation* p 68. Braudel, F *Civilisation and Capitalism 15 to18 Centuries Volume II—The Wheels of Commerce* p 153. Kamen, H *Spain 1469–1714—A Society of Conflict* p 89
11. For a ruler who was so meticulous, so conscientious in fulfilling every administrative task of the vast empire, and so insistent upon micro managing, it seems paradoxical that he had little appreciation of and was apparently unwilling to give attention to finances and the mounting debts. Davies, RT *The Golden Century of Spain 1501–1621* pp 126–136 points out that Philip was indeed hard-working and unwilling to delegate, but he also had a clearer grasp on the issues and wider affairs than many of his Councils. Clearly this was not the case in the issue and Council of Finance. In fairness to Philip, Davies points out that the Dutch Revolt took him completely by surprise and that, therefore, he could not have anticipated the spiraling costs needed in suppressing it
12. Kamen, H *Imperial Spain 1477–1715* p 167
13. Braudel, F *Civilisation and Capitalism 15 to18 Centuries Volume II—The Wheels of Commerce* pp 479–524

14. Koenigsberger, EG "Western Europe and the Power of Spain" in *The Cambridge Modern History Vol III—The Counter Reformation and the Price Revolution* p 257

15. Martin de la Gazbela to Zuniga 9 November 1575, cited in Parker, G *Imprudent King—A New Life of Philip II* p 226

16. One of the doyen historians of the period, Parker, G in his *The Army of Flanders and the Spanish Road 1567–1659*, in a comprehensive and informative chapter, deals with the mutinies of the Army of Flanders. It points out that the majority of mutinies were resolved by negotiations, during which the leaders of the mutineers imposed rigid discipline on "their" commands. The negotiations were sometimes heated but resulted in a settlement of back pay, with comparatively few cases of retribution against the mutineers or even their leaders. Most of the grievances were genuine and concerned excessive delays of pay, and the main motivation of the mutineers was to settle these, not to disrupt the army or create havoc and desert. Significantly, troops who had remained loyal usually refused to fight or take action against their mutinous comrades, sometimes assuming that the issues would be settled and that they would all be reunited as comrades. For their part, the senior commanders of the Army were loathe to resort to combat but chose to work towards a settlement; the mutinous troops were genuinely experienced and skilful soldiers who were too valuable to lose, and usually their loyalty would be fully restored with the settlement of pay. In short, the overall damage of the mutinies was not a loss of troops but disruption in the war effort and financial damage in having to speedily find large-scale funds to arrive at a settlement

17. Wedgwood, CV *William of Orange* p 156

18. Hamilton, EJ *American Treasure and the Price Revolution in Spain* p 34

19. Research by Hamilton, EJ cited by Spooner, FC in chapter "The Economy of Europe 1559–1609" in *The Cambridge Modern History of Europe Vol III—The Counter Reformation and the Price Revolution in Europe* p 25

20. This was part of a cycle known as the "Potosi curve", according to Moreya Paz-Soldan, M *Historia Vol IX*, cited in F Braudel *The Mediterranean World in the Age of Philip II Vol I*

21. Elliott, JH *Europe Divided 1559–1598* p 270

22. Mattingly, G *The Defeat of the Spanish Armada* pp 387–388

23. Researches of Spooner, FC cited by Braudel, F *The Mediterranean World in the Age of Philip II Vol I* p 479

24. Boxer, CR *The Dutch Seaborne Empire 1600–1800* p 23

25. Geyl, P *The Revolt of the Netherlands 1555–1609* p 208

26. De Wit, D *Public Gebet 1663–1664 Vol I* p 200, cited by Israel, J *The Dutch Republic—Its Rise, Greatness, and Fall 1477–1806* p 286

27. Price, JL *The Dutch Republic in the Seventeenth Century* p 17

28. Jonker, MJ and van Zanden, JL *A Financial History of the Netherlands* p 34

29. Wallersten, I *The Modern World System Vol I* p 211, cited by Braudel, F *Civilisation and Capitalism 15 to 18 Centuries Vol III—Perspectives of the World* p 206

30. Archives Nationales Marine, Paris, B7463fo30, cited by Braudel, F *Civilisation and Capitalism 15 to 18 Centuries Vol III—Perspectives of the World* pp 190–191

31. William Temple *Observations on the Provinces of the United Netherlands 1720* p 126, also cited by Braudel, F *Civilisation and Capitalism 15 to 18 Centuries Vol III—Perspectives of the World* pp 190–191

32. Letter of Jacques della Faille 23 April 1594, cited in Boxer, CR *The Dutch Seaborne Empire* p 21

33. Defoe, D *A Plan of the English Commerce* p 92
34. Crossman, EH chapter XII 'The Low Countries' in *The New Cambridge Modern History Volume the Decline of Spain 1609–1659* p 365
35. Boxer, CR *The Dutch Seaborne Empire* pp 22–29
36. See also Appendix II
37. Wedgwood, CV *William the Silent* pp 101–106
38. Wedgwood, CV *William the Silent* p 112
39. Parker, G *The Dutch* Revolt p 148
40. Wedgwood, CV *William the Silent* p 119
41. Wedgewood, CV *William the Silent* p 123
42. Harrison, F *William the Silent* p 168
43. William of Orange to John van Nassau 20 February 1570, van Prinsterer, G *Archives ou Correspondence Inedite de la Maison Nassau-Nassau*, cited in Elliott, JH *Europe Divided 1558–1598* p 189
44. Polisensky, J *Tragic Triangle—The Netherlands Spain and Bohemia* pp 184–185
45. Wedgwood, CV *Richelieu and the French Monarchy* p 55
46. van Deursen, A in his *Maurits van Nassau* argues that Maurits in the later years was far less effective than when he was in a working relationship and part-nership with Oldenbarneveldt and that in his quarrel with Oldenbarneveldt, whilst Maurits may have been the winner, he was ultimately the loser. How-ever, in his wide study *De last van veel Geluk—de Gescheidenis va Nederland 1555–1702* p 216 he fully acknowledges that in the 5-year period of danger and threats, 1621–1625, Maurits's obtaining the Treaty of Compiegne—and the financial subsidies—was undoubtedly his best achievement
47. Interview with Professor Judith Pollman, History Department, University of Leiden June 2018
48. Kamen, H *Spain 1469–1714* p 139
49. Israel, J *Empires and Entrepots* p 22
50. See also Appendix I
51. Israel, J "The Politics of International Trade Rivalry During the XXX Years War" pp 517–518
52. Limm, P *The Dutch Revolt* p 66

Part III

Later Revolts and Insurgencies

14 Revolts and Insurgencies Over the Next 3 Centuries

Let us turn to later revolts and insurgencies occurring in territories then possessed by European powers and carried out by groups or organisations with the object of making their territories independent and would-be nation states. We will look at a period of approximately 300 years after the final recognition of Dutch independence, i.e. from the 1648 Treaty of Westphalia and the Peace of Münster. Three of these insurgencies failed; the rest were successful. All are instructive when compared to the Dutch Revolt as to "our" factors of a successful revolt or insurgency for independence.

Catalonia Rebels Against Hapsburg Spain, 1640–1645

Within Spain, in the same period as the Dutch Revolt and the Eighty Years' War, the province of Catalonia revolted and attempted to break away. There was a strong feeling of Catalan identity, and the Catalan province provided much of the wealth of the medieval Kingdom of Aragon, long before there was a united kingdom of Spain. The immediate cause that resulted in hostilities was economic. As we have seen, in 1621 the Duc of Olivares came to power in Spain as the first minister of the newly crowned King Philip IV. Philip had a strong sense of Spain's imperial mission and longed to restore the greatness of the Spanish Empire. Olivares, conscientious, hard-working, and fair-minded, saw the necessity of raising more revenues with all parts of Spain and the Empire contributing to the Treasury. The current situation was that the burden of raising both monies and manpower for the army fell excessively on Castile.

Accordingly, the Union of Arms was promulgated to ensure more equitable arrangements for all parts of the Spanish Empire. Under its provisions, Portugal and Catalonia would each furnish and pay for 16,000 troops. Immediately the Union of Arms was opposed by regional *Cortes* or *parlements*, although Valenica and Aragon did eventually undertake to make regular contributions. However, the Catalonian parliament, the Disputacio, was proud of its traditional and long established rights and service to the province. It enjoyed certain privileges, and it rejected the

Union of Arms. Two successive Viceroys of Catalonia were sent in turn by King Philip to resolve the situation. By their tactlessness, perceived high-handedness, and lack of respect for Catalonian customs, both failed in either raising contributions or in calming the situation. Catalonian national feelings and pride had been aroused to violent levels.

By 1635 Spain was at war with France, as part of the complex and changing alignments of the ongoing Thirty Years' War. France invaded Catalonia in order to conquer two of its border counties. Olivares sent Spanish troops to Catalonia, hoping to rally a united front against the external enemy. However, the main part of the fighting on the Spanish side was carried out by Castilian, Flemish, and Italian troops; the Catalonian levies were conspicuous by their lack of activity. In 1640 the Spanish troops were ordered to remain in Catalonia for the foreseeable future in order to re-engage the French during the campaigning season the following year. Tensions mounted between the Catalan nobility and gentry and the Catalan agricultural workers on the one side and the Castilian troops based and billeted in Catalonia on the other. Tensions finally boiled over into an insurrection, whereby armed Catalonian mobs invaded Barcelona. Barcelona quickly came under the control of the insurgents, and other towns were equally quickly subdued or suborned, and almost the entire province was in armed revolt. At this stage there was unease amongst the Catalonian nobles about the excesses of the armed mobs, but the insurgency still held together and was unstoppable. The leaders of the various Catalan insurgent forces, all guided by a cleric named Pau Clario, declared an independent republic. They appealed to and placed themselves and the republic under the protection of France. By 1645, Catalonia was entirely under French control, Olivares had been dismissed by Philip IV and had died in disgrace. However, the Catalans chafed under French rule, and the Catalan nobility were expressing open dissatisfaction with the French occupation and the excesses of the Catalan rebels. Amongst the latter groups, egalitarian and quasi-anarchic elements were gaining influence, and schemes involving land and wealth redistribution were being proposed.

By 1650 Philip IV was free from the draining struggle with the Dutch, who had officially been acknowledged as fully independent by the 1648 Treaty of Münster as part of the overall European peace settlements of the Peace of Westphalia. The dissatisfaction with French rule by the Catalan nobility and merchants had risen to the extent where they were openly preferring and advocating a return to Spanish rule. In 1651 Philip IV sent one of his commanders, Don Juan of Austria, to recover Catalonia by force. His Spanish troops, upon crossing the border into Catalonia, were received with little hostility and soon approached Barcelona, which was besieged. Barcelona surrendered in 1652. Catalonia reconciled itself to Spanish rule, having had some its provincial rights and privileges restored. France had withdrawn its troops and agreed to a peace settlement with Spain whereby one of the Catalan border counties and part of another were ceded to France.

Analysis and Comparison With Dutch Revolt

The Catalan revolt, whose immediate cause was a combination of economic factors and affronted national pride, failed due to divisions and conflicting ideologies between the rebels and a failure to exploit international events. The Dutch Revolt was undoubtedly in its early stages caused by economic factors, with Alva's insistence upon imposing taxes. The Tenth Penny was particularly hated, and the Gueux de Mer significantly adapted into their flags and pennants a design incorporating ten coins. But in the long term, the excessive class divisions that hampered the Catalan revolt were mostly avoided in the Dutch Revolt, thanks to William of Orange's constant unifying counsel and efforts. Like the Dutch, the Catalans had—and still retain—a strong sense of national identity and cause that Philip and his vice regents ignored and brushed aside at Spain's cost. However, in terms of exploiting international events, the one coup the Catalans was to appeal for the protection of a foreign power that was a traditional enemy. This compromised any aspirations to independent sovereignty. It is indeed true that the nascent Dutch Republic placed itself under English protection in the early 1580s. However, thanks to Jan van Oldebarneveldt and the States-General, this was not a complete abrogation of sovereignty and when the protector—Leicester—appeared to be attempting to gain too much power, he was opposed and ultimately defeated. The Catalans were not allies of the French, who looked upon them with disdain but were occupied and eventually subordinated to them.

Portugal Revolts Against Spain and Wins Independence, 1640–1668

The revolt in Catalonia against Spain touched off a Portuguese revolt against Spain. Since the early 1580s, Portugal had been part of the Spanish Empire. However, before that, it had been an independent kingdom since the Thirteenth Century, with long national traditions, customs, law, and its own language. During the Fifteenth Century, its explorers had rivalled those of Spain in the global voyages of discovery, gaining territories and flourishing trade through its own overseas possessions. The incorporation of Portugal into the Spanish Empire had been through dynastic events. The reigning Portuguese house of Aviz came to an end, and Philip II gained Portugal through his mother, who was the daughter of King Emmanuel I of Portugal. Philip II's accession to the Portuguese throne was conditional on two important undertakings. Firstly he undertook to maintain Portuguese customs, liberties, and privileges. Secondly, any Viceroy of Portugal had to be chosen from the Portuguese royal family or nobility. These conditions were adhered to by Philip II, and he faithfully upheld his promises. However, the bustling and busy commercial activities of Lisbon declined due to competition with the Spanish port of Cadiz, and Spanish and Castilian nobles and administrators migrated to Portugal and gained profitable positions, ousting the Portuguese. Portugal's overseas commerce and trading post possessions in Asia were encroached upon and attacked by the Dutch. To the Portuguese, it appeared that Portugal had given much and that the only gain was the hostility of the common enemy, the rising Dutch Republic.

During the reign of Philip IV, economic discontent in Portugal rose. With the rising costs of Spain engaging in the Thirty Years' War, taxes were increased. In 1619 the Portuguese had contributed 1 million cruzados to Spain's war effort; in 1634 Spain demanded a further 3 million cruzados, which caused resentment and outcry. In 1637 a 5% property tax was imposed in Portugal. The revenues being raised from this tax, it was stated by Madrid, was for the defence of Portugal, but this claim was widely disbelieved, and the tax caused particular hardship, including serious tax riots in two of the provinces of Portugal. The Spanish government of Portugal as a whole was generally resented. Viceroy Margarita of Saxony, the sister of Philip IV, was conciliatory and moderate, but the representative in Portugal of Spain's chief minister Olivares, Miguel de Vasconcellos, was particularly hated and opposed by the Portuguese nobility and lower classes alike. As we have seen, Spain and its Empire were governed by the chief minister and the ministers through several councils and through viceroys; in 1638 Olivares abolished the Council of Portugal, inaugurating more direct rule from Madrid through Vasconcellos.

In the late 1630s, an insurrection was planned and developed by certain families of the Portuguese nobility, with Joao of Braganza as the individual designated to take over Portugal upon its success. Joao of Braganza was a descendent of the former Portuguese ruling family of Aziv. In Spain, Olivares, on discovering the plot, tried to decapitate it by luring Joao away with offers of lands and government positions. For a while there was stalemate while both sides tried to work out the other's intentions and when to move. Then in 1640 the Catalonian revolt broke out, and Joao of Braganza was ordered by Madrid to leave Portugal with some troops and serve in quelling the Catalonian revolt. He refused and quickly and quietly retired to his estates. This was the trigger of the revolt, and in December 1640 the conspirators acted. The viceregal palace was taken over, Margarita of Saxony fled across the frontier into Spain, and Miguel de Vasconcellos was murdered.[1] The Lisbon populace rose and proclaimed Joao of Braganza as King Joao IV of Portugal, a proclamation fully endorsed and confirmed by the Cortes of Portugal. Apart from one enclave, Ceuta, all the overseas territories of Portugal speedily recognised the new regime and dynasty.

Initially the Spanish were preoccupied with Catalonia and with the wider arena of the Thirty Years' War. Also, Richelieu had sent a French Navy unit to monitor and assist the rebellion; supplies were landed, and a French presence gave succour and encouragement to the insurgents. It was not until the end of the Thirty Years' War that Philip IV turned his attention to the Portuguese, who meanwhile had grown stronger in resolve, organisation, and military numbers. In 1659 Philip ordered Spanish units into Portugal to subdue the rebellion, which by now had evolved and developed into a *de facto* independent state. Also, Portugal was assisted by a formal alliance with England, King Charles II marrying the Portuguese Princess Catherine of Braganza. Three defeats were inflicted against the Spanish armies by the allies during the years 1665–1667; these were not major engagements, but they reinforced the reality that Portugal had a functioning army and that the Spanish armies—already suffering defeats in Europe—were not the invincible formations that they formerly were. In early 1668, Spain agreed to negotiate with the Portuguese as equals, and by the treaty of that year, Portugal was formally recognised by Spain as independent.

Analysis and Comparison With Dutch Revolt

Of the 4 factors, two were crucial in the success of the Portuguese revolt, a national identity and the exploitation of international events. Portugal, as we have seen, had been an independent kingdom in its own right and indeed had forged an overseas empire. Its people's national sense of identity had never been lost, and at the crucial moment of rebellion a noble family, the house of Braganza, was present to act as both leader and royal titular head of the national revolt.

International events worked in the favour of the revolt and were exploited by the insurgents. Up to and during the rising, French support under Richelieu's policy was available; however, the revolt never became entirely dependent upon French support, nor, in contrast to the Catalonian revolt, did it become a vassal statelet to France. Spain had to leave the Portuguese rebels alone, being distracted with the Catalonian revolt and the wider Thirty Years' War. Both revolts were evidence of what had been occurring for some time and what was one of the international factors that enabled the Dutch Revolt to succeed: "imperial overstretch".[2] The Portuguese were able to raise and equip an army unhindered. Also, with the passage of time, Pope Urban VIII formally received and accredited their ambassador at the Vatican, implying full recognition of the Portuguese state.[3] The Pope was anxious in the ongoing struggle of the Counter-Reformation in the Thirty Years' War to have two principal Catholic powers reconciled and this appeared the swiftest and easiest way of settling the issue. When Philip IV, with Spain's involvement in the Thirty Years' War having ceased, finally turned his attention and armed forces to regaining control of Portugal. In the 1660s, Portugal was supported by a strong alliance with England, a combination that prevented Spain's efforts and that assured independence, which Spain officially recognised at the 1668 Treaty of Lisbon.

Britain Loses the American Colonies, 1770–1783

In 1763 Britain emerged victorious from the Seven Years' War, mainly fought against France. Britain's empire included India, western Canada, and the 13 Atlantic seaboard colonies of America, as well as numerous trading and overseas territories across the globe. Twenty years later, Britain had been forced to the peace conference table at the Peace of Paris, where it acknowledged the sovereign independence of the 13 colonies as the United States. After 8 years of hostilities, Britain had been humiliated by a successful revolt by a substantial part of her empire, the American colonies.

The immediate cause was the escalating disputes over taxation, but long-term factors were also driving the colonies apart from Britain. The attitude of the British establishment was that the colonists were rather uncouth backwoodsmen, whilst the colonists regarded the British as overall full of flummery and nonsense. Each colony had its own elective assembly legislating for the colony. These were held in high respect by the colonists, conscious of the traditions of liberty and why their ancestors had emigrated to America; British politicians regarded these colonial assemblies as little more than local town councils, absolutely subordinate to the Parliament at Westminster. By the economic wisdom of the time, colonies complied with the international terms of trade, which meant they provided the mother country with raw materials that were manufactured by the mother country and then exported. The mother country traditionally always had by far the better end of the deal. The commodity trade by the colonies was regulated by London with various customs duties; the colonists resorted to smuggling and illicit trade on a large scale, which became fully consensual and an accepted way of life. Any attempt by faraway London to impose duties or even legislation was derided and resented by turns. The whole issue of the vast American colonies, even during the hostilities and open warfare, was never given sufficient consideration in terms of America; all considerations were taken by the British in the context of how the various events and decisions would impact and play within Westminster politics. As the dispute escalated, some politicians, notably the Earl of Chatham, Colonel Barre, and the radical John Wilkes, spoke up for the colonists. They appealed to the British government to act with moderation and reason and to see the colonial viewpoint, but they were an ignored minority.

The initial dispute arose over taxation when the British Minister Grenville and Parliament passed the Stamp Act in 1765, along with some other duties. (Stamp acts had been an incorporated and formed part of the taxation system of the Dutch Republic for over a century.) This resulted in widespread disturbances. Britain repealed the duties, but at the same time passed the Declaratory Act, emphasizing Westminster Parliament's overriding authority over the colonies.

Then in 1767, again as part of Westminster's political moves, the British Minister Townsend introduced and parliament passed the Revenue Act, which imposed a tax on tea and some other duties. Opposition in the colonies to what were perceived as uneconomic and crippling duties imposed in a high-handed manner by Westminster grew rapidly. Disturbances occurred in the early 1770s, including the taking over and burning of a customs revenue vessel, the vandalizing of a whole cargo of tea from a ship in Boston port (the famous Boston Tea Party), and demonstrations resulting in a unit of soldiers firing on a threatening crowd (the Boston Massacre, after which the officer in charge was, in a scrupulously fair trial acquitted of murder, defended by John Adams, one of the future signatories of the Declaration of Independence).

Colonial politicians made openly seditious speeches and made moves to resist, and *ad hoc* armed militias proliferated. In 1775, British forces made preemptive moves to seize and confiscate arms and ammunition and engaged armed rebel colonists at Concord and Lexington. They achieved their objective but sustained heavy casualties. A pitched battle then took place when the British took and occupied Boston, dispelling a large American force at Bunker Hill. Again they sustained heavy casualties, and the colonist troops had stood their ground.

By then, the situation had escalated to open hostilities. On 4 July 1776, the Americans issued the now famous Declaration of Independence. The colonists were led by a Continental Congress, with General Washington as commander in chief. Washington's main strategy was to recruit, expand, and forge an army, occasionally inflicting small defeats upon the British but with the main priority of keeping the army in being. The army was constantly beset by severe problems of supply, pay, equipment, arms, even basic clothing and uniforms. In the winter of 1776 Washington and 12,000 troops took shelter in the area of Valley Forge, where they suffered severe hardships and privations. Morale was low, and desertions occurred. This was the nadir of the Americans' struggle. However, the colonists' army held, and the revolt continued.

The following year, in 1777, the British military attempted a new strategy, that of dividing the colonies by cutting off what was seen as the main centres of rebellion, the New England colonies. One plan was to engage in a pincer movement, one British army moving down the Hudson River from the north, whilst another army would move upwards from New York. In this way, the New England colonies and the city of New York would be divided and cut off from the other colonies and the main centres of rebellion contained. Another plan, advocated by General Howe was that of a single swift and decisive stroke to take Philadelphia, striking hard at a principal centre of rebellion. The British with their resources could attempt one or the other; what they could not do was to attempt both, yet this is precisely what, in a roundabout way, they tried to do. General Howe was given authority to take Philadelphia but was warned that this was a sideshow; the main strategy was that of the two army pincer movements up and down the Hudson River. Howe was instructed that his main priority was to support the main strategy of linking up from a south-north direction with General Burgoyne, who would be advancing southwards down the Hudson.

Burgoyne's army set off advancing down the Hudson River and made good progress at first. Howe made a speedy drive and took Philadelphia, where he remained. Then Burgoyne's army encountered increasing resistance from American forces, who waged a constant attritional guerrilla war. Soon Burgoyne's advance came to a halt, and at Saratoga he was outnumbered and surrounded. Howe bestirred himself from Philadelphia, far too late for the southern pincer of the two armies to be effective. On 17 October 1781, Burgoyne surrendered with honourable terms. A decisive defeat had been inflicted upon British forces by the American colonists. It was a turning point.

It was also a turning point in the international situation. France, up to then had been discreetly supporting the colonists. In 1778 after Saratoga, it engaged in open warfare with Britain, made a formal alliance with the Americans, and recognised their independence. Spain, in alliance with France, engaged in open warfare with Britain. Other European powers formed an alliance of neutrality but hostility to Britain. Britain had been engaged in quelling a revolt and was now having to wage a global war.

Meanwhile, on the American continent the British continued, convinced that a single pitched battle, if won decisively, could settle the whole issue. Britain still relied on the strategic assessment that the main rebellion stemmed from the New England colonies. Instead of trying to isolate these colonies, the British under General Lord Cornwallis decided to strike at and then strike from the southern colonies, move up northward through them into Virginia, and possibly on to New England. He could gain victories in the south, deny the Americans the use of the Atlantic ports, and exploit the anticipated support from the Loyalist elements, and even recruit some of them.

Accordingly, Cornwallis and British forces, supported by the British Navy, took Charleston, South Carolina, and made 5,000 American troops prisoner. For the Americans, this was the heaviest defeat of the war so far. Cornwallis then advanced, ever in pursuit of the decisive battle. He was determined to advance, despite his troops suffering from the climate and supply problems. Loyalist support and recruits had failed to materialise in any significant numbers. Insisting upon advancing, he suffered defeats at Kings Mountain and at Cowpens on the border between

South and North Carolina. Moving into North Carolina, he gained a Pyrrhic victory at Guilford Courthouse, costing the British even more casualties. However, he pushed on into Virginia and made his way and base at Yorktown, an enclosed port on the southern part of the Chesapeake. This was a vulnerable position, but the British forces were secure there with naval support.

However, the British were not the only forces enjoying naval support. In 1781 the French Admiral de Grasse sailed from the West Indies making for the Chesapeake River complex with 28 ships and 3,000 soldiers to support the Americans. Washington abandoned any plans he had to retake New York, speedily marched south, and effected a link-up with the disembarked French forces. Both armies quickly marched farther south and speedily surrounded and invested Yorktown. At precisely this period, the British Navy had failed to pursue de Grasse and returned to guarding British possessions in the West Indies. Britain had lost control of the seas around the American seaboard. Cornwallis hunkered down and defended. But by October 1781, he realised there was no prospect of relief. On 19 October 1781—almost 4 years to the day since the turning point of the British surrender at Saratoga—Cornwallis surrendered with honourable terms. He and his 7,000 men were allowed to depart.

The following year, the British Navy regained its position with a massive victory over the French Navy under de Grasse at the Battle of the Saints. Also for the next two years in their naval war with the Dutch, they gained significant victories. However, the main issue of the American colonies, the struggle for independence, was already decided. A year later, after negotiations at the international Treaty of Paris, the United States was recognised as a sovereign independent nation. The American colonies had won their struggle for independence.

Analysis and Comparison With Dutch Revolt

Like the Dutch Revolt, the American colonies had a strong self-identity. There was a strong feeling of separatism from Britain, a feeling caused and accentuated by distance. That identity included the deeply held values of independence of action and thought, self-reliance, and determination when facing the physical challenges of the continent and carrying out commodity trading. Like the Dutch provinces, the differing colonies were often at odds with one another and the central authority of Congress during the War of Independence. (And indeed the interstate quarrelling in the immediate post-independence period was the despair of many US government ministers and officials.) However, the colonies overall were united in their separatism from the distant Westminster government and, when hostilities broke out, united in the aim of independence.

Considering the second factor of adequate armed forces, the American rebel forces in the initial stages encountered major difficulties in recruiting, maintaining discipline, and retaining forces. The winter at Valley Forge marked the nadir of the independence struggle as far as the numbers and quality of troops of the rebel forces. However, if the Americans had problems in numbers, the British were faced with far more serious challenges of having enough forces. The sheer size of the 13 colonies meant that the troops available could not be everywhere and completely quell the revolt throughout the colonies.

More importantly, the British Navy, magnificent in rising to the occasion of so many tasks as it was, was inadequate to patrol the American seaboard and enforce the blockade and to keep supplies and reinforcements from Britain continuing across the Atlantic, in addition to combatting the French and Spanish navies. The American Navy was miniscule in comparison, but with resourceful captains like John Paul Jones, their ships ranged far and wide and inflicted individual defeats on British warships and damage to British merchant shipping. By 1781 Russia, Sweden, and Denmark had formed the Armed Neutrality of the North, fending off British warships from stopping and searching their neutral vessels suspected of breaking the blockade. After 1780 the navy of the Dutch Republic was ranged against the British, and although the British were considered to have won this Fourth Anglo-Dutch War, waging it was still an unwelcome distraction and additional stretch on British naval resources.

With such a daunting remit, it was an achievement of the British Navy to have carried out so much, especially the victory over the French fleet in 1782 at the Battle of the Saints. However, the year before, the British Navy had lost control of the seas of the seaboard of America. Such periods of loss of control were inevitable. However, this particular lapse coincided with the vital stage of the July to October 1781 siege of Yorktown, where Cornwallis's troops were hemmed in by French-American armies. With no chance of evacuation, Cornwallis surrendered, and a decisive battle in the American War of Independence had been won by the Americans. The British Prime Minister Lord North immediately recognised the significance of this event. On hearing of its news, he publicly exclaimed, "O God, it is all over". It was. The factor of insufficient British forces had finally taken its decisive toll.

The factor of having a favourable international situation involved several European powers. The Dutch Republic, although its *government* did not give official recognition to the United States as a sovereign independent state, was nonetheless the first to show official recognition. On 16 November 1776, a single act was significant. On a Dutch Caribbean island, the garrison received an official salute from a ship of the tiny American Navy formed by Congress, the *Andrew Doria*, flying the flag of Congress when it entered the harbor. The Dutch garrison gave the official return salute, with the correct cannon fire. In doing so, it afforded official recognition to the American flag, the American warship, and the nascent nation of the United States.

Spain accepted an envoy from Congress, John Jay, and entered negotiations with him, though diplomatic recognition only came later.

Spain, a traditional enemy of Britain, was not the only European power or the first to see an opportunity to harm Britain. As early as December 1775, French Foreign Minister Gravier, Comte de Vergennes sent French envoys to the Continental Congress to explore the possibility of cooperation and alliance. The Congress responded two months later by sending Silas Deane as a representative to France. The main remit of Deane was to plead for funds. Less than a year later in December 1776, Congress sent Benjamin Franklin as its official representative, as official ambassador to France. Franklin was to reside there for years and, by his persuasiveness and incisive arguments, great personal charm, and his intellectual pursuits, greatly advanced the American cause. Initially, Vergennes was careful to balance any aid. He did not wish to give enough support that would result in an American victory, nor did he wish to ensure that the position of the Americans would be so strong that Britain would seek a reconciliation. Rather, he was content to give the Americans aid but only to the extent of ensuring that they were able to continue the struggle and therefore keep Britain distracted and economically impacted by the distant rebellion. The principal aim was to impact on Britain in order:

to ruin commerce and sap strength.[4]

Officially, France remained neutral, but throughout 1775 some discreet financial aid was sent, and French volunteers, from both the regular army and civilians, were assigned to join the American forces. Smuggling commodities and supplies, breaking the British blockade, was discreetly encouraged and organised. The British ambassador to France, Stormont, was aware of this and protested at the extent to which France was engaged in this to Vergennes, who tersely stated that the French government could not totally stop smugglers, to which Stormont indignantly replied:

Do smugglers go in fleets, Sir?[5]

After the arrival of Benjamin Franklin, American pleas and persuasions for more substantial aid and recognition intensified and became more convincing. With the British forces' significant defeat in 1777, when Burgoyne surrendered to American forces at Saratoga in October, Vergennes committed France to full support. In February 1778, France made two official treaties with the Americans: the Treaty of Alliance and the Treaty of Amity and Commerce. These treaties officially recognised the United States as a sovereign independent nation and pledged aid and support, as well as trade and commercial ties.

Franklin, whilst still ambassador to France in 1781, attempted further international support by going to Vienna and pleading the American cause at the court of the Austrian emperor. The following year, in March 1782, after Britain had declared war on the Dutch Republic, the Dutch officially recognised the United States as a sovereign independent nation. Spain did not officially afford official recognition to the United States until the international Peace of Paris (where Britain and the United States concluded peace) but had made an alliance with France in April 1779 at the Treaty of Aranjuez. By this, the Bourbon "ruling family compact" was affirmed and an alliance made against Britain. Spain declared war against Britain in June 1779.

In terms of the international affairs factor, there was much interest by foreign powers in the involvement in the American struggle for independence, interest to which the Americans were not slow in responding and exploiting.

In the case of the factor of finances, as with the Dutch Revolt, in the early stages of the American revolt and War of Independence, the insurgents' armies were woefully short of equipment, arms—and finances. Throughout the struggle, the nascent United States was scarcely ever free of financial risk. Even after the victory of Saratoga, with the Americans supported by France and Spain, and with the British Navy having to contend with France and Spain and the Armed Neutrality of the North, and with the sheer size of the continent with constant guerrilla warfare taking its toll on the British forces, there was still a significant fall in financial confidence in Congress. Throughout late 1780 to 1781—less than a year before the crucial event of the British surrender at Yorktown—there were an extreme fall in financial confidence and a dramatic shortage of credit in Congress, and the French general in America, Rochambeau, predicted that the American currency would:

fall to non-value.[6]

A key factor was that of financial aid and funds from foreign sources to the nascent United States. From 1775, France, in addition to permitting and facilitating volunteers and arms to be sent and commodities to be smuggled, clandestinely sent finances. As clandestine finance facilitator, Pierre-Auguste Caron de Beaumarchais filled the role. Beaumarchais started life as a watchmaker. He then rose in society by marrying into property, purchasing a royal appointment that privileged him to a title, and then, acquiring the title by engaging in court intrigues and politics. Known to literature for his plays and books, including *The Marriage of Figaro*, he was sent by Louis XVI to London on a minor secret service errand. Staying in London during the early 1770s, he made himself an expert on the deteriorating situation of the American colonies. He sent regular reports (some inaccurate) back to the Court of Versailles. On his return to France, he was instructed by Vergennes to ensure that discreet finances and aid were sent to the Americans. Vergennes discreetly credited Beaumarchais's account. Beaumarchais then formed a front company registered in Spain as Rodriguez Hortales and Co., through which he purchased arms and equipment from the French government arsenals and military suppliers. These purchases were then exported through the port of Le Havre, Beaumarchais being present there under a false name and pretending to be a mere agent of the company. The goods were sent to the Dutch neutral island of St. Eustatius (the same island whose garrison had returned the official salute to the American warship the *Andrew Doria*) and then on to a Connecticut-based import company owned by Silas Deane. Monies were also transferred from Hortales and Co. to Deane's company. Due to the efforts of Beaumarchais and Deane during this discreet phase of supplying the colonists, France supplied 200 cannon, 25,000 muskets, 2000,000 pounds of gunpowder, 20 mortars, and tents for 25,000 troops.[7]

After Saratoga, France made two formal treaties of alliance with the United States, as it would between two sovereign states, and declared war on Britain. From then on, troops, aid, and supplies from France to the Americans were increased and sent openly, and then in 1781 they further increased due to the urging and persuasions of Franklin at Versailles.

John Jay was sent as an official representative to Spain. Although Spain avoided giving him official accreditation and recognised the United States as sovereign and independent only in the final stages of the Treaty of Paris in 1783, Jay did receive and was able to facilitate financial payments from Spain to the American insurgents.

A significant amount of foreign finances came from the Dutch Republic. John Adams was sent by Congress as a representative to the Netherlands. Britain, since the days of its Glorious Revolution and King William III, was the traditional ally of the Dutch Republic and its stadhouder. However, as we have seen, provincial sovereignty and the commercial interests of the Regent class in the towns was not always akin to those of the stadhouder. From the mid-1770s, Dutch entrepreneurs issued credit to start trading—and breaching the British blockade—in exports to the Americans of cloths from Leiden, gin and liquor from Rotterdam, and clothing from Haarlem, in exchange for imports of sugar, rice, coffee and rum, some of which served for re-exporting. Amsterdam financiers also invested in the expanding land markets around the Ohio River. When John Adams arrived in the Netherlands, he was well prepared with a list of contacts of potential financial backers and investors in the success of the American Revolution. These included the regents of several towns, representatives from the banking house of Lalande and Fijnje, and the chief official, or pensionary, of Amsterdam. In 1782, a financial consortium advanced the Americans a 5-million-guilder loan, at a reasonable rate of 5% interest—and they gained a 4.5% brokerage fee, repayable over 15 years. Other loans followed in the immediate post-independence period in 1784, in 1787, and in 1788, advancing another 9 million guilders, which proved invaluable to the finances of the nascent United States.

Foreign financial backing had been available to the Americans and was a vital factor. In the Dutch Revolt during the Eighty Years' War, a significant part of the finances had been generated by the Dutch through their exponential economic growth.

Vendée Regional Revolt Against the French Revolutionary Government, 1790s

The French Revolution broke out in 1789 and was to convulse France with fanatical and fratricidal political struggles, eventually leading to European-wide wars and only ending with Napoleon's final defeat at Waterloo in 1815. It awoke strong revolutionary passions and nationalist aspirations throughout Europe. However, in the west of France in the Vendée and part of Brittany and in other neighbouring provinces, it provoked an opposite reaction. Under royalist France, the duchy of Brittany had been traditionally a separate entity within France but with a large degree of autonomy. It was a compact entity centring around Rennes, which was the seat of one of several provincial *parlements*, all of whom had bedevilled French constitutional politics and hampered effective government during the Seventeenth Century Wars of Religion and in the years of crisis leading up to the outbreak of the French Revolution.

During the French Revolution, the Vendée Revolt itself centred upon the extreme south eastern area of Brittany, the outer districts of the neighbouring province of Anjou, parts of the provinces of Poitou and Touraine. In these areas, the peasantry had more of an affinity with the local aristocracy than peasantry in other parts of France. The local aristocracy resided there, unlike their counterparts in other regions of France, and were in general the poorer echelons of the aristocracy, possessing small holdings that they divided and rented. They often experienced some degree of hardship as did the peasantry. The extravagant, rich, and uncaring absentee nobleman was not a characteristic of this region.

The western power base consisted of traditional royalism, that is the local aristocracy supported by the conservative and Catholic peasantry. This combined with some parts of the better off peasantry and the working classes of the small towns. The last two were hostile to any form of titles and elites, but the common hostility towards distant revolutionary Paris rule generally ensured a united insurrection. Apart from agriculture, the other major economic sector was sea fishing and related fish processing based around the port of Nantes; the workers in these parts were also innately conservative. The region was strongly Catholic, and both the local clergy and the distant Catholic hierarchy had the devotion of the peasantry. The revolutionary government in Paris, through the Constituent Assembly, passed the Civil Constitution of the Clergy:

the most ambitious piece of political architecture the Constituent Assembly attempted.[8]

The Constitution nationalised the Catholic Church, sold off church lands and their benefices, and required all clergy to swear an oath to the Revolution. Nearly all the clergy in France refused. Whilst some of the peasantry in the west welcomed the sale and redistribution of church lands, all in the region were totally alienated by what was viewed as the revolutionary oppression of the clergy and the beloved Catholic Church. Passive resistance to the "new" revolutionary clergy was carried out by the communities, with locals hindering the newly appointed state clergy in their devotions and functions. The resistance was not only that of the lower poorer peasants but also that of farmers and village traders-innkeepers, blacksmiths, haulage and cart owners, whose counterparts in other regions of France were generally in favour of the egalitarian and levelling doctrines of the revolutionary government in Paris.[9]

Resentment and anger rose amongst the suspicious peasantry against the distant Paris government and the increasingly revolutionary ideology and policies being promulgated and adopted by the government there. The anger and disaffection broke out into open insurrection, caused by the government now sitting as the Convention and imposing conscription. The decree of universal conscription in August 1792 called up all males fit for military service. Then the government, through the Minister of War Carnot, decreed a *levée en masse* in February 1793 and a further *levée* in August 1793.

News of the uprising in the Vendée reached the government in Paris, which was preoccupied with the Prussian invasion to the east of the country and which was now threatening the fortress of Verdun by late 1792.[10] Action from the Paris government was delayed. By early 1793, the numbers of insurgents in the Vendée were in their thousands, and they rose further[11] with the news of the Paris government decreeing the *levée en masse*. The insurgents advanced on the port of Rochefort, with the objective of capturing it and giving access to a British invasion force. By the time the full extent of the revolt was understood by the revolutionary government in Paris by March 1793, the key towns of Cholet, Chemille, and Fontenoy-le-Compte had been taken by the insurgents. Four provincial aristocrats, former soldiers with the royal army and all with military training, were leading large insurgent formations. By April 1793, almost the whole of the Vendée was under insurgent control. Parish committees were established to collect arms and supplies, as well as royalist currency assignat notes whose design was the head of the son of the guillotined Louis XVI, the boy entitled Louis XVII. Even field hospitals were established.

However, the tide of victory turned in June 1793 with the failure of the insurgents to take Nantes, a key regional town and vital port.[12]

The Revolutionary government in Paris was able to deploy, increasing the numbers of republican troops, who as time progressed were better trained and equipped, in addition to being well led under the ruthless republican General Turreau, whose scorched earth policy deprived the insurgents of supplies and sanctuary. Then a fanatical representative of the government, Jean Baptiste Carrier, arrived in Nantes and purged the city of royalists and rebels (and many innocent individuals) by mass execution. The able revolutionary general, General Hoche, then took over military command in the region and eradicated the rest of the insurgent forces, skilfully employing counter-insurgency tactics, whilst keeping his troops disciplined yet tolerant and respectful to the general population. By 1796 the Vendée Revolt was over.

Analysis and Comparison With the Dutch Revolt

In comparing the Vendée insurgency to the Dutch Revolt, several interesting factors, including our 4 factors, are apparent. The objective of the Dutch Revolt was firstly to rebel against several aspects of Hapsburg rule, but by 1572—an early stage in the Eighty Years' War—a Dutch national identity and national cause had been created. An independent nation completely free from Spanish rule was the aim, albeit firstly it was to be compromised in that the southern provinces were to remain loyal to and under Spanish rule thanks to the enlightened rule of the Archduke Albert and Isabella at a crucial stage of the Eighty Years' War and secondly within the northern United Provinces, provincial sovereignty was an essential constitutional element. Nonetheless, by 1572 the Dutch Revolt was an aspiring nation fighting for its independence. By contrast, the Vendée insurgency was a rebellion against Paris revolutionary rule and an attempt to revert to the former regime of paternalistic, aristocratic rule under and within a France ruled by a French monarchy, with the Catholic clergy restored to their pivotal position in society. Such a prospect could be realistic only if other regions and provinces of France rose in rebellion against the revolutionary government; it could not be achieved by Vendée alone.

Turning to two of the other factors, having adequate armed forces and finances, whilst the Dutch insurgents were at times struggling for finances, the financial strain on their Spanish opponents was more severe and constant. Also, the Spanish had to overcome the constant logistical difficulties of transporting and deploying troops to the Netherlands. By contrast, the initial difficulties of the French revolutionary government had to do with raising enough troops to meet the different military threats to the regime, including that of the Vendée. The 1793 *levée en masses* was implemented. These were carried with difficulties and flaws in implementation, but thanks to the superb organizing and improvising ability of Carnot, the *levée en masse* nonetheless delivered large numbers of potential soldiers. Once this was in motion, large numbers of troops could be continuously deployed to quell the Vendée. Revolutionary generals like Jourdan and Hoche quickly adapted their large untrained formations and made them effective fighting units, by a combination of revolutionary fervour, *esprit de corps*, improved supplies and ammunition, and, in the case of Hoche, new counter-insurgency tactics. One of the first defeats of the Vendéens, that of Chatillon in July 1793, was due to revolutionary General Kleber skilfully deploying veteran French revolutionary troops who had learned their fighting and tactics on the eastern front around Mainz. By contrast, the Vendéens could rely only on levies raised in a small territorial area, whose base centred on Cholet with an outer base area of a quadrilateral 60 to 70 miles wide. Also, though the levies raised were large in numbers, they were led by different commanders who often were at odds with one another, resulting in divided counsel and leadership. La Rochejacquelin, who was to have a prominent role in a subsequent Vendée revolt, was a brave and tenacious fighter but was doctrinaire with little sense of pragmatism or adaptability. At the crucial battle for Nantes in 1793, there was poor coordination among the 4 main formations of insurgent forces, causing one of the leaders, Cathelina, make a serious tactical mistake in which his forces suffered severe casualties, and he himself was killed. The rest of his forces promptly withdrew from the battle.

In the factor of international dimension, in the case of the Dutch Revolt, as we have seen, Spain was distracted by other threats, the Turkish threat and the volatile situation regarding France and the latter's internal wars. These forced Spain to fight on two fronts, and in the case of the intervention in France, there was also English support for the Dutch forces. Later, thanks to Maurits's diplomacy, foreign alliances were made, in one instance ensuring a massive financial subsidy. In the case of the Vendée revolt, at first the revolutionary government in Paris was certainly distracted. The serious international threat in 1792 from combined Prussian forces that invaded to restore a royalist regime preoccupied the revolutionary government so much that the Vendée Revolt was allowed to expand and gather strength. At the decisive Battle of Valmy, to general astonishment, the invading Prussian forces were held by French revolutionary troops and then retreated back to Prussia. It was only after this, from October 1792 onwards, that the revolutionary government in Paris begin to assess other threats and give attention to the Vendée. However, after that they were able to deploy increasing numbers of troops. The Vendéens, for their part, hoped for foreign assistance when the international situation intensified with the British–French Republic conflict. Within Britain, the Vendée Revolt had engendered much sympathy amongst certain society circles in Britain but produced little actual help. Seaborne landings were projected off the Breton coast, but only one with any likelihood of success was carried out, that of Quiberon

Bay in 1795, which was easily dealt with and repelled by the able French General Hoche. None of the other anti-French coalition powers gave any assistance to the Vendée insurgents.

A final factor that may be of interest in this revolt is the government reaction. The Spanish reaction to the Dutch Revolt under Alva was harsh repression, and then, under Requesens, a form of reconciliation was attempted. However, the attempt at reconciliation was completely disrupted by the events of the Spanish mutinies. The French Revolutionary government too, when it started regaining control of the region, instigated unmitigated terror. In late 1793 and in mid-1794, the revolutionary general Turreau pursued a campaign of vicious repression and destruction. One of his despatches to the War Ministry in Paris stated simply:

[M]y purpose is to burn everything.[13]

This was accompanied a short time later by one of the revolutionary *representatives en mission* from Paris, Jean-Baptiste Carrier. On his arrival in Nantes, he took control and purged the city of any insurgents, royalists, or indeed any whom he deemed anti-revolutionary in a series of mass executions, first by firing squads and then by mass drownings in the river Loire.

However, sheer repression was not the only policy. General Hoche, skilled in counter-insurgency tactics, when the territory had been recaptured and the region was mostly under control, signed truces with the remnants of the insurgent guerrillas, both those from Vendée and those from Brittany. Having restored order, Hoche granted local freedom of worship for non-juring, non-revolutionary priests and clergy,[14] measures that greatly reconciled the region. By 1796 the Vendée Revolt was over. Repression and reconciliation had made an effective combination.

1815 Vendée Revolt—Thwarted

In February 1815, Napoleon escaped from exile in Elba, landed in France in a whirlwind of events involving a march on Paris, ousted the restored Bourbon regime, and re-established himself as ruler of France—all within just over a month. France was in turmoil, though generally supportive of Napoleon.

The Allies were still in Congress at Vienna and held together. They issued a declaration outlawing Napoleon and formed a military coalition to intervene. Napoleon, having had his peace offers rejected out of hand, made speedy and wide-sweeping measures for raising, forging, and equipping an army to counter the Allies. His focus and that of his ministers and his generals was to the north-east. However, the Vendée and parts of Brittany were hostile. An initial period of apparent calm was deceptive.

The western power base of the Vendéens still consisted of traditional royalism, conservatism, and Catholicism, as well as support of the old aristocracy. The better off peasantry and working artisans were hostile to any form of titles and elitism, but the common hostility to revolutionary Paris would ensure a united insurrection in the region. By April 1815, no less than 11 royalist leaders had met, formed a conspiracy, and formulated plans and a strategy. A command structure had been worked out with a united command, learning the lessons of the failure of the 1790s. The aristocratic brothers La Rochejaquelin—one of whom was prominent in the 1790s revolt—were in command, and recruits were being enrolled in clandestine insurgent units. In the second week of April 1815, coordinated royalist attacks were carried out against gendarmerie and army bases and garrisons in 11 different locations throughout Vendée and Brittany.

By mid-May 1815, the insurgents numbered 15,000, and a small arms shipment had been smuggled in and landed consisting of 20,000 rifles. The government forces in the region numbered a maximum of 4,000. Further attacks were made against 7 garrisons and barracks. The local army commander compared the situation to that of 1793 in an urgent and desperate report to Paris.[15] Ministers in Paris, though, preoccupied with the allied coalition being renewed against Napoleon and France, were alarmed, and Napoleon was prevailed upon to send a force of 20,000 troops to the region. These included a Guards regiment and artillery. The insurgents lacked artillery.

However, one government individual who remained calm was the legendary Joseph Fouche, appointed (yet again) to his post as Minister of Police by Napoleon. Fouche, with an impeccable sense of timing and his wide network of contacts of all political persuasions and parties, arranged a meeting with one of the aristocrats of the Vendée, Comte de Martillac. Martillac was a former royalist officer of senior rank. This rendered him legally, according to both the former revolutionary regime and the present restored Napoleon regime, an outlaw. Fouche met Martillac in a discreet meeting and persuaded him at length with a powerful analysis of the then current situation. Fouche's argument ran that if the Vendée and the west of the France continued on their path to insurrection, then this would enable Napoleon to be granted more powers to raise further forces, and these additional forces would reinforce those deployed against the advancing anti-French coalition and make his defeat less likely. Hostilities against the coalition in the north-east would not take place until June—here Fouche's prediction was very accurate—which would give Napoleon plenty of time to ruthlessly deal with the Vendée in the west and then quickly switch the forces to the north-east front. And, Fouche continued, the success of any Vendée revolt, as was proven in the 1790s, did not depend on what happened in the west but rather how events unfolded in the north-east and to what extent the Paris government would be too preoccupied with the external threat of invasion to deal with the internal Vendée revolt. Martillac was at first bewildered by these well presented and articulate predictions but was finally convinced.

Fouche, being Fouche, whilst negotiating with Martillac on behalf of the restored Napoleon regime was also in constant contact with officials and politicians who had been ousted when Napoleon regained power. He was also in contact with representatives of the allies of the anti-French coalition, to whom he was predicting the eventual defeat of Napoleon.

Martillac was finally convinced by Fouche. He and two like-minded Vendée conspirators were given safe conduct passes by the French army and travelled deep into Vendée, where they met insurgent commanders who were far advanced in their preparations for the revolt, which in some areas had already started. When these commanders were informed of the meetings with Fouche and his informed analysis, they agreed to halt preparations and to cease hostilities. The principal Vendée commander La Rochejacquelin refused to agree, but his commanders held to their decision not to start a conflict, and they issued a statement to their followers that ordered no hostilities at present. La Rochejacquelin stubbornly insisted on going ahead and carried on fighting with much reduced forces and was killed in a skirmish with the French army in early June 1815. The Vendée revolt in the west petered out.

Analysis and Comparison With the Dutch Revolt

The second Vendée revolt of 1815 failed; it could be argued that it never really started. It failed to reach serious hostilities due to negotiations and dialogue. On Fouche's part, these were somewhat duplicitous proposals, as he was playing several sides simultaneously. However, the analysis presented to Vendéens was sound, the negotiations held, and both sides engaged fully in them and were willing to keep to their parts. This was unlike the Dutch Revolt, which in the early stages and during the governorship of Requesens, the Spanish king Philip II maintained and would not move from certain rigid positions, namely those on religion. Also, Philip was never reconciled to anything except the Dutch returning to be under Spanish sovereignty. Whilst at times Philip initiated feelers towards negotiations, these were only for deception. On the Dutch side, William of Orange never trusted Philip and could see only limited value in negotiations with the Spanish.

In the 1815 Vendée revolt, Fouche's negotiations and proposals effectively divided the insurgents at crucial points, firstly in Fouche working on Martillac and then from him to the other commanders. In the Dutch Revolt, William ensured, with difficulty, a united front by his constant, tireless efforts at conciliation and talking and ministering to the different concerns and interests of the various groups within the Dutch Revolt.

Greek Revolt and Gaining Independence From the Ottoman Turks, 1821–1828

In the Nineteenth Century, the territorial entity of ancient Greece formed part of and was under the sovereignty of the Ottoman Empire. This Empire held sway over the Balkans up to what is now modern Croatia and bordered the Hapsburg Empire. The Ottomans also held territories along the North African coast, including Egypt. However, it was an empire in decline, and the revolutionary fervor of the tumultuous years of the French Revolution and Napoleonic Wars had aroused nationalist aspirations all over Europe, including amongst the Greeks. A secret society existed, the Hetairia Philike, whose objective was Greek independence, that had been in existence for several years. Its members included wealthy Greek merchants living and trading in European ports, Greek communities in Odessa and Moscow in the Russian Empire, and Greek businessmen and their associates living and working in Paris and London. The prominent members of the society corresponded with one another, planned, and organised the recruitment of new members to the Hetairia Philike.

The first outbreak of revolt occurred in 1821, led by a Russian army officer who was well placed on the staff of the Czar. The officer, Alexander Ypsilante, attempted to start a revolt against the Turks in the northern parts of Greece and in the Danube provinces. He appealed to the local populations but received little support. Disowned by the Czar and the Russian government alike, he fled abroad and was subsequently imprisoned. Other revolts broke out in Hellas and spread to Attica and the Peloponnese. The response of the Turkish government was violent repression, deploying troops, defeating some of the insurgent forces, and engaging in reprisal killings. The Greek Orthodox Patriarch of Constantinople was seized and publicly hanged. However the insurgents were not defeated everywhere; at the Battle of Dervenalia in the Morea, Turkish forces were repulsed

The Turks allocated more and more resources and troops to the struggle, but groups of Greek insurgents held out and went to ground. Also the insurgents had financial backing from expatriate Greek merchants, some of whom had been involved in planning a revolt, and all of whom donated generously. There were also many sympathisers throughout Europe, conscious of having an affinity with the classical Greek past. Prominent intellectuals such as the French poet Lamartine and the English poet Lord Byron (who symbolically died during the revolt at one of the major sieges at Missilonghi), the French writer Victor Hugo, King Ludwig of Bavaria, a royal patron of arts, all gave their vocal support to the Greeks. Funds from a group of sympathisers were coordinated by a Genevan banker, and in 1823 a loan for the Greek insurgents was raised in the City of London. The loan was to be dispersed in two instalments.

The struggle remained one-sided in terms of numbers, and further resources were deployed by the Turks. In 1824 Mehmet Ali, the Sultan's governor and near autonomous ruler of Egypt, was requested by the Sultan to give assistance in quelling the revolt. Troops, infantry, cavalry, and artillery, numbering over 16,000 landed in Crete and Cyprus, then in the Peloponnese itself, at each stage methodically and ruthlessly defeating the insurgents, cowering the population, and quelling the revolt. By 1825 the insurgents were in retreat, seeking to go to ground, with little sign of more help available.

However, further finances followed. A Greek delegation nearly obtained a loan from France, contacts with the French bank Lafitte, but negotiations failed. Turning to Britain, they managed to contact a British Greek committee of a pro-Greek association. They attended a series of meetings, one of which was attended by the British Foreign Secretary George Canning, and eventually a loan of 800,000 sterling was obtained on the securities of certain properties in Greece. Two instalments of 40,000 sterling were made immediately available to the insurgents, with an understanding that further payments would follow when a contract had been signed by the provisional Greek government and that the lenders, through the Greek London committee, had satisfied themselves that this government loan was viable, in that it—and the revolt—would survive.

Up to 1822 the 5 great powers—Austria, Prussia, Russia, and Britain, together with France under its restored royalist government—were committed to upholding and maintaining the 1815 Vienna Settlement, with no territorial changes. Indeed, between 1815 and 1822, disturbances, revolts, and revolutionary activity in various parts of Europe had caused the great powers to further international congresses where they reaffirmed the *status quo* and had supported two of their number to engage in armed intervention to quell revolts in 3 countries, Austria intervening in the Kingdoms of Piedmont and Naples and France in Spain.

Greece was discussed at one of these congresses at Laibach in 1821, and one of the decisions was that the Greeks were rebels and should be left to their fate. This was despite the Czar Alexander's strong sympathy for the Greeks. The other powers persuaded the Czar to eschew any support for the Greeks, in exchange for their sanctioning intervention in Spain.

Britain felt growing unease at this continued intervention by the great powers in the internal affairs of the smaller states. When Foreign Secretary Castlereagh, one of the dominant Foreign Ministers at the Congress of Vienna, died, he was replaced by George Canning. Canning was hostile to what he perceived to be repressive intervention by the great powers. In 1823 he recognised the Greeks as belligerents. Russia began to support the Greeks, partially due to Alexander's sympathy for them but also as an opportunity to hasten the decline of the Ottoman Empire and make territorial gains down through the Balkans.

In April 1826, Britain and Russia signed an agreement, which proposed a large measure of autonomy for a new Greek state. The following year, in July 1827, an Anglo-French-Russian treaty was signed. This stated that the powers would mediate in the whole question of the revolt, and that, in the event of any rejection to their assistance by Turkey, they would establish commercial and consular relations with the Greeks; any opposition by Turkey to their arranging an armistice would be met by military action. To support this, all the countries deployed warships to the region.

The Treaty was couched in mild terms, but the allied naval commanders on the spot interpreted the terms as intervening in favour of the Greeks and engaged in a naval battle with the Turkish fleet at Navarino Bay. The outmatched Turkish fleet was annihilated. The British attempted to treat this, in the words of then Prime Minister Wellington, as "an untoward incident". However, Russia took the opportunity to declare war on Turkey and advanced through the Balkans. Britain took alarm at Russia's belligerent behaviour, and relations between the two powers rapidly deteriorated. France mediated between the two. Russia was indeed winning her war with Turkey but was experiencing unexpected resistance and setbacks. It was agreed that Russia should act only in the Danube provinces, whilst Anglo-French navies would act in the Mediterranean. Following this, Serbia, liberated by Russia, would be autonomous whilst the French prevailed upon Mehmet Ali and his forces to evacuate the Morea, and the liberated Greek territory would be autonomous. By the Treaty of Adrianople in 1828, Greek autonomy was confirmed in a narrow area, and a year later at the Treaty of London, after this Greek entity had been slightly reduced further in size, Greek independence was recognised. The Revolt had succeeded, and a small state of Greece had gained independence.

Analysis and Comparison With the Dutch Revolt

Compared to the successful Dutch Revolt and the Eighty Years' War, the Greek Revolt was successful after a comparatively short struggle. The Greeks fought bravely and tenaciously, but the military balance clearly favoured the Turks. However, arguably, the resources and military strength of the Turks were less in proportionate terms compared to the military strengths of the Dutch insurgents ranged against the Spanish Empire of Philip II, Philip III, and Philip IV.

Also, as with the early stages of the Dutch Revolt, there were divisions between the insurgents. The Hetairia Philike had been skilled at conspiracies and clandestine communications among differing groups across Europe but had achieved little in organising and creating centralised fighting forces.[16] In early 1824, serious divisions broke out within the Greek insurgents. The members of the Hetairia Philike—who were conscious that it was they who conspired and planned for years towards the revolt—together with members of the Greek nobility of Achea, all felt sidelined and ousted by the Peloponnese aristocracy who had taken over the leadership of the revolt and had formed the provisional government. For a brief period, there was actual fighting between members of the two factions, and there were more fundamental divisions. The upper classes of Greek societies wished for an end to Turkish rule but for the social hierarchy to remain the same; several of the insurgent leaders from differing parts wished to create for themselves warlord zones where they alone could hold sway; the agrarian workers and lower classes looked forward to the end of Turkish rule, resulting in drastic reductions of taxes and the redistribution of land. The military balance favoured the Turks, and when Mehmet Ali and his Egyptian forces had been deployed, had the struggle lasted longer, Turkey would have successfully quelled the revolt.

This was prevented by international intervention by the European powers. This contrasts with the Dutch Revolt where international intervention, either with the well meaning efforts of the Holy Roman Emperor to resolve the issue in the early stages or during the governor-generalship of Leicester in the mid-1980s, only convinced the Dutch that they were better off fighting the Revolt alone. In the Dutch Revolt, international events did not assist the Revolt by having a European power directly intervene to settle the question but rather by the turn of international events distracting Spain and making Spain fight on more than one front.

In the Greek Revolt, Britain, led by Foreign Secretary Canning, was determined to halt the trend of repression by the European powers and their constant intervention in order to maintain what he saw was the rigid and doctrinaire Congress System of maintaining the status quo. Russia, by recognising the Greek state, saw an opportunity in gaining influence and eventual territory at the expense of Turkey. Less than a decade later, Russia was to seize a further opportunity through a turn in international events in the region. In this, Russia gained the long-term objective of full access through the Dardanelles by befriending an isolated Turkey in a Russo-Turkish alliance.[17] France, apprehensive about the forward Russian policy in the region and British open hostility to this Russian policy, mediated and obtained common ground amongst the European powers for a Greek state. Finally Austria, under Chancellor Metternich, the driving force behind the Congress System, steadfastly opposed any armed intervention on the side of the Greeks. However, he and Austria acquiesced in the Treaties of Adrianople and London, which established an independent Greece, but the new state was confined to the narrowest of boundaries.

The Greek Revolt had started by Greek initiative and Greek collective bravery and tenacity, and it survived and succeeded because of the main factor, international intervention. All the European powers had their differing motives and strategic priorities, but all recognised that an independent Greece was part of a common solution. The Russian threat in the Balkans was contained, the declining Ottoman Turkish Empire was maintained, and the status quo remained reasonably intact.[18]

Belgium Revolt, 1830, and Gaining Independence From the Kingdom of the Netherlands

The Belgian Revolt of 1830 is an insurgency worthy of consideration as it is possibly history in reverse with the Netherlands the possessing power.

As we have seen, during the Dutch Revolt, the politicians in the States-General—under the cajoling and remonstrances of Maurits after Nieuwport—finally accepted the territorial limitations of their successful Revolt. The southern provinces loyal to Spain could not be conquered, and the whole of the former Spanish Netherlands was divided into the Dutch Republic and the loyal Spanish Netherlands, along the lines of the Unions of Utrecht and Arras. Under the wise rule of Albert and Isabella, any rebellious elements in the southern loyal provinces became reconciled (or had fled north) to Spanish rule. The provinces developed and prospered economically, though in a different economic direction to that of their northern neighbour.

During the late Seventeenth and early Eighteenth Centuries, there was a period of European Wars, including the War of Spanish Succession, in which parts of the Spanish Netherlands were taken and annexed to France under Louis XIV. This war was ended by the 1713 Treaty of Utrecht; as part of the peace settlement, a follow-up treaty, the Treaty of Rastadt, transferred the Spanish Netherlands from the Spanish Hapsburgs to Austria Hapsburg rule. They remained Austrian territory until the French Revolution. During the French Revolution and Napoleonic era, both the Austrian Netherlands and the Dutch Republic were occupied as part of France. The Dutch entity (Stadhouder William V having fled to England) was a separate client kingdom with Dutch politicians forming a pro-French administration and its king being Napoleon's brother Louis. (Louis, whilst loyal to his brother and to France, had a strong empathy with the Dutch.) The Austrian Netherlands were annexed outright as sovereign French territory. During the Wars of Liberation against Napoleon and France fought by a coalition of Britain, Austria, Prussia, and Russia, a joint Dutch-Belgian brigade fought as part of the Allies and formed a component part of Wellington's forces at the Battle of Waterloo. After Napoleon was defeated, the major powers at the massive peace conference of the Congress of Vienna were faced with the problem of balancing the 3 priorities: to restore the map of Europe, to avoid merely reasserting the forces of reaction of the Ancién Regime, and to prevent any future aggrandisement by France.

It was this last priority that impacted upon the Austrian Netherlands and the Dutch Republic. To prevent further aggression by France, a chain of barrier states bordering France was created, hemming France in and restricting France to the borders of 1792. The historic republic of Genoa, small and vulnerable, was given to the Kingdom of Savoy; the major powers collectively guaranteed the inviolability and neutrality of Switzerland; the Rhine Provinces, formerly a group of semi-independent territories, all became part of Prussia; finally, the former Austrian Netherlands were united with the Dutch Republic in a Kingdom of the Netherlands. The Prince of Orange ascended the throne of the new kingdom as King William I. Article 6 of the First Treaty of Paris—part of the series of treaties of the peacemaking of the Congress of Vienna—prepared against any possible annexation of the Austrian Netherlands or the Dutch entity by France in stating:

> Holland, placed under the sovereignty of the House of Orange, will receive a territorial enlargement. The title and exercise cannot, in any case whatsoever, belong to any prince wearing or who might be called to wear, a foreign crown.[19]

The ruler of the new kingdom, King William I, was the grandson of the previous Dutch Stadhouder William V. He had been brought up in exile in England and educated at Eton, and he had served under the Duke of Wellington against Napoleon. He welcomed his new domain. He was well meaning towards his new subjects, trying to establish a type of Greater Netherlands. Economically, the unification led to advancing the industrialisation of the south, and investment from the Dutch was forthcoming and generous. Extensive public works in the south were funded. A Société Générale was formed, a bank whose remit was specifically capital formation for Belgian economic expansion.

However, differences in cultures were resolved with simplistic solutions. Dutch was made the official and sole working language, and government officials and civil servants in the Flemish and southern provinces were given a fixed time to master the Dutch language or transfer to the Walloon provinces (where there was no guarantee of an equivalent position or salary). Lawyers who could not speak Dutch were barred from pleading in the Dutch courts and in the Flemish provinces in the south. Also, the Dutch education policy caused conflict with Belgium whose population was predominantly Catholic. The Dutch tried to limit the Catholic Church's influence and hold on education, antagonising all sections of the population. Conscientious to a fault, King William proposed to find a *de facto* "national" Catholic Church, which would be the established church of the kingdom. There were also plans for secular theological universities and therefore state-controlled curricula on religious teaching, which would replace Catholic seminaries.

In the economy, overall most commercial interests were content with the economic tariff system and the levels of taxation in the expanded kingdom. Generally, Dutch and Belgian businessmen were content with the personal union of the crowns, which left the economic unity of Belgium and the Dutch kingdom untouched. However, there was a growth of a Belgian national consciousness. In 1828 there was a campaign involving a multitude of petitions, all calling for an end to the personal rule of William I.[20] These petitions and any other demonstrations were ignored by the Dutch ministers and administrators.

The Revolt started spasmodically on 25 August 1830 in Brussels, following a rousing theatre production based on the Seventeenth-Century revolt of Naples against the Spanish. Roused and angry crowds rioted, called for an uprising, surrounded the residence of the Dutch minister in Brussels, and rioted around the various ministries and prominent newspaper premises. The insurgency spread to Liege and other cities, where the police lost control. By the end of August, the insurgents had increased in numbers but were of two types. These were, firstly, those enrolled in the Garde Bourgeois, a middle-class, hastily formed militia, conservative and conscious of protecting property, and, secondly, the agrarian and industrial worker, who was egalitarian with a wide social reform programme and contemptuous of titles and nobility. Both types were united in their detestation of Dutch rule.

A group of Belgian insurgents drew up a petition and travelled to The Hague to place their grievances before King William I, who referred it to the States-General for consideration. At the same time, the Dutch sent 6,000 troops to Brussels. However, deploying them in close combat was decided against, given how many of the population were supporting the Revolt. The Prince of Orange attempted to mediate but without success. By October 1830, groups of insurgents had raided various premises in Brussels and gained money and arms, and throughout Belgium the insurgent numbers continued to increase and to form themselves into units. On 4 October 1830, a provisional government formed from the leaders of the insurgent groups and made a formal declaration of independence. Independent ministries were formed, including a Foreign Ministry. King William despatched thousands more of troop reinforcements to be ready for action. At the same time, he appealed to the 4 Great Powers—Britain, Austria, Prussia, and Russia—to intervene. The Belgian self-declared Foreign Ministry also made a representation to the powers. The Belgian Revolt had become an international issue for eventual international settlement.

From then on, it was long and hard negotiations on an international level with the Belgian side proving themselves stubborn, skilled and determined. At one stage, in August 1831 the Dutch, frustrated by what they viewed as Belgian intransigence, invaded and swept aside the Belgian insurgent forces but were driven back shortly after by a French counter-invasion, which was supported and sanctioned—and carefully watched—by Britain, Prussia, Austria, and Russia. Britain was particularly anxious as the issue involved the security of the English Channel. A truce was brokered, and long diplomatic negotiations resumed. The final settlement, after several interim treaties were agreed and signed, was arrived at with the 1839 Treaty of London,[21] in which Belgian independence was recognised. The new state was confined to narrow territorial boundaries, and the yearly interest on the former national debt of the former united kingdom was to continue to be paid by Belgium. Belgian neutrality—the subject of the infamous phrase by a German diplomat in 1914, "the scrap of paper"—was guaranteed by all the powers.

Analysis and Comparison With the Dutch Revolt

There are significant aspects to comparing and contrasting the Belgian Revolt of 1830 to the Dutch Revolt. One important aspect is that of national identity. The Dutch Revolt was, in the first stages, a revolt against the changes involved in the restructuring of the bishoprics and the modernizing of the miscellaneous territories and jurisdictions then comprising the Netherlands. The differing provinces and regions jealously guarded their traditional rights and customs. The imposed changes, combined with the religious aspects of increased activity against heresy, were the initial cause. William of Orange united the 7 northern provinces against the Spanish and in doing so created a national consciousness but only by tirelessly negotiating and reconciling differences and disputes among the provinces and among some insurgent factions. The struggle of the Revolt was hampered by their differing interests. One of Leicester's tactics in the 1580s, whilst governor-general in his power struggle with Oldenbarneveldt, was to negotiate with and attempt to deal separately with the Sates of Overijssel. During these talks, discussions were explored by which Overijssel could maintain constitutional links with—and gain privileges from—the Holy Roman Empire.[22] The Dutch Navy, essential to the economic well-being of the Republic, was divided into 5 Admiralties with 5 separate administrations, two of which had been created not for reasons of operational efficiency but to settle inter-regional and provincial jealousies amongst the maritime provinces.[23] And by contrast, the representatives of the inland provinces showed little interest in the Navy, giving the Army both their priority and the bulk of their financial contributions.[24]

Within the Belgian entity of 1830 there was a strong sense of national identity. Since the Union of Arras in 1579, the southern provinces had remained loyal to Spain and had benefitted under the wise rule of Archduke Albert and his wife Isabella, and with the transfer of sovereignty to the Austrian Netherlands in the Eighteenth Century, they had developed economically, with rapid progress in agriculture.[25] After the occupation and annexation by French revolutionary forces and the egalitarian and nationalist sentiments stirred by the French Revolution, Belgium in the first decade of the Nineteenth Century had a strong sense of national identity and Francophile sympathies. Significantly, upon the outbreak of the Revolt and the subsequent debates in September 1830, when the Belgians realised Dutch reluctance to negotiate a compromise, they insisted on independence or, failing that, union with France.[26]

The religious and economic aspects need to be considered in comparing the two revolts. Like the Dutch Revolt, the Belgian Revolt had a strong religious cause. The attempted education reforms were widely seen as an attack on the Catholic Church. This, together with the language issue, was seen as disrupting the way of life for many, and in the case of government employees and lawyers, it involved substantial disruption and loss of earnings. Unlike the Dutch Revolt, the economic grievances were not prominent. As we have seen, every effort was made by King William I and his ministers to stimulate economic growth in the Belgian part of the new kingdom, with some good results. Unfortunately, the year 1830 was one of economic crisis, and in the Walloon provinces several banks failed, there was an industrial fall in performance and share returns, and two successive bad harvests occurred in the agricultural sector.[27] Unemployment rose, and several factories in Brussels were destroyed by unemployed workers, forming part of a pattern of industrial unrest and violence in several parts of Europe. William and the Dutch could scarcely be blamed for this temporary economic crisis in Belgium, but its timing was a catalyst to the revolt.

In comparing reactions by the respective possessing powers to the insurgency breaking out, there is a difference. The Dutch Revolt in its first stages was severely quelled by military force, followed up by harsh judicial repression under Alva. By contrast, the outbreak of the Belgian Revolt met with an apparent willingness to negotiate, motivated by the potential to divide the insurgents or as a delaying process in order to be in so much the better position for military intervention. Dutch armed forces were deployed but kept back in reserve. When the Dutch did invade, it was out of frustration with the unfavourable terms emerging from the negotiations, and they defended their invasion as "negotiations supported by military measures". The Dutch campaign was a success in that it defeated the insurgent levies, but the invaders were forced to withdraw by the French counter-invasion. However, the action did serve Dutch interests in that it demonstrated that the Dutch were still a force and that the final terms had to be acceptable to them as well as to the insurgents.

In one sense, the European powers, in facilitating and indeed dictating, that Belgium be separate from the Netherlands, were undoing their own mistake in the settlement of the Congress of Vienna. There the British Foreign Secretary Castlereagh insisted on the two entities being united. Castlereagh had been planning this with the Prince of Orange as early as 1813 as he was initially convinced that both the Belgian and the Dutch entities would welcome this development. From then on, official British

Foreign Office documents referred to the Prince of Orange as 'the Sovereign Prince of the Netherlands'. However, by early 1814, it became clear to Castlereagh that the large majority of the population of the former Austrian Netherlands were totally opposed to union with the Dutch Republic and that they were willing to accept union with France or revert to Hapsburg rule. Castlereagh chose to ignore this[28] and prevailed upon the other European powers to create a union of the Kingdom of the Netherlands. This was to form the necessary buffer state against future French aggression. This latter imperative caused the other powers to also ignore popular opinion in the former Austrian Netherlands.

To summarise, after the initial outbreak, the real struggles throughout the Belgian Revolt were fought over lengthy and complex international negotiations in which both insurgents and the possessing power negotiated with other large European powers in an international context. The final settlement was resolved in an international dimension.

Ireland Gains Independence From Britain, 1916–1921

Ireland under British rule had been the subject of several movements and armed rebellions attempting to gain independence, all quelled by Britain. However, by the start of the Twentieth Century, Ireland was comparatively quiescent. Reforms by the British administration in land tenure, education, local government (in which, completely against contemporary political norms, all women were also entitled to vote), and economic investment had improved overall standards of living. The situation was by no means ideal—Dublin housing conditions remained appalling, and unemployment amongst skilled labourers was high—but compared to the previous century, Ireland was transformed.

In the first decade of the Twentieth Century, the militant movement, the Irish Republican Brotherhood, was moribund. The main thrust for self-determination was in the political arena, through the Irish National Party whose MPs attended Westminster and Sinn Fein in Ireland. After two previous failed attempts in the past, finally, in 1912, the British government was to grant Ireland a form of self-determined autonomy in the Home Rule Bill. However, at a late stage this was frustrated by the Unionists of Ulster, in alliance with the British Conservative Party, who wished Ireland to remain entirely under British rule. Arming themselves with illegally imported arms, the Ulster Unionists threatened rebellion, ironically to preserve the *status quo*. In 1914, the Home Rule Bill was finally passed with difficulty but not implemented due to the outbreak of the First World War. Ireland was disappointed but overall remained patient.

However, a small minority group of militant Irish nationalists in 1916 organised and staged an uprising, seizing the principal buildings in Dublin. It was a forlorn, doomed attempt, and British troops quelled the uprising in a few days. By executing 12 of the insurgents, however, the British made martyrs of them, and public opinion in Ireland veered increasingly against Britain and toward gaining freedom by violence. Elections in 1917 resulted in a landslide for Sinn Fein, whose representatives, instead of taking their seats in parliament in London, remained in London, and formed a breakaway parliament, the Dail, and a government. Meanwhile, the armed militant wing of Irish nationalism, the Irish Volunteers (later in the struggle to become the IRA) were arming and organising. Guerrilla war ensued from 1919 to 1921.

The British were not defeated; the sheer difference in numbers, arms, and equipment on both sides were heavily in favour of the British forces. At any one time during the struggle, full-time IRA operatives were estimated to be not more than 3,000, but they had the overwhelming support of the population. By 1921, a truce, or ceasefire, was arranged, followed by negotiations in London with representatives from both sides. This resulted in the signing of a treaty creating the self-determining entity, the Irish Free State.[29]

Analysis and Comparison With the Dutch Revolt

The Irish insurgency shared one important aspect with the Dutch Revolt: there was a delay in its becoming a national armed uprising. As we have seen, the initial causes of the Dutch Revolt were religious with the anti-heresy crackdown and the reorganisation of the bishoprics, then the economic grievance caused by Alva's attempted repressive taxes. It took some time and indefatigable hard work by William of Orange to unite the differing groups and interests of the Dutch rebels into a true national movement.

The cause of Irish nationalism was a clearly identified one with a single objective of a self-determined, independent Ireland. However, the various groups and associations—the linguistic and cultural Gaelic Athletic Association and the Gaelic League, the parliamentary Irish National Party, Sinn Fein—all these pursued the struggle for independence through peaceful means up to 1914. Ireland had for decades remained "peaceful, patient and hopeful".[30] Even the militant and armed Irish National Volunteers were formed under the passive gaze of British authorities as a force to defend Ireland against Britain's enemies. The majority remained loyal to Britain at the start of the First World War, many of them volunteering for British army service in the war. Those of the minority group who had formed themselves into the anti-British force, the Irish Volunteers, even after the 1916 Rising, largely regarded themselves as a defensive force to fight only if conscription was introduced in Ireland. It was due to Michael Collins and the secret Irish Republican Brotherhood, which had infiltrated the Irish Volunteers, that the Irish Volunteers finally took the offensive in 1919 in continuous guerrilla warfare.

Both the Irish insurgents and the Dutch forces tended to avoid open, pitched battles in the early stages of the Dutch Revolt. Louis of Nassau's victory was the exception; invariably, in pitched battles during the early stages, the well trained and experienced Spanish forces prevailed. Maurits's victory at Nieuwport was due to his reforms and training of the Dutch armies, as well as his tenacity and that of his troops, combined with his superb sense of timing in unleashing his reserves. However, it was a skilful victory that rescued him and his forces from a position in which he had had no desire to be and one that had been forced upon him (for the last time) by politicians with a strategic political agenda.

Maurits's alternative to pitched battles was skilled strategic manoeuvring, sudden strikes at towns, and sieges. The Irish alternative to pitched battles was guerrilla warfare and ambush attacks, supported and facilitated by successful waging of an intelligence war combined with targeted assassination.

Regarding assassination, in the Dutch Revolt it was the Spanish who achieved the greatest success, killing William of Orange in 1584. Philip II proclaimed William an outlaw and had placed a bounty on his killing. After some failed attempts, a fanatical Catholic managed to gain entry to William's quarters in Delft and shoot him, inflicting fatal wounds. The assassin was caught, tortured, and executed, but Spain ensured that his wife and family were granted a substantial pension. The assassination was effective in that it was an undoubted blow to the Dutch Revolt, eliminating the focal rallying and essential leader, and impacting upon the morale of the Dutch. Predictably, it made a martyr of William, generated rising anger, and strengthened the ideal of a Dutch nation. All of this was foreseen by Parma when he opposed targeted assassination and constantly counselled Philip against using it.

High-profile assassination was attempted by the IRA, in that an attempt was made on the life of the new Governor-General Sir John French shortly after he had arrived in Ireland; also, the wholesale assassination of the entire British Cabinet by an attack in London was discussed amongst the IRA and "ministers" of the clandestine Irish government but was eventually rejected as counterproductive. The Director of Intelligence and leader of the IRA guerrilla campaign, Michael Collins, forcefully pointed out that it would not eliminate the British leadership in a single blow as some were rather simplistically predicting. By far, the greater part of assassinations and murders carried out by the IRA were directed at lower-level targets. As such, the assassination and murder campaigns were a part of the intelligence war strategy.[31]

During the course of the Dutch Revolt, intelligence and spying were practiced by both sides, and indeed by all the European powers in the complex and changing alliances of the period. As early as 1565, Philip II had two spies[32] at the estates of Count Hoorn at Veere, reporting back on the Count even whilst the latter was respectfully advocating to Philip conciliatory and peacemaking proposals. The England of Elizabeth I had an efficient and ruthless espionage service under Sir Francis Walsingham, which frustrated several plots to assassinate Elizabeth as part of a

Catholic uprising.[33] Walsingham had at last one agent travelling about the Low Countries who, whilst plying his precarious trade as a general merchant, was sending reports to England on the movements of Spanish troops and updates regarding the Armada and the possibility of the invasion of England.[34] Dutch authorities and agents were in close contact with their English counterparts with Walsingham. In mid-1584, tipped off by Walsingham's suspicions, Dutch authorities intercepted a ship in the North Sea and detained one of the passengers. This was an individual named Creighton. Just before Creighton was taken, he tore up papers he was holding and threw them overboard, but the wind blew back the fragments, which were retrieved by his captors and pieced together. The Dutch handed Creighton over to the English. Creighton was carrying messages to Scotland as part of a conspiracy by English Catholic exiles to assassinate Elizabeth and start a rebellion. Maurits and the Dutch cooperated closely in intelligence matters with England during the mid-1580s, and Maurits and the Dutch forces throughout the Revolt could generally rely upon local populations to provide ground-level intelligence about Spanish units and troop movements. There are incidents of women in the Netherlands during the Dutch Revolt, having been made destitute by fortunes of war, becoming the close companions of Spanish soldiery yet still quietly passing on information to Dutch forces. One famous (and much embellished) incident is that of Magdalena Moons, a woman of a comparatively wealthy Dutch lawyer family, becoming the close companion and lover of the commander of the Spanish troops at the siege of Leiden. She used various arguments, charm, and wiles to persuade the commander to delay the final assaults on Leiden, and this delay coincided with the time needed for the floodwaters to rise to sufficient depth for the relieving troop-carrying barges of Boisot's forces, thus enabling the relief and victory in 1574. How far Moons was in collusion with the Dutch forces is a matter of much speculation.[35] However, the delay in the Spanish forces pushing home their assaults on Leiden, for which she undoubtedly was responsible, did give the Dutch relieving forces the vital time necessary for the floodwaters to rise and transport the relieving forces.

Compared to the Dutch Revolt, the Irish in their War of Independence used intelligence to a different extreme and more intensively, and their war was more an intelligence war.

The IRA, by murdering police officers, eliminated intelligence sources because police officers were the eyes and ears of the British administration within the Irish communities. Accordingly, a campaign of intimidation and murder was waged against the Royal Irish Constabulary (RIC), eventually resulting in many of the surviving members of the force to resign. Collins and the IRA did not expect the police to shirk their police duties or be turncoat informers; however, those RIC members who showed too much zeal in anti-insurgency or political activities were first warned off. If they ignored the warning and persisted, they were shot. It was a salutary lesson to all the RIC.

Under the control of Collins and the IRA, the Irish insurgency was no longer infiltrated by informers; quite the reverse, the insurgents were the infiltrators, gaining the intelligence.[36] Collins and the IRA had several informants within the police forces, individuals who were fully sympathetic to the struggle for Irish freedom and were active as Collin's agents. Each one was allotted a handler by the IRA intelligence section, a section specifically created by Collins. Besides the RIC, the other major police force was that of the capital, the Dublin Metropolitan Police (DMP). Collins and the IRA gave strict instructions that uniformed members of the DMP engaging in normal, non-political policing duties were not be harmed, let alone killed. The main targets for assassination were those DMP members serving in G Division, which was engaged in anti-subversion, i.e. countering the activities of the IRA. These individuals were ruthlessly targeted and killed.

Targeted assassination was also used by the IRA to ensure the security of their finances. As will be shown, the IRA had accumulated significant funds before the guerrilla war started. The British had countered this by employing a tenacious and able financial expert[37] to trace and intercept the funds. His inquiries were coming dangerously close to locating the some of the funds and identifying the methods of clandestine transfer. Collins authorised a well organised assassination of the financial investigator, and IRA operatives abducted him on the tram during his commute to work, forced him to get off, and shot him several times. This was carried out in the morning of a weekday in full view of other commuting passengers. As well as eliminating the threat to the insurgent finances, the assassination sent yet another intimidating message.

As well having as informers in the police during the War of Independence, the IRA and its political wing Sinn Fein had Irish trade unionists working for them. The railwaymen were particularly useful in terms of reporting troop movements, in conveying messages and supplies, and in disrupting trains used by British forces. Hotel porters and staff, restaurants and bar staff were useful sources of information, as well as, very importantly, the post office workers and telephonists in an age where postal mail and the telephone were the only means of speedy long-distance communication. To Sinn Fein and the IRA, intelligence was an absolute priority in terms of allocating skilled operatives and resources and money. Its effectiveness was such that the Irish Consul in Dublin informed the US State Department:

> [N]o event occurs in Ireland that the wonderful espionage of Sinn Fein does not cover. . . . [N]o conversation can be conducted over the public telephone without it being known and reported to Sinn Fein.[38]

A final, important factor in comparing the Dutch Revolt and the Irish insurgency is that of finance. As we have seen in the early stages of the

Dutch Revolt, the insurgency was supported by *ad hoc* methods of financial support, and at times the financial situation was critical. The later stages of the Revolt, in Maurits's period, a national functioning economy emerged, thanks to the wealth of the province of Holland. As we have also seen, the struggle with Spain caused an extreme economic strain on the Republic but an even more extreme strain on Spain, which economically broke first. By contrast, the Irish insurgency, while not enjoying unlimited or luxurious funds, was overall adequately funded from the very start of the armed conflict.

As soon as the Irish elections were completed in 1918 and the Irish representatives opted to form their own parliament or Dail in Dublin, instead of attending the British parliament at Westminster, a clandestine government was formed within ministries. It was announced that a National Loan would be floated throughout Ireland to raise funds for the "Irish government" (with Michael Collins resolving that this would be funds for the forthcoming armed struggle). Collins, as clandestine Minister of Finance, organised the selling of the loan bonds, raising, collecting, transporting, and secretly storing the funds. Some of the cash funds were painstakingly—in multiple small transactions—converted to gold and stored at secret locations in Dublin, ensuring that the clandestine Irish government, through its Ministry of Finance, had gold bullion reserves. It was a remarkable achievement by Collins, and the amounts raised exceeded the projected target. The Irish "Prime Minister" de Valera made an extended tour of the United States, and part of his activities was raising donations from the population of the United States for the Irish freedom struggle. These too were successful, although for various complex, nefarious reasons, de Valera did not send all the collected funds to Ireland, keeping a substantial proportion in the United States.[39] The result, nevertheless, was that almost a year before the armed guerilla war started, the Irish had accumulated a substantial war chest.

As the struggle continued, Collins, as Minister of Finance, managed to favourably balance the finances of the clandestine Irish government, and in 1920 he could ensure that funds were available for both paying the workers or "government servants" and funding the armed struggle.[40] However, by the time of the Truce, both the IRA and the clandestine Irish government were hard stretched for funds and supplies. Financially, the Irish insurgency had held out—but only just. But that it had survived was due to finances being raised, clandestinely moved, and concealed and available well in advance of the conflict. This contrasts with the Dutch Revolt, which in the early stages was seriously short of financial support.

France Loses the Overseas Territories in Vietnam, 1948–1954

French possession of their south-East Asian territories began under the Empire of Napoleon III, with several areas around the Mekong Delta being conquered in the 1860s, as part of the imperial forward foreign policy. As part of the French recovery after their disastrous defeat in the Franco-Prussian War (and the internal coup against the Emperor whose regime was replaced by the Third French Republic) and in keeping with the atavistic expansion of many European countries, the Third Republic expanded these territories. In 1880 the Tonkin area was acquired for France by conquest. By 1890 the French overseas possessions included virtually the whole of what is now modern Vietnam.

The French regime in Vietnam, like other contemporary colonial regimes of the European powers, was exploitative. Rice, coal, rubber, and silks were harvested, mined, or produced and exported at large profits, whilst the demand within the Vietnamese domestic economy was manipulated for French products. French bureaucrats and French businessmen enjoyed a rich lifestyle, and below them a small class of Vietnamese assistants, interpreters, administrators, and minor civil servants enjoyed a modest living and status. The majority of the Vietnamese population, predominantly rural, maintained a precarious existence. The French named their regime *mission civilization*, but it gave back little in the way of providing public services or infrastructure. Public health facilities were minimal, and the education system, while benefitting small numbers of the Vietnamese who went on to become minor administrators and bureaucrats, left the majority of the Vietnamese population semi-literate.

There were attempted revolts. In the 1880s and in 1916, two unsuccessful risings occurred against the French. These uprisings were sponsored and supported by the Vietnamese emperors, formerly the ruling royal families of Indo-China. The revolts were suppressed with harshness, and members of liberation groups or organisations, nationalist or left-wing or extreme communist were imprisoned. In 1919, Ho Chi Minh, accompanied by a self-appointed Vietnamese delegation, tried to attend the international Versailles Peace Conference in order to plead for Vietnamese self-determination. They were refused entry.

The French continued to suppress any nationalist or liberation groups and to imprison their members. In the 1930s the left-wing Popular Front was elected in France, and an amnesty was granted and the prisoners freed. By 1939, a Vietnamese nationalist movement, the VietMinh, had been formed and was active. With the Fall of France in 1940 and the victory in Europe of the Axis powers, the Japanese invaded and occupied Vietnam, despite VietMinh resistance. When the United States entered the Second World War in 1941, they sent OSS (Office of Strategic Services) agents to work with the VietMinh resistance groups in their struggle against the Japanese. At the end of the Second World War, President Franklin D. Roosevelt, as representative of one of the most powerful of the victorious Allies, was deeply committed to scaling down colonialism and to smaller nations eventually achieving self-determination, if not outright independence. In 1943 he confided to his Secretary of State Cordell Hull that Indo-China should not revert to French rule. However, with the rise, expansion, and perceived danger of the Soviet Union and the complex problem of who should actually take power in the liberated colonies, Roosevelt grew more favourable to restoring the French to Indo-China as trustees to gradually move the Indo-Chinese toward self-government. Roosevelt's successor, President Harry Truman, was alarmed by the Soviet Union's power and assertiveness. In August 1945, he confirmed the restoration of France's possessions in Indo-China. When the Japanese surrendered, a VietMinh congress in Hanoi proclaimed the Democratic Republic of Vietnam. The declaration used phrases similar to those used in the United States 1776 Declaration of Independence. Ho Chi Minh, suspicious of France, also transmitted a message to the United Nations, stating that if their independence went unrecognized, then they, the VietMinh, would keep fighting until independence was conceded to them.

The "independence" lasted a month. US planes ferried British troops and some French units into Saigon. The VietMinh commander attempted dialogue with the British commanders, but he and his forces were forcibly expelled. A French government was installed, and over the next few months, divisions of French troops arrived. The remaining US OSS operatives were recalled, and over US$1 million worth of equipment was placed at the disposal of the French forces.

Popular Vietnamese opinion was virulently anti-French and expressed in widespread popular demonstrations and placards in many cities and regions. French attempts to make incursions and to occupy areas in the north of the country were met with both passive and active resistance. French intelligence officers and diplomats were prolific in their lobbying of US officials and politicians with apparent signs of alleged direct links between Ho Chi Minh and the Soviet Union. Some French intelligence units received financial support from the United States to continue monitoring these links.

On 6 March 1946, Ho Chi Minh and the French authorities came to an agreement. France gave a sort of recognition to Vietnam as a "free state" but "a free state within the French Union" and agreed to withdraw its troops from the northern half of the country by 1952 in 5 phases of evacuation. The VietMinh agreed to cease guerilla activities in the south. The country was effectively divided north and south of the 17th parallel.

Ho Chi Minh continued, through VietMinh General Giap, to negotiate regarding the future of the southern part of the country, but later in 1946 the French announced that the south would be a "free republic" also "within the French Union" under the old name of "Cochin-China". Negotiations broke down, and in November 1946 the French bombarded the port of Haiphong in the north, and the fighting spread to Hanoi. Giap's forces, after fighting a rearguard action, retreated into the Trong Son mountain ranges near the Chinese border, where they had already constructed bases, hideouts, and supply caches. Guerrilla war was to continue for the next 8 years.

The VietMinh was not just a guerrilla army of combat fighters but a large political organisation with a military wing. The VietMinh was a large grouping of organised male and female peasants, workers, and youths. It encompassed literary and cultural organisations, intellectuals, and professions. If VietMinh members were unfit or too old to engage in combat, they could certainly be relied upon to give clandestine logistical support and/or form local defence groups.[41] The VietMinh was a national organisation throughout Vietnam, numerous and widespread. The Hanoi city defence corps of the VietMinh alone numbered tens of thousands of individuals. The combat fighters themselves were well organised in a disciplined military formation with commanders and units, and the fighting arm was integrated politically within the whole organisation. Army units were commanded by a military officer, but each unit also contained a political officer. Opposing them were the French regular army units. These were numerous, but they could not cover and contain the whole country. Their actions and operations were essentially random and reactive. Generally in the rural areas, the VietMinh held sway. It was a struggle between a strong military force against a strong political organisation.

In October 1950, Giap launched a major counteroffensive. His forces were equipped with heavy mortars from China. They targeted a group of French fortresses and strongpoints in the north, then Giap switched tactics and escalated the attacks into a general offensive on a wider front with many objectives. They suffered defeats and losses, resulting in any potential future offensives being estimated as not possible for at least two years. But in inflicting the defeats on the VietMinh, the French suffered more than 6,000 casualties in that single month. A French historian described this as:

> the greatest colonial defeat since Montcalm died at Quebec

and identified this point in the struggle as when the French lost the war in Indo-China.[42]

The French continued their so-called search and destroy missions but were faced with a nationwide underground VietMinh movement with an ever active guerrilla army. By 1953, France was deploying 190,000 troops in Vietnam; they had already sustained 74,000 losses. They had made little progress in taking control of the rural areas, and the casualties mounted. Continued financial aid to France came from the United States. With the events of the Korean War having unfolded and ending in a truce dividing that country, China was now perceived by the United States to be the principal threat, and it was deemed essential to support France in Vietnam to "contain" the perceived spread of militant communism in Southeast Asia.

The French High Command then settled on a solution. This was to manoeuvre the VietMinh into a large conventional set piece battle where superior French military training, skill, and equipment would prevail. Blocking the VietMinh supply routes would inevitably draw out the Viet Ming into giving battle. The strategic area of Dien Bien Phu was chosen and fortified accordingly. Some 10,000 French troops were deployed at the strategic choke point of Dien Bien Phu, and another 5,000 troops were placed in reserve. The valley centre was gutted of all old houses and buildings, and bunkers and a fortified command centre were built and an airstrip constructed.

In military terms, it was a good strategic decision, given the position of Dien Bien Phu deep in the rear of the VietMinh forces and based on the French assessment that the VietMinh had no trucks and would be unable to bring up weapons and supplies. The one apparent French weak point was the dependency of the whole position on supplies being flown in by air and the distance the supplying planes would have to fly on a round trip from Hanoi to Dien Bien Phu. During the forthcoming conflict, serious errors in French strategic thinking were to be exposed. By indefatigable activity and feats of organisation and improvisation, the VietMinh brought up supplies and equipment. One large auxiliary force cleared the jungle routes to the Dien Bin Phu area, then quietly brought up and stored supplies, whilst the regular military forces of the VietMinh force marched to the area and deployed. Throughout the north of the country, mobilised civilians culled, gathered, and gave a steady supply of rice and vegetables. Specially adapted bicycles ("iron horses") were laden with supplies and wheeled through hundreds of miles of jungle. Each transport and supply unit had its own "bicycle repair officer".

The VietMinh also managed to bring up strong artillery. Some 48 105 mm howitzers and 105 lighter artillery arms were in place on the now lethal hills and mountains surrounding the French strongholds in the valley. The VietMinh under General Giap had artillery superiority of 3 to 1, and in March 1954 the siege of Dien Bien Phu started—not the set piece, open battle the French originally had envisaged. By late March, the central airstrip was effectively closed due to intense artillery fire, and the French troops were cut off from being further supplied. Their losses mounted steadily. The French held out with great tenacity and bravery, but the final result was never in doubt. On 7 May 1954, the French surrendered, the VietMinh acknowledging a worthy foe by agreeing that the surrender could be made without any raising of the white flag. The French losses were 3,000 with a further 3,000 permanently disabled and 8,000 taken prisoner.

From May to July 1954, an international conference assembled in Geneva, and it was decided that a temporary partition of Vietnam would take place (along the 17th parallel). In October 1954, Ho Chi Minh and Vietnamese officials entered Hanoi and took their posts. The United States had refused to sign the Geneva Accords, had formed an alliance with South Vietnam, and officially recognised and supported only the South Vietnamese regime. But for the French it was over. The VietMinh insurgency had won.

Analysis and Comparison With Dutch Revolt

First is the factor of the insurgent's motivation and the concept of freedom and national identity and cause. As has been seen, the Dutch Revolt initially evolved out of religious grievances. These were in combination with outrage at perceived constitutional violations of the Netherlands' provinces' freedoms, practices, and privileges. Then, with Alva's imposition of the 3 sets of taxes (especially the hated Tenth Penny), economic factors stimulated the Revolt. The feeling of a free nation state was developed slowly by the tireless efforts of William of Orange (or, in this context, perhaps better named "William the Silent", the Dutch term for silent in fact meaning a combination of discretion and wisdom), who, with tact and skill, kept together—just—the insurgents nobles, lower classes, and differing religious factions. When the north-south divide of the Netherlands became more pronounced and remained during the Revolt and was accepted by the Union of Arras and the Union of Utrecht, the southern provinces eventually reconciled to Spanish sovereignty, and the northern or Dutch provinces commenced fighting to be a nation state.

By contrast in the Vietnamese insurgency, from the very start of the post-1945 period, the whole of Vietnam wished for freedom, for the French occupiers to leave. This was due to both nationalism and a strong feeling to end the French colonial economic system, which was grossly unfair to the majority of the Vietnamese. As has been seen, from the outset, representatives from Indo-China attempted to obtain nation state recognition. A form of national identity had been present and had been pursued by Vietnamese representatives since the era of the Versailles Peace conference and arguably long before, stretching back to the pre–French colonial era.

On several occasions in 1946, the French made overtures to the Viet-Minh offering various forms of autonomy. However, they failed to realise that outright nation state status was the aim and the single-minded wish and objective of the Vietnamese. Consequently, their overtures and proposals fell on deaf ears. The United States, when supporting France and fighting on its own after the French withdrew, gave repeated "assurances" and official pronouncements about freedom from communism. But the majority of the Vietnamese wished for freedom from foreign exploitation, both French and their own collaborating minority. The agrarian aspect was important. Ho Chi Minh, in the overall struggle, could not manage to gain the same popular support in the south as Giap and his victories did in the north. However, one crucial element in his gaining support in the south was his consistent and clearly proclaimed policy and promise of land redistribution.[43] This promise that the rural population would own their own land was inestimable in furthering and forging a sense amongst the Vietnamese population of national identity.

In terms of the military and military resources factor, there are some similarities between the Dutch Revolt and the VietMinh insurgency. There were few set piece battles, and manoeuvres and deployments leading to successful sieges were the main conflict activities. The French attempts at forcing open battles all failed, and the strategy evolved into surprise attacks and search and destroy missions, usually with poor results. Paradoxically, the major French attempt to draw out the VietMinh into an open engagement or decisive battle ended in a major siege in which the French lost. However, even this attempt to force a decisive open battle was a last push to gain a victory, not to crush or set back the insurgency but to gain a strong negotiating position in any peace talks. Even before the French troops were committed, the senior officer General Navarre had admitted that the war could not be won.

Both the Dutch insurgents and the VietMinh, as their respective liberation struggles continued, evolved from irregular forces to organised national armies, with military units and structure. Arguably the Viet-Minh evolved over a longer period, whilst the radical military reforms of Maurits and William Lodewijk resulted in a near transformation. The VietMinh, when clandestinely reinforced by Chinese troops and "advisors", cooperated well with their allies. By contrast, relations between Dutch troops and English troops in joint campaigns against the Spanish were often strained. Far better was the naval cooperation between the English fleets and the Dutch fleets during the engagements against the Armada (notwithstanding the temporary breakdown in communication between Howard and the Dutch).

Turning to the factor of finances, the sinews of war, during this period the French had massive financial resources from the United States. Subsidies and grants from the United States for France to suppress the Viet-Minh insurgency were approved starting in 1946, and by the time of Dien Bien Phu, these had amounted to over US$2 billion. The VietMinh relied upon *ad hoc* methods of financing and supplies. The majority of the Vietnamese constantly and collectively donated large consignments of rice and other foodstuffs to the fighters. Equipment was rudimentary but used and adapted to good effect, such as the converted bicycles, or what were to become the iconic jungle sandals of the VietMinh troops made from vehicle tyres. After 1952 China provided a steady stream of various supplies to VietMinh units. During the Battle of Dien Bien Phu, while the besieged French troops were eking out their diminishing rations and ammunition, China was sending 4,000 tonnes of supplies a month to Giap's forces.

As we have seen, in the early stages of the Dutch Revolt, William of Orange relied upon a myriad of *ad hoc* payments and financing, captured equipment, and hand-to-mouth loans from sympathisers. Then, during the later stages, the economic wealth of the province of Holland and to a lesser extent the province of Zeeland, both protected by the victories of Maurits, ensured money flow to the Revolt. Also at certain times during these later stages, timely foreign subsidies as a result of alliances ensured that the Revolt was adequately financed. By contrast, Spain throughout the Revolt, as we have seen, was faced with mounting debts and severe cash flow problems.

The final and fourth factor considered in this comparing and contrasting of the Dutch Revolt and the VietMinh insurgency is that of the impact of international events. As has been seen, international events and diplomacy had their effect upon the Dutch Revolt by preventing Spanish strategy from focussing solely on quelling the Dutch Revolt and resulting in Spain's having to fight on two fronts in more than one vital period in the struggle. For a period, England gave active military assistance to the Dutch, and there was naval cooperation between England and the Dutch against the Spanish armada.

In the VietMinh insurgency, international developments also had an impact. First the increasing suspicion of the Soviet Union by the United States resulted in President Roosevelt changing his wishes for Indo-China (and other former colonies) to become independent. Then the advent of the Cold War engendered the threat of communism, and so French control of Vietnam had to be supported against the VietMinh, who allegedly had links to the Soviet Union. Then, after the Korean War, China and its alliance to the VietMinh meant that continued United States' support to the French was perceived as an essential barrier to the "spread" of communism.

However, international events and developments occurring during the VietMinh insurgency had an impact in another way, this time on France. The international events of the Vietnam War and the French defeat caused, stimulated, and spurred in France, especially in the French Army, a continuous sense of national shame and loss of national honour that needed to be restored. This manifested itself across French politics in an unquestionable imperative that although—or because—Vietnam was lost, Algeria would always remain French. French politician and future President Mitterand wrote in 1957:

> When the war in Indo-China broke out, France was able to believe that the 1940 defeat was nothing more than a lost battle, and that the armistice of 1945 was going to restore its power at the same time as its glory.[44]

Then the catastrophe of Dien Bien Phu occurred. Therefore Algeria irrevocably had to remain if for no other reason than to stop the cycle of decline. The historian Raymond Aron write in 1958, commenting on the French national sentiment:

> The Algerian War offers us one more occasion for France to meditate on decadence. Algeria lost, and France is on the slippery slope down which Portugal and Spain slid.[45]

The international event of the French loss of Vietnam impelled France to continue to repress any Algerian moves for self- determination and to engage in a war against Algerian independence. It is to this comparative insurgency we next turn.

Algeria Gains Independence From France, 1956–1962

As early as 1837, a great French political scientist and philosopher, observing the French in Algeria, warned:

> It is not enough for the French to put themselves alongside the Arabs if they do not succeed in establishing a lasting bond with them . . . forming the two races into a single people.[46]

The French settlers as a whole never mingled or integrated but remained a superior, occupying class. By 1948, the indigenous Algerian population had doubled since 1896, whilst the French population, the *pieds noirs*, in Algeria scarcely rose. Algerian peasants migrated to the towns to low-paid jobs, and urban deprivation increased.

A political party for the Algerians had come into being since 1945, the Parti Progressive Algeriénne (PPA). Banned by the authorities in 1945, it re-emerged as Mouvement pour le Triomphe des Libertés Démocratiques (MTLD), militant in its demands for Algerian identity and nationalism. At the end of the Second World War, on VE day itself 8 May 1945, the Algerians rose in revolt in the small town of Setif. They were crushed with considerable severity. Some reforms were implemented, but these were insufficient—too little and possibly too late—for they still ensured the perpetuation of power by the French *pied noir* minority. Then, after the French humiliation at Dien Bien Phu in Vietnam, a more organised revolt began in November 1954, which started the Algerian War of Independence.

In the aftermath of the Setif rising in 1945 and in the years leading up to November 1954, the Algerian national movement had undergone changes. The MTLD had been affected by a breakaway movement, the Comite Révolutionnaire d'Unité et d'Action (CRUA), whose committee included two future leaders of the Algerian resistance and which was a movement fully committed to armed struggle.

The committee convened a wider meeting consisting of all the revolutionary leaders throughout Algeria, and from these it formed the Algerian revolutionary movement, the Front de Libération Nationale (FLN). The FLN's military wing, the Armée de Libération Nationale (ALN), began the war. It was a war that was to continue until independence was finally granted to Algeria after 6 long and bitter years.

The FLN first targeted military and armed force personnel, army barracks, and police stations (the IRA designated such targets as "legitimate", as opposed to attacks on civilians, which they officially forbad). Then the FLN expanded its attacks to include Muslim civilians and Algerians, whom they bitterly designated "friends of France", that is Algerian servants, estate workers, vineyard workers, and those in domestic work, all employees of French nationals or companies, local government officials, and local police officers. The FLN also imposed with dire penalties a ban on smoking and drinking any alcohol for all Muslims.

The French deployed more troops. These were both battle-hardened and experienced from guerrilla warfare in the Indo-China campaign. Amongst the French armed forces the paratroop regiments and the Foreign Legion were heirs to a long and proud tradition in the armed forces and were revered by popular opinion in France. These units engaged in counter-insurgency warfare that produced success but at a price. The paratroops—the legendary *les paras*—were indeed revered and vaunted in the French media, but they engaged in the systematic torture of suspects in custody to gain intelligence. By 1957:

> the paratroops resembled less the warriors of antiquity than an especially nasty police force.[47]

Yet despite the involvement of large regular forces (two-thirds of the entire Foreign Legion was in action in Algeria) and calling up reservists and French national servicemen and deploying them to Algeria, the military situation for France did not improve. Throughout 1956, the attacks by the ALN continued, and the FLN itself grew in numbers. The FLN convened a summit in Souman, Tunisia, where objectives were debated and clarified and a military hierarchy within the ALN was implemented. Algeria was divided into 6 zones, or 6 *wilaya*. Each *wilaya* commander was given discretion and was flexible in how the military conflict was to be pursued within his *wilaya*. The *katiba*, or company, of 110 fighters was made the standard operational fighting unit. A Conseil National de la Révolution Algérienne (CNRA) was formed. Its title was deliberately made similar to that of the national wartime French resistance organisation. The CNRA was held to be the sovereign Algerian parliamentary body with delegates meeting on a regular basis.

The following year, the famous Battle of Algiers occurred, an almost year-long campaign by the FLN for control of the city of Algiers. The battle was fought by a network of over FLN 1,400 operatives who engaged in a bombing campaign. Bombs were planted and detonated in cafes and restaurants, and selected assassinations of collaborating Algerian officials were carried out. An attempt was made to persuade or coerce the populace into a general strike. Paratroop regiments were brought into Algiers from outlying country areas and deployed in breaking the strike by forcing shopkeepers to remain open and by rounding up and forcing children back to school. Rigorous searches were carried out, and there was "intense investigation" of suspects. A second round of bombings occurred in May 1957 to which the French responded with swift countermeasures, effective in that many of the operatives, including the leaders of the bomber cells, were killed or captured. The overall result of the Battle of Algiers was a series of defeats for the FLN. The remnants of the fighter cells managed to escape and make their way to the comparative safety of Tunisia. The FLN strategy of large-scale terrorist attacks in the cities was abandoned.

The following year, a new development occurred that gave a new dimension to the conflict. In January 1958, after a decade of researching and prospecting, the first oil deposits of the Sahara desert were brought up and flowed towards France. Some 5 million tonnes were drawn in the first year, and French oilmen made projections and forecasts that within a generation, the oil from the Sahara would meet the total demand and needs of France for oil. This coincided with the aftermath of the disastrous Anglo-French intervention in Suez of 2 years before, and the Sahara deposits would nullify the post-Suez threat to French oil supplies. Therefore, after 4 years of struggle, in the words of a distinguished historian:

[Q]uietly France now found herself with a new motive for winning the war that went beyond any consideration of a million *pieds noirs*.[48]

By 1958 the conflict had become international. The French Army had constructed a veritable border fortress system along the Algerian-Tunisian border. This system, the Morice Line, was a massive electrified fence supported by fortresses and strongpoints. It was efficiently patrolled and proved an effective barrier against FLN fighters who, sheltering in the sanctuary of Tunisia, frequently attempted to cross into Algeria to carry out attacks. The FLN were being supplied by international arms dealers. The French, in turn, engaged in intelligence counter-operations to nullify the deals and eliminate the dealers. Even ever neutral Switzerland was impacted. An extremely efficient assassin of the French Secret Service (SDECE) and his network of operatives had their movements in Switzerland made public. More lasting and unfortunate publicity came when the Swiss Attorney General was implicated in authorizing and passing to the assassin's network secret information about the FLN arms smugglers. The "informal" gathering of such intelligence had involved the telephone tapping of the Egyptian Embassy in Berne. In March 1957 the Swiss Attorney General committed suicide.

The Tunisian leader Habib Bourguiba, besides affording sanctuary to FLN fighters, was tireless in his efforts for international recognition of Algeria as a sovereign, independent state. The world's media were becoming increasingly attentive in covering the French executions of convicted bombers, and in journalists investigating use of torture by security forces on captured suspects. Adverse scrutiny and censure came from international human rights organisations. Anti-war feeling amongst popular opinion in France increased significantly. As early as 1955, the FLN, incredibly, had managed to engineer the Algerian issue to be scheduled for discussion at the United Nations. Then, in July 1957 a certain young US Democratic opposition senator, John F Kennedy, rose to speak in the US Senate. He challenged the Eisenhower administration to intervene and implement US efforts to achieve an international solution to the Algerian question. He emphasised that such a solution had to include Algerian independence. Significantly by 1958, when on every occasion the Algerian question was tabled for a motion at the United Nations, the US, instead of supporting France, abstained.

Army morale, apart from in the elite units such as the French Foreign Legion or the paratroop units, was depressed. But France persisted. In 1959 the ALN was still able to make attacks within Algeria, blowing up trains or ambushing army convoys. A new strategy was developed by the French forces under a recently appointed Commander in Chief Air Force General Maurice Challe. Up to now the quadrillage system had been adopted, whereby Algeria was divided up into rectangular areas, with each area being patrolled and policed by a specific army unit. This was replaced by, and units were deployed into, *commandes de chasse*. These separate holding forces would react to an attack, engage, and then continue the engagement, pursuing the attacking FLN unit relentlessly, hunting them down, seeking out their lairs and bases, and eliminating them. This new strategy had its successes, and some of the local Algerian population regained their confidence and trust in the French army. In 1960 Challe was posted back to France; the successes of Challe's new strategy was to be the zenith of French military success in Algeria.

Back in France, since 1958 Charles de Gaulle had come to power as a result of a complex tumult in French politics. He had been enigmatic, as ever, but had been watching and studying all the elements of the situation—Algeria as an external part of France, the extreme stance and clinging to power of the minority *pieds noirs*, the conditions of the majority of Algerians, the military resources and strategy of the French army fighting against the stubborn and apparently indefatigable FLN. In September 1959, he made a highly publicised speech. He advocated Algerian self-determination but ruled out "secession". For the following two years, from 1960 to 1962, de Gaulle remained enigmatic. In early

1960 a leading French politician voiced all public opinion when he rhetorically asked:

Where will he lead us, this prince of ambiguity?

However, de Gaulle had already realised that some form of Algerian self-determination was inevitable, given how debilitating the armed struggle was to France, the apparent tenaciousness of the FLN, and the increasing unpopularity of the war in France.

Increasingly alarmed, the extreme groups of *pieds noirs* staged demonstrations that escalated into revolt in Algiers in January 1960. In a week of barricades and confrontation, paramilitary groups of *piers noirs* killed 14 gendarmes and wounded 125. French paratroop regiments stationed nearby were strangely inactive. The following year, 4 French generals, including Air Force General Challe, engineered a political coup in Algiers and declared that Algeria would always remain French. The generals appealed to the army and were followed by many officers in the paratroop regiments. However de Gaulle, in a skilful and memorable address by radio, appealed to France and to the army. The mass appeal was listened to by the troops, who all possessed or had access to personal transistor radios. The conscripts and the reservists serving in Algeria heeded his appeal. De Gaulle's address included that he, as president, absolved all the troops from all disciplinary requirements and regulations owed to their seniors—in effect an appeal by the head of state to the troops over the heads of their senior officers. It broke the attempted coup. The signals units of the army remained loyal and refused to send communications between rebel units; arms were seized, and wavering officers were prevailed upon by their conscript soldiers to remain loyal. De Gaulle had not been intimidated by the extreme loyalists, nor was he any less determined in his resolve to deal with the FLN. The guerrilla war was continuing, but a peace process had started.

The extreme *pieds noirs*, together with remnants of the paratroop regiments, formed a movement called the Organisation de l'Armée Secrète (OAS) whose sole object was to keep Algeria French by terrorism and ensuring that it would be impossible for de Gaulle's governmental representatives to govern Algeria. It was led by two of the failed coup generals who were living in exile but who were still in contact with and coordinating loyalist *pied noir* resistance. From early 1961, French traitors and Muslims were targeted in attacks, assassinations, and bombing campaigns similar to those carried out by the FLN. The FLN, besides continuing its offensives against French troops, retaliated with murders and assassinations in a terrible spiral of violence and counter-violence. The OAS then started attacking targets in metropolitan France.

During this intense period of violence, the peace process started. In June 1960 representatives from the FLN unsuccessfully approached de

Gaulle. The following year, during a two-month period, delegates from both sides attempted peace negotiations at Evian, but these ended inconclusively. A second round of talks in March 1962 yielded a more positive result. This was a signed agreement that itself resulted in, on 19 March 1962, a lasting ceasefire between the French armed forces and the FLN.

However, the final end of the struggle was untidy and extremely violent. On the French side, there was the bringing to account those involved in the attempted "generals' coup". More pressing was the need to curb and finally defeat the OAS, who were continuing their pointless and nihilistic attacks. This was a struggle of clandestine terrorism and counter-insurgency, a struggle that caused many deaths of French forces, military and police officers, and of former French soldiers who had transferred their loyalty—and their deadly training and skills—to the OAS. On the Algerian side, those Algerians who had remained loyal to France, especially the military units forming part of the French forces, were hunted down, tortured, and killed by the FLN. Politically, the Algerian leadership underwent quarrels and splits with several of the insurgent leaders going into exile. One of these fleeing leaders took with him millions of FLN funds; he was eventually hunted down and murdered in Europe.

However, the overall result was that the FLN had won. The Algerian insurgency had succeeded.

Analysis and Comparison With Dutch Revolt

One common factor in both the Algerian struggle for independence and the Dutch Revolt was the inability until late into the conflict of France in the former case and Spain in the latter to recognise the genuine constitutional and political grievances of the insurgent populations. In the Dutch Revolt Alva, with the approval of Philip II, emphasised the alleged heretical nature of the rebels, whilst ignoring the constitutional grievances and traditional time-honoured privilege and customs that had been peremptorily swept aside. Requesens attempted to redress these but was overtaken by military and financial events. In Algeria after the Setif uprising had been crushed, political reforms were inaugurated in the 1947 Statute that proposed 5 basic reforms. These had been demanded by the Algerian population for some years. Unfortunately, the constitution still retained the dual electoral college system. The Algerian MTLD refused to recognise the right of the Assemblée Nationale in Paris to legislate the Statute, whilst the *pied noir* minority, using their grotesque advantage of the dual electoral college system, blocked the statute by inserting a clause stating that the 5 major reforms had to be approved by a majority in the Algerian National Assembly. But this approval would never happen as long as the dual electoral college system prevailed. In a later period, one of the enlightened French governors of Algeria, Jacques Soustelle, attempted reform by concentrating on the integration of the two communities and by rectifying some of the inequalities of the dual electoral colleges. At the same time, he granted economic aid of 5 million FrF to reduce unemployment by creating public works. However, he was pressurised by the *pied noir* minority to increase the power of the military to deal with FLN attacks and to enact repressive measures that inevitably fell heavily on and alienated the Algerian population. Throughout, French strategy:

> failed to address itself to the political side of the solution—the side that was paramount.[49]

Another comparative factor between the two insurgencies was that of militant loyalism. During the struggle in the period of William of Orange, William was beset with various divisions amongst the Netherlands rebels, particularly those of the nobility of the southern provinces who had decidedly differing views on whether to break totally with Spain. It is to the eternal credit of William that he held the Revolt together for so long.

However, once the Unions of Utrecht and Arras were formed and certainly after the unsuccessful invasion by the Dutch forces into Flanders in 1601, the division of the area of the Netherlands was inevitable: the southern provinces were reconciled to Spanish rule. They provided some willing levies to Parma's armies in the pre-1598 advances into the United Provinces. Though there was little militant loyalism in the south stridently and actively advocating continued union with Spain, the southern provinces remained eventually, after the events of the Revolt up to 1579 had run their course and staying under Spanish rule was pragmatically making the best of the situation. There was no equivalent of the *pied noir* extremism that occurred in Algiers and that manifested itself in the mobbing of French Premier Mollet when he visited Algiers on 6 February 1954 or of the firefight of the "days of the barricades" of late January 1960. In the words of one eminent historian (writing in the 1970s) of the Algerian revolt, the *pieds noirs* goal was:

> was not Algerie Francaise; what the majority wanted was a *pied noir* regime ranging between South Africa at its best and worst, but under the umbrella of French protection.[50]

The effects of extreme French settler *pied noir* militancy were twofold. In the early stages, it revealed to a shocked French government the depth of feeling against Algerian independence by the minority and caused pressure on the government to deploy more resources and troops and to adopt a hard line. This made impossible negotiations with the Algerians about reforms or some sort of self-government. However, blind obedience to the *pieds noirs* alienated some elements of the French army. In 1960 troops had to be brought back from the outlying desert areas of Algeria to help contain the *pied noir* "barricades" at the very time when the

French Deuxieme Bureau was reporting that the FLN campaign was faltering and may even have been at the breaking point.[51] *Pied noir* intransigence also made de Gaulle even more determined, once he realised the need for Algerian self-determination to pursue this policy through. *Pied noir* violence and terrorism against this policy increasingly alienated the population back in France.

Turning to the important factor of finance. As we have seen, in the early stages of the Dutch Revolt led by William of Orange, finances were almost hand to mouth with various methods and sources of funding, mainly loans of sympathetic supporters and rulers and goodwill promises. Under Maurits, Dutch trade and commerce developed exponentially, and there was regular state financing for the economy of the nascent Dutch Republic, although rising costs and tax increases caused difficulties during the second decade of the Seventeenth Century. Throughout this century, the nascent Dutch Republic battled it out economically with Spain. The Dutch economy suffered and was impacted. However, it was Spain that gave up the struggle for economic reasons; Spain broke first.[52]

By contrast, the Algerian FLN did not have a nascent state economy to support its struggle; indeed, its leaders constituted a self-styled government that was a government in exile. But since 1957 a supportive financial network had been organised and was operating effectively. This ensured that the FLN and the Algerian independence movement were continually funded. The FLN imposed order amongst the Algerians living in France. It formed an innocent sounding organisation, the Fédération de France, which purported to be a confederation of Algerian social and cultural societies and centres in France but in fact was a disciplined revenue-raising organisation. An Algerian FLN member, Lebjaoui, was sent to France to recruit and organise support cells and to make available at short notice a picked group of FLN killers who could carry out selected reprisal murders within metropolitan France and who could continuously "collect" funds. Lebjaoui started on these tasks but was arrested within two months by French police. His FLN colleague sent to replace him, Omar Badouad, built upon the rudimentary networks established by Lebjaoui. However, Badouad prudently focused less on forming murder squads and concentrated on fundraising. From mid-1957, funds started flowing to the FLN. The Fédération de France operatives collected contributions—either voluntary, or by peer pressure, or by extreme threats and extortion—from the Algerians in France. Bars, cafes, restaurants, business premises, private addresses, all were "visited", and a sliding scale of contributions was fixed. Algerian students paid up to 500 FrF a month, workers up to 3,000 FrF a month, and there was "minimum level of contribution" of 50,000 FrF a month for small businessmen and shopkeepers. Soon, within the first year, the total takings amounted to over 2.5 million FrF, and the total was rising.

There are two essentials to terrorist or insurgency financing: raising the monies and transferring the monies. Raising the monies, whilst requiring organisation and some pressure on occasion, had the security advantage of involving mostly ethnic Algerians collecting from ethnic Algerians. This advantage worked against transferring the monies. For Badouad and the Fédération de France to move the collected cash by using Algerian couriers would inevitably risk their being stopped and searched. Fortunately for the FLN, an ally was at hand.

The individual was Francis Jeanson, a Marxist professor and writer. During the Second World War, he had attempted to travel and join the Free French Forces in Britain but was arrested whilst travelling through Spain. He was jailed for a period, and his health was permanently damaged. Sickening and frail yet a passionate advocate of Algerian independence, he undertook to assist the FLN by physically smuggling large amounts of the collected cash out of France. Jeanson acted with no direct orders from the FLN but was in contact and close liaison with their operatives in France. He established his own network of 40 sympathetic and like-minded French individuals (who when physically couriering the money through French customs would attract less attention than would Algerians). One writer specializing in terrorism suggests that by 1960 the Jeanson network numbered up to 3,000 operatives.[53] For 3 years the collected cash "donations", in used notes carried in worn suitcases, were discreetly couriered by Jeanson and his couriers out of France to Switzerland, travelling overland by rail or coach. In one year alone, 10 billion FrF was smuggled out. The monies were deposited in Swiss banks, earning interest whilst there (Badouad's left-wing principles made him uncomfortable with this "unearned income") and then were used to purchase arms and equipment for the FLN.

The rebel nascent Dutch nation state, through its economic effort, provided finances for the struggle. In stark terms, the Dutch used commerce as an international instrument of war in its struggle for survival.[54] The FLN used and exploited the Algerian population abroad to provide the funds and were helped by Frenchmen and women sympathetic to the insurgency to move the funds where they could be deployed for the struggle.

Finally, a similarity between the Algerian insurgency and the Dutch Revolt lay in the final recognition by the possessing power that the struggle was no longer sustainable. Spain realised this because their economy could no longer afford the struggle. The French—or de Gaulle—realised that political reality dictated recognition of Algeria as an independent state, and, once having decided, de Gaulle steadfastly kept to this course. In realising the futility of continuing to enforce French rule on Algeria as a part of France, de Gaulle was like the Archduke Albert of the Spanish Netherlands, who readily saw the impossibility of reconquering the northern United Provinces and was for cutting Hapsburg losses and trying to make good the well-being and economy of the Spanish Netherlands. This realisation also reached the Spanish Court (but cutting losses did not include the cessation of economically damaging hostilities in the post-Truce period). De Gaulle initially held a determination that Algeria should remain French. However, as he became more familiar with the realities of the conflict, the determination of the FLN, and the obduracy of the *pieds noir* community, he changed his view and realised the long-term good for France. As early as April 1958, he informed the journalist Arthur Rosenburg of the certainty that Algeria would become independent.[55]

> Unlike some of his followers, he believed in abandoning lost causes, not in promoting them.[56]

The debt of France to de Gaulle in his political realisation and holding firm to it was recognised and voiced in former Prime Minister Michel Debre's assertion:

> It was a miracle that we didn't collapse into civil war over Algeria, and this we owe to de Gaulle.[57]

Notes

1. As with the Hapsburg imperial councillors in Prague at the start of the Bohemian Revolt, Vasconcellos was thrown from a high window in the palace. Unlike the three imperial councillors, the fall killed him instantly
2. Wilson, PH *The Thirty Years War—Europe's Tragedy* p 655
3. However, in his detailed and comprehensive *A History of Portugal* H Livermore points out that the Portuguese ambassador's accreditation to the Vatican was of a year's duration. During that period, Spain exerted intense pressure against this accreditation through the Spanish ambassador and through Spanish representation at the College of Cardinals. After a year, the Portuguese ambassador left without official farewells from the Vatican, and he departed as a private individual in his capacity as Bishop of Lamego. Nonetheless, official accreditation and recognition had been granted, and a Portuguese ambassador had been in residence
4. Hardman, J and Price, M (eds) *Louis XVI and the Comte de Vergennes correspondence* p 250, cited in Jones, C *The Great Nation—France from Louis XIV to Napoleon* p 305
5. Cronin, V *Louis and Antoinette* p 168
6. Tuchamann, B *The First Salute—A View of the American Revolution* p 212
7. Cronin, V *Louis and Antoinette* p 167
8. Jones, C *The Great Nation* p 432
9. Schama, S *Citizens—A Chronicle of the French Revolution* p 696
10. Hibbert, C *The French Revolution* p 169
11. Hibbert, C *The French Revolution* p 194
12. Schama, S *Citizens—A Chronicle of the French Revolution* p 787
13. Wallon, H *Les Representants en mission et la justice Revolutionnaire dans les departements de lAn II Vol I* p 220, cited in Jones, C *The Great Nation* p 485

14. During the early stages of the French Revolution the revolutionary government in Paris passed the law of the Civil Constitution of the Clergy, which in effect made all clergy in France answerable to the revolutionary regime as well as to their religious vows. The law stipulated all clergy swear an oath of allegiance to the revolution. A substantial number of clergy refused to swear the oath. Those clergy who refused were known as "non-jurors". Non-jurors were regarded by the revolutionary regime as subversives and were replaced in their parishes and communities by state-appointed clergy. Many suffered violence, even execution. In royalist and traditional Vendee, however, non-juring clergy were supported and given sanctuary and continued their functions as local priests, whilst the state appointed replacements were ignored, isolated and expelled by the local community. Hoche's policy of tolerating the non-juring clergy and his laissez faire was a significant factor in pacifying the Vendee

15. Houssaye, H *1815 la Premiere Restoration, le Retour de l'Isle de lElba, les Cent Jours* p 567

16. Dakin, D *The Greek Struggle for Independence* pp 70–78

17. Turkish-Russian Treaty of Unkiar Skelessi, 1833

18. Berenger, J *A History of the Hapsburg Empire 1700–1914* p 139

19. de Maartens, F *Receuil des Principaux Traites depuis 1761 jusqu'a present*

20. Rude, G *Europe Between Revolutions 1815–1848* pp 231–232

21. A detailed and admirably comprehensive and clear account of the twists and turns of the negotiations in the years leading up to this treaty is to be found in Fishman, JS *Diplomacy and Revolution—The London Conference of 1830 and the Belgian Revolt*

22. Israel, J *The Dutch Republic—Its Rise, Greatness, and Fall 1477–1806* p 226

23. Prak, M *The Dutch Republic in the Seventeenth Century* pp 62–74. See also Appendix II

24. Prak, M *The Dutch Republic in the Seventeenth Century* pp 62–74. See also Appendix II

25. Ogg, D *Europe of the Ancien Regime 1715–1783* p 105, 208. Geyl, P in his partisan *History of the Dutch-Speaking People 1555–1648* outlines the repressive nature of the Archduke's rule, but he fully acknowledges "the prosperity of agriculture" p 313

26. Rijks Gescheidkundije Publicatieen Gedenstrukkender de Algemeine Gescheidenis van Nederland 1795–1840 XXX/128

27. Zamoyski, A *Phantom Terror—The Threat of Revolution and the Repression of Liberty 1789–1848* p 364

28. Zamoyski, A *Rites of Peace—The Fall of Napoleon and the Congress of Vienna* pp 138–139, 206–208

29. The document was not given the title of "treaty" as this would imply Ireland was already a sovereign nation and that two nations were negotiating as equals. The official title of the signed document was "Article of Agreement for a Treaty between Great Britain and Ireland"

30. Ridley, N *Michael Collins and the Funding of Political Violence* p 13

31. A full account of the intelligence war waged by the IRA during the War of Independence is given in Ridley, N *Michael Collins and the Funding of Political Violence* chapter 7 "Collins' Intelligence War"

32. A metal worker and an Augustinian monk, Villavicenzio

33. An admirable and clear account of the various plots and their frustration by the counter-espionage agents is given in Neale, JE *Queen Elizabeth I* chapters 11, 12, and 16

34. Mattingly, G *The Defeat of the Spanish Armada* p 123

35. Kloek, E *Kenau en Magdalena—vrouwen in de Tachtigjarige Oorlog* pp 220–266 gives a balanced account and interpretations of this incident, distinguishing between fact and myth. It is also a neoclassic balanced and comprehensive work on the roles of women on both sides during the Eighty Years' War, including a sympathetic account of Margaret of Parma and an account of Kenau, the hero of the siege of Haarlem. It is a valuable contribution to the scholarship of the Eighty Years' War. A comprehensive, balanced and sympathetic study of Margaret of Parma is also written in Steen's, CR *Margaret of Parma—A Life*, including describing how she stubbornly contested Philip II of Spain's hard-line approach and attempted conciliation during the early stages of the disturbances and the Revolt

36. Dangerfield, G *The Damnable Question—A Study in Anglo-Irish Relations* p 313

37. Alan Bell, a retired police officer and a magistrate. Bell also had links to British intelligence. Ridley, N *Michael Collins and the Funding of Political Violence* pp 99–101. Coogan, TP *The Twelve Apostles* pp 133–136

38. US Consul in Dublin, reports to Washington 2 January 1920 and 14 January 1920, cited in Mackey, J *Michael Collins* p 134

39. For an account and discussion of de Valera's activities in the United States and the issues of the finances he raised, see Coogan de Valera, TP and Coogan, TP *Michael Collins*. Ridley, N *Michael Collins and the Funding of Political Violence*

40. For a full account of the raising of the National Loans and Collins as Minister of Finance, see Ridley, N *Michael Collins and the Funding of Extreme Political Violence*

41. Maclean, M *Vietnam—The Ten Thousand Day War* p 36

42. Fall, B *The Two Vietnams*

43. Hastings, M *Vietnam—An Epic Tragedy 1945–1975* p 32

44. Horne, A *A Savage War of Peace, Algeria 1954–62* p 175

45. Horne, A *A Savage War of Peace, Algeria 1954–62* p 175

46. de Tocqueville, A *Oevres Completes Vol 3* p151

47. Talbott, J *The War Without a Name—France in Algeria* p 69

48. Horne, A *A Savage War of Peace—Algeria 1956–62* pp 241–242

49. Talbot, J *The War Without a Name—France in Algeria 1954–62* pp 44–45

50. Horne, A *A Savage War of Peace Algeria 1954–62* p 245

51. Horne, A *A Savage War of Peace—Algeria 1954–62* p 382

52. Limm, P *The Dutch Revolt* p 298

53. Crenshaw, M *Revolutionary Terror—The FLN in Algeria 1956–1960* p 98

54. Plumb, JH Introduction, in Boxer, CR *The Dutch Seaborne Empire* p xxi

55. William, PM *Wars Plots and Scandals in Post War France* pp 140–114

56. Talbott, J *The War Without a Name—France in Algeria* p 138

57. Horne, A *A Savage War of Peace—Algeria 1956–62* p 548

Part IV

Maurits of Nassau

15 Maurits of Nassau
His Achievement

Maurits of Nassau, brought up in an era of revolt and liberation struggle and religious turbulence, at an early age sustained the shock of his father being assassinated and then was shielded from political power due to his age and lived in the shadow of an outstanding statesman leading the States-General. Yet he took the military lead of the Revolt, fought and held the finest generals leading Europe's most powerful armies, and ensured the survival of the Revolt. Then in a period of peace, he settled a dangerously divisive internal religious schism within the Dutch Republic and on the outbreak of war, ensured—just—the survival of the Revolt, handing on the baton, flag, and sword of the fight for freedom to Frederick Henry.

Maurits's break with that outstanding statesman—Oldenbarneveldt—has been the subject of much discussion by historians. At least one school of historical thought holds that Maurits would have been a lesser force without Oldenbarneveldt. Johan van Oldenbarneveldt was undoubtedly an outstanding statesman, and the Dutch Republic was well served by him. In the 1580s his placing the Republic under England's protection and then his handling and restraining of Leicester when the latter attempted to gain too much power and influence was masterly. Later, his skill, perception, and clear-sightedness during the negotiations leading up to and resulting in the Twelve Years' Truce achieved a fine balance. The outcome balanced, on the one hand, a diplomatic coup in that Spain recognised the Dutch Republic as a sovereign independent nation and, on the other hand, the prevention of those within the Dutch Republic opposed to concluding any truce from pushing the Republic into further economically damaging war.

Maurits had opposed the Truce negotiations but had realised that there was no alternative, as renewal of hostilities was not feasible. After both England and France had made their positions clear in that they would not support the Dutch if they abandoned the peace talks and renewed the war, Maurits fully appreciated that the Dutch could not fight such a war alone. Far better to keep England and France as allies in peace and agree to the Truce—but still remain ever mistrustful of Spain and ensure that the army was in a state of readiness. He realised the wisdom and skill of Oldenbarneveldt in these negotiations.

However, Oldenbarneveldt was not infallible. His insistence on the 1600 invasion of Flanders was a serious misjudgement. The situation was retrieved only by Maurits's military skill and the results of years of hard work by Maurits and Willem Lodewijk in creating a disciplined, well formed Dutch Army.

During the religious Arminian controversy of 1610–1619, Oldenbarneveldt committed serious misjudgements. Perhaps it is indicative of how politically out of touch he was—or how desperate—that he insisted upon action whilst the province of Holland, his power base, was itself divided. In recruiting *waargelders* on a provincial basis and attempting that their sole allegiance was to the provincial States, Oldenbarneveldt was threatening the very unity of the Dutch Republic. Furthermore, in attempting to subvert the loyalty of the regular army troops from the Republic to that of the provincial States, Oldenbarneveldt was threatening the very institution that had ensured the success of the Dutch Revolt and that would guarantee the future security of the Republic. Earlier, in 1609 Oldenbarneveldt had indeed secured a beneficial truce, and Maurits had been reconciled to it. However, Maurits's opposition to the Twelve Years' Truce had been due to his fear that when the Truce was ended, he would be too old to be a military leader and that the army would have deteriorated through lack of combat experience and the softening effects of a lengthy period of peace. He accepted the Truce whilst making every effort to ensure that the army did not deteriorate, yet here was Oldenbarneveldt diluting the nation's armed forces with hired soldiers of dubious quality and subverting the loyalty of the regular troops away from him, as stadhouder and prince, and from the Republic. In taking on Oldenbarneveldt and his supporters in 1618–1619, Maurits had no choice. Once the decision was made, he followed it through with care, skill, and ruthlessness.

During the early 1620s, Maurits was criticised for his lack of drive and decision, when there were civic disturbances and tax riots in several towns. However, perhaps it is understandable that an individual of advancing years—in 1620 he was 53 and in poor health—who had for 19 years engaged and led continuous fighting, leading a revolt against arguably the most powerful European country of the era, followed by a half decade of preventing divisive theological controversies from escalating into civil war, was now slowing down and was less active and less in touch than before. But he certainly showed drive and urgency in the penultimate year of his reign in pushing for and ensuring the alliance with and vital financial aid from France.

In considering the 4 factors of a successful insurgency, Maurits overall fulfilled them.

As for the factor of a national identity or a national cause, Maurits fully upheld this. In doing so, he was extremely resourceful and able.

Cautious and long-headed, even though he was, when necessary, capable of swift and incisive action, he was absolute in his conviction of the Dutch nation. He was also a realist:

> He did not look for his people, as his father did, in the southern Netherlands.

He realised that the division of the Hapsburg Low Countries encapsulated in the 1579 Union of Utrecht and Union of Arras was permanent. Hence his reluctance to engage in the 1600 near-disastrous invasion of Flanders, vaunted by some in the States-General as the start of reversing Parma's gains and reconquering the south. Maurits realised that the southern provinces were reconciled to remaining loyal to Spain. They became so and even recovered economically under the regency of Albert and Isabella, who also were prepared to leave the northern provinces alone and peacefully coexist. This strong and genuine desire for peace by Albert was recognised by Maurits and later exploited by him. Maurits did indeed recognise the reality that the Dutch Republic would consist of only the northern provinces, but accompanying this realisation was his strong sense of duty and purpose to the nation, the new Dutch Republic:

> [H]e stood guard at the cradle of the nascent nation of the northern Netherlands".[1]

With regard to the factor of adequate armed forces, it was he, together with Willem Lodewijk, who gave almost his life's work to raising and creating a professional and efficient Dutch Army capable of resisting the powerful armies of imperial Spain. This army as we have seen, was fit to take on and defeat the powerful armies of imperial Spain. His leadership and able generalship in the use and deployment of this army gained victories that would ensure the survival of the Revolt.

With regard to the factor of finance, as has been stated, Maurits can scarcely be credited for the exponential economic performance and growth of the Dutch Republic during the late Sixteenth and early Seventeenth Centuries. However, overall he used the economic resources of the Republic well. He encouraged and supported the VOC, making an alliance with the Sultan of Atjeh in December 1600,[2] assisting the VOC to advance in that region. He encouraged the economic activity of the regents yet was never their political servant. He kept the regency oligarchs in check, ensuring that sectional and provincial commercial interests did not prevail over the wider interests and well-being of the Dutch Republic. In his final years—the penultimate year of his life—his speedy diplomatic efforts ensured in 1624 a timely alliance and vital foreign subsidy for the Dutch Republic.

Maurits has a fully justified reputation as an able military leader and general. However, he was perceptive in international affairs, and in "our" international affairs factor, Maurits showed adroitness and perception. He was quick to exploit Parma's enforced about-turn of the Spanish offensive, from the Low Countries to advancing into France to intervene in the French civil wars of religion. It could be argued, less charitably, that to exploit this did not take much perception and that indeed any leader of the Dutch Revolt who failed to take this opportune semi-gift would be justifiably condemned. However, the manner in which Maurits effected his counterstroke was near perfection. Firstly, his tactic of striking at the south near Breda and then to the east, then backward and forward, combining manoeuvres leading to a series of highly successful sieges, certainly deserves acknowledgement and praise, and in this context Maurits can be judged to have fully exploited the international situation.

As has been described, he acquiesced in the Truce negotiations, fully realizing that due to the international situation concerning England and France, the Dutch could not on their own sustain a renewal of war with Spain.

In 1618 he supported the Elector Palatine Frederick V in the latter's bid for the Bohemian crown. In this he gave due support to the grandson of William of Orange, as well as supporting a German ruler in a bid that, if successful, would have tilted the balance of the electoral college of the Holy Roman Empire heavily in favour of the Protestant cause. When the rebellion failed, he gave the defeated young (and now deposed) elector and his family sanctuary in the Dutch Republic and ensured their sustenance and well-being. However, no more subsidies or support was given to the cause or to the Protestant Union. The Dutch could not afford to become the paymaster of Protestant Europe in their struggle against the Hapsburg Empire and Hapsburg Spain. The Truce was expiring, and the immediate danger was Spain quickly renewing the war.

As the Truce was coming to an end, Maurits manipulated the international situation, exploiting the Archduke Albert's wish to continue the peace. In this, by using the same strategy that Oldenbarneveldt did in the preliminary talks in the 1600s leading to the Truce, that of unofficial discreet dialogue and contacts with both Albert and using various unofficial intermediaries between Brussels and The Hague, he spun out the possibility of maintaining the peace, hoodwinking Albert and even King Philip III and his ministers in Spain. The result was that the Dutch Republic gained valuable time and that, in the renewal of the war, Hapsburg Spain was shown clearly to be the aggressor.

Maurits ably fulfilled and carried out all 4 factors for a successful insurgency.

William of Orange, rightly judged "father of the patrie", by his tenacity of purpose, combined with patience, reliability, and conciliation, created from the Dutch Revolt a nascent country. Frederick Henry added considerable territory to the Republic and led it through the final stages of the Eighty Years' War, resulting in the Dutch Republic gaining official recognition from imperial Spain at the 1648 Treaty of Münster.

Between their two periods of leadership, Maurits of Nassau for over 30 years, combined military ability with superb tactical skills, with perception of the wider strategic issues, with an able grasp of international affairs, and with decisive action when needed.

He ensured the survival of the Dutch Revolt and the nascent Dutch nation.

Notes

1. Kikkert, JG "Maurits van Nassau" pp 98–99
2. Archief Stadoudersljike Secretaire (the Treaty itself displayed in Nationaal Achief The Hague. 2017)

Appendix I
The 1620s Spanish Trade Embargo Against the Dutch Republic

There is little doubt that Spain made tremendous efforts and allocated considerable resources to establish its trade embargo against the Dutch Republic during this period.

An interesting difference of opinion is to be found amongst two eminent historians regarding the effectiveness of the Spanish trade blockade.

Fernand Braudel, a doyen of economic history, is doubtful about the feasibility of Spain enforcing a full blockade and the effectiveness of the blockade. In one of his many monumental works, in which the interplay between the Spanish preoccupation with the Mediterranean and the Turkish threat on the one hand and the northern European affairs of the Dutch Revolt and the Thirty Years' War on the other is analysed, he states:

> [I]t was foolish to try and enclose the *pays d'en bas* when they made their living from the entire world and were indispensable for the life of the rest of Europe.
>
> (*The Mediterranean and the Mediterranean World in the Age of Philip* II vol II p 1014)

However, Jonathan Israel, in a focused and detailed work on Dutch economic history, points out the results of the Spanish embargo, not by concentrating upon how effective it was—it was effective, but illicit trade did continue—but by pointing to:

> the very lengths to which Dutch entrepreneur were forced to go in their efforts to evade the Spanish ban.
>
> In this Israel cites merchants resorting to transporting goods by mule across the Pyrenees and Navarre, and the hiring and commissioning to carry their good—at exorbitant rates—of French Scottish and Hanseatic shipping.
>
> (*Dutch Primacy in World Trade 1585–1740* p 132)

Appendix II
The Governance of the Dutch Navy: The 5 Admiralties

The first admiralty of the Low Countries was formed in the Fifteenth Century by order of the Hapsburg ruler and was based in Veere, in Zeeland. With the rise of the Dutch Revolt and the importance of the fledgling navy under the so-called Sea Beggars, differing fleets were commissioned and became active, particularly by contributions from the merchants and commercial classes of Amsterdam

By the 100 Instructions issued by the States-General in 1597, the Dutch Navy was governed by 5 different admiralties.

The 5 Admiralty colleges were located in the 3 seaborne provinces, Holland Zeeland, and Friesland. Three out of the 5 admiralties were based in Holland, one was based in Zeeland, and one was based in Friesland. The admiralties in Holland were at Rotterdam, Amsterdam, and Hoorn (in the north quarter of Holland), in Zeeland at Middelburg, and in West Friesland at Dokkum (the admiralty in the north quarter of Holland, Hoorn, alternated with Enkuizen as the headquarters of this admiralty).

The flag of each college indicated that it was part of the United Provinces, that is part of the Dutch state, but also that it had its own collegiate emblazoning; each admiralty college had its own coat of arms. At the Battle of Gibralter in 1607, when 27 Dutch ships engaged a larger Spanish fleet and won, the Dutch fleet was commanded by Admiral Heemskerck, Admiral of Amsterdam, and the second in command was Vice Admiral Alteras, Admiral of Zeeland. The flag of the Dutch Republic flew on the front mast of the ships, but on the mainmast of his flagship Heemskerck flew the flag of the Amsterdam admiralty, while on his flagship Alteras flew the flag of Zeeland.[1]

More practically, each admiralty, through its college, was responsible for its own supplies, maintaining its own shipyards, stores, and arsenals and keeping its own accounts. Each admiralty recruited its own officers and seamen and decided on its shipbuilding programme.

The famous admiral and Dutch patriot, Michael de Ruyter, was vice admiral of Zeeland admiralty at the start of the Anglo-Dutch Wars, then in 1654 transferred as vice admiral to the Amsterdam admiralty.

Admiralties were also the subject of inter-provincial rivalry. One of the Admiralties was formed of necessity by Oldenbarneveldt as a compromise solution to regional bickering involving Amsterdam and West Friesland.

The 5 admiralties were far from well financed and were frequently in debt. The admiralty of Rotterdam was a particularly poor and delaying paymaster. Towards the end of the stadhoudership of Maurits, a scandal came to light involving the Rotterdam Admiralty in which the Advocaat-Fiscal and councillors were found to have embezzled 175,000 guilders of the Admiralty revenues. Throughout the Sixteenth and early Seventeenth Centuries, only the Amsterdam Admiralty managed to remain solvent and to regularly build new ships.

In 1665, the VOC paid for, equipped, and maintained a fleet of 20 ships, which it placed at the disposal of the Dutch Republic. It became known and semi-officially recognised as "the sixth admiralty", and this may be seen as evidence of the expanding power of the VOC. For a time, the VOC maintained and expanded "its", fleet but the main preoccupation of the VOC was overseas commerce, and it failed to adapt the ships in step with the 5 official admiralties, and its role as the "sixth admiralty" ceased after some years.

The 5 admiralties system continued as the governance and command structure of the Dutch Navy until 1795, when the Dutch Republic was invaded by French Revolutionary forces. The stadhouder had fled to England. A pro-French revolutionary regime founding the Batavian Republic was established, and the States-General reorganised the governance of the Republic (including abolishing itself for a National Assembly). In this reorganisation, a more centralised state was created, in the face of much opposition from some of the provinces. Part of the reorganisation was the abolition of the 5 admiralties, which brought the Navy under one command. Significantly, one of main causes of opposition to the new centralised Republic from Friesland and Zeeland was the abolition of their admiralties.

Appendix III
The Regents and the Dutch Republic

The regents in the Dutch Republic were a bourgeois oligarchy. The use of the term "bourgeois" may appear misleading. In the Dutch Republic, unlike other countries in Europe at the time, the aristocracy and landed gentry were not so powerful. Whilst the titled gentry and nobility did wield some political influence, collectively they were not a class above or wealthier than the bourgeois Regents.

The Regents were a group of successful businessmen, many of whose ancestry was of minor nobility in the mediaeval era when the various territories and jurisdictions of the wider Netherlands were part of disparate territories of Burgundy. Just as these individuals had grasped business opportunities, so they had grasped opportunities caused by the Dutch Revolt to seize political power in town and local communities, in the provincial States, and in the States-General.

Delineating class structures is an inexact exercise, with so many societal variables and changing events. However, it can be safely stated that the Regents became the upper class in the Dutch Republic. Parallel to them but without the same influence were the noble and titled families; below the Regents were the middle classes, the merchants, the businessmen, and the professionals who were unable to become regents, being either unable to break in or unwilling to expend the time and energy on public duties. Should they wish, these individuals could always aspire to lower and middle positions in municipal government, subject to regent favour and patronage. (In Amsterdam, there were 400 petty broker jobs within the gift of the city regents.[2]) Below these were the skilled workers of the towns and wealthier agricultural workers, often with their own small trade or landholding. Below these were the unskilled workers, the labourers in the country and manual workers in the towns, and the dockers and workers in the ports, often working on a casual basis. These last had no political power but could not ignored and their opinions mattered. Several outbreaks of popular unrest and disturbances and riots in the Seventeenth Century served as a reminder and a stark warning to the Regents that they could not ignore these elements of the population and their opinions.

During the late Sixteenth Century and early to mid-Seventeenth Century, the Regents evolved—deliberately—into a closed oligarchy. They monopolised directorships on the boards of banks, finance houses, and trading companies. Parallel and linked to this development was the general trend of many Regents withdrawing their capital and energies from active business and becoming rentiers and investment monopoly share and bond holders. This enabled them to spend more time to lead in politics and in national and local administration.

Political power within the Dutch Republic lay in the States-General. The members were representatives from the provincial States. States could send as many representatives as they wished, but in voting on matters in the States-General, each State had only one vote. Unanimity was necessary to pass a resolution or law. Usually the representatives from the provincial States spoke in debates and voted according to the policies or mandates laid down by their respective States. The provincial States themselves were comprised of members who were representatives from the town and communities within the province. In Friesland, the State representatives were from rural estates, grouped by villages. The Gelderland States convened in a joint meeting of representatives from the 3 parts of the province, a total of 6 representatives. The Utrecht States consisted of an equal number of representatives from the nobility, from the towns and from the clergy. The important States of Holland had one representative from the nobility and representatives from 18 towns within the province. Given the extreme urban nature of the Dutch Republic, and the near predominance of the States of Holland, the town representation—in effect the Regents—was crucial. One historian has pointed out that power in the States-General rested with the individual provincial States who themselves were dominated by the towns, and

> effective power rested with 57 towns,

which were under the domination of 2000 Regents.[3]

By the Eighteenth Century, they had increased in numbers to between 8,000 and 10,000 but had formed a tightly closed oligarchy within the government and the institutions and financial sector financial. Their sons were nominated as their "successors" in various offices and were brought up accordingly, in an education whose ethos was to govern and serve. The British ambassador to the Dutch Republic wrote of the Regents:

> [A] people differently bred and mannered from the traders, though like them in modesty of garb and habit and parsimony of living. The youth are generally bred at schools and at the Universities of Leiden and of Utrecht in the common studies of human learning but also in civil law which is that of their country. . . . The chief end of their breeding is to make them fit for the service of their country in

magistracy of the towns. And of these kind of men are civil officers of this government generally composed, being descended of families who have many times been constantly in the magistracy of the towns for many years, and some for many ages.[4]

A neoclassic example of the hereditary trend of the Regent power is found in the de Witt family, originally from Dordrecht. Cornelis de Witt, a successful wood and timber merchant, in the crucial years of the Dutch Revolt and the Twelve Years' Truce was burgomaster of Dordrecht. He was also a representative of the province of Holland in the Zeeland Admiralty College in the 1590s and in the early 1600s the largest subscriber in the Zeeland chamber of the VOC. The son of Cornelis, Jacob de Witt gained his father's place on the Dordrecht town council, became the representative of Dordrecht in the States of Holland, and one of the States of Holland's representatives in the States-General. Between 1698 and 1748 in Amsterdam, the senior governing posts in the city were monopolised by only 40 Regents;[5] for over 75 years in the town of Hoorn, the Breedhoff family held the positions of postmaster plus the principal town governing positions; in the States-General, the important post of greffier was held for several generations by members of the Fagel family.[6]

By the mid- to late Eighteenth Century, the ethos and power of the Regents declined with the overall decline of the Dutch economy, and the ethos of regency itself became less public service orientated, and those in power became more desirous of comfort, luxury, and extravagant personal possessions. Also, the political power struggle mitigated against them. Traditionally they had opposed or at least kept at bay the power of the stadhouder. This was based upon the strategy that the Republic was safe from attack by land, therefore the Regents in the States of Holland, due its economic paramountcy dependent upon seaborne trade and industry and Holland's over 60% contribution to the national budget, would be dominant. Together with the other provincial regents, the Regents of Holland would lead. However, once Louis XIV of France's atavistic territorial ambitions and advances embroiled the major powers of Europe in land-based wars, the stadhouder, as captain general of the armies, was urgently called to power due to the crisis. Symbolically—and horrifically—the Witt bothers, after many years of public service, fell from power and a short time thereafter were murdered by the urban mob in The Hague, as part of this power change from Regents to the stadhouder

During the period of this book, Maurits was not opposed to the Regents as a powerful class. However, during his long period of office, he kept the Regents in check and, after his successful struggle against Oldenbarneveldt, tended to increase the influence of the titled nobility and rely on certain individuals from this class for important duties. In the later periods, they aspired to more power or to prevent any increase in power of the stadhouder.

During the period when they were at their most dedicated to public service with an ethos of modest personal wealth combined with that of public service, they were a remarkable asset to the Republic. In this they facilitated and enabled the Dutch Republic's remarkable rise to economic wealth and internal efficiency, and they maintained the liberties and sovereignty of the differing provinces. In the words of one Dutch historian, they constituted:

> the most remarkable social phenomenon in the Netherlands during the Seventeenth Century.

Further:

> Sober and dignified, level-headed and lucid, not amiable but bold and steady, such were the burgher regents at their best.[7]

Notes

1. The battle is captured in the painting by van Wieringen. The painter did portray the differing flags of the admiralties on the command ships but was also careful to place in a prominent position on Heemskerck's flagship the royal arms of Prince Maurits
2. Schama, S *Patriots and Liberators—Revolution in the Netherlands 1780– 1830* p 51
3. Parker, G *Europe in Crisis 1598–1648* p 141
4. Cited in Boxer, CR *The Dutch Seaborne Empire 1600–1800* p 35
5. Schama, S *Patriots and Liberators—Revolution in the Netherlands 1780– 1830* p 50, citing the extensive genealogical researches of Elias, JE *De Vroedschap van Amsterdam*
6. Schama, S *Patriots and Liberators—Revolution in the Netherlands 1780– 1830* p 50
7. Geyl, P *The Netherlands in the Seventeenth Century Part II 1648–1715* p 191

Bibliography and Works Consulted

Koninklijke Bibliotheek (Netherlands National Library)

Accario de Serionne, J *Les Interets des Nations de l'Europe developpe realtivement au commerce* Vol I 1776 Koninklijke Bibliotheek (Special Collections) The Hague

Berichten over 80 jaar oorlog-de Nederlandse Opstand tussefeit en fiction (Symposium 22 November 2018, guidance and presentations on assessing contemporary source material)

Bingham, J *Aelian Tactics-The Tactics of Aelean or the Art of Embattling an Army After ye Grecan Manner* 1613 Koninklijke Bibliotheek (Special Collections) The Hague

de la Pise, J *Tableau de l'Histoire de princes et principaute de l'Nassau* de l'impremerie Th Maire The Hague 1639 Koninklijke Bibliotheek (Special Collections) The Hague

de Parival, J *Les Delices de la Hollande* 1662 Koninklijke Bibliotheek (Special Collections) The Hague

de Klerk, ES *History of the Netherlands East Indies Vol 1* W and J Busse NV Rotterdam Netherlands 1938, Koninklijke Bibliotheek (Netherlands Collections) The Hague

Mulder, L *Journaal van Anthonis Duyck* 1866 Martinus Nijhoff Koninklijke Bibliotheek (Netherlands Collections) The Hague

Nationaal Archief (Netherlands National Archives)

Aantekeningen Resoluties van Holland de aanstalling van de leden der Admiraliteit ter Amsterdam 1598–1728

Archives Spanish Netherlands Regeringin Brussels

Archief van het College ter Admiraliteit in Friesland

Archief van het College ter Admiraliteit in Zeeland

Colenbrander, HT *Jan Pieterz Coen. Bescheiden Omtrent zijn Bedrief in Indie Vol I* Martinus Nijhoff 1919 (Netherlands National Archives, Library Section)

Heeres, MJE *Corpus Diplomaticus Nederland-Indicum* 1596–1650 Martinus Nijhoff 1907 (Netherlands National Archives, Library Section)

Japikse, DN (ed) *Resolutien der Staaten General 1576–1609* Rijks Gescheidenkundige Publication Martinus Nijhoff 1930 (Netherlands National Archives, Library Section)

Ten Raa, FG and de Baas, F *Het Staatsch Leger Vol I 1568–1588* Vol III Breda/
The Hague 1911 (Netherlands National Archives, Library Section)
Regeringin archivein Geunieerde Provincien (Leycester)
Resolutien der Staten-General 1576–1609

Provincial Archives Noord-Holland, Haarlem

Miscellaneous documents regarding the fall of Haarlem

City Archives Delft

Miscellaneous documents of the earlier period of the Revolt.

Regionaal Archief Dordrecht (Regional Archives Dordrecht)

Het Utrechts Archief (Provincial Archives of Utrecht)

Scheepvaart Museum (Netherlands National Maritime Museum, Reference Library)

*De Eerste Shipvaart der Nederlanders naar Ost-Indie onder Cornelis de
Houtman Vol III Verdere Becheiden Bettergende de Reis* Leershoten Ver-
eening 1929
de Vivero, R *An Account of Japan 1609* (translated and introduced by C Stone)
Hardinge Simpole 2015
Scheurleer, DF *Onze Mannen ter Zee in dicht en bled Vol I 1572–1654* Martinus
Nijhoff 1912
van de Woude, J *Coen-consequent koopman* HP Leopolds Den Haag 1937

British Library

Orders, J and van Hestens, H *The Triumphs of Nassau . . . A Description of
All Victories . . . Granted to God . . . to the Estates Generall of the Vnited
Netherlands Provinces Vnder the Control and Command of Prince Maurice of
Nassau.* London Adam Islip 1613

Articles

Israel, J 1986 "The Politics of International Trade Rivalry During the XXX Years
War" *International History Review* Vol 8, issue 4
Odegard, E 2014 "The Sixth Admiralty. The Dutch East India Company and
the Military Revolution at Sea 1639–1667" *International Journal of Maritime
History* Vol 23, issue 4
Wilson, CH 1973 "Transport as a Factor in the History of Economic Develop-
ment" *Journal of Economic History* Vol II, issue 2

Books

Allen, P 2000 *Philip III and the Pax Hispanica 1598–1621-The Failure of Grand Strategy* Yale University Press Conn USA

Arnold, T 2001 *The Renaissance at War* Cassell London UK

Aston, T (ed) 1967 (reprinted 2012) *Crisis in Europe 1560–1660* Routledge UK

Ballesteros y Beretta, A 1947 *Figurales imperials—Alfonso VII, el Emperador, Colon, Fernando el Catolico, Carlos V, Felipe II,* Espasa Calpa SA Spain

Berenger, J 1997 *A History of the Hapsburg Empire 1700–1918* Longmans London UK and New York USA

Boxer, CR 1959 *The Dutch in Brazil 1624–1654* Clarendon Press Oxford UK

Boxer, CR 1969 *The Portuguese Seaborne Empire 1415–1825* Hutchinson & Co University of Texas Texas USA

Boxer, CR 1988 *The Dutch Seaborne Empire 1600–1800* Pelican Books London UK

Brandi, K 1970 *The Emperor Charles V* Jonathan Cape London UK

Braudel, F 1982 *Civilisation and Capitalism 15th to 18th Centuries Vol II—The Wheels of Commerce* William Collins London UK

Braudel, F 1985 *Civilisation and Capitalism 15th to 18th Centuries Vol III—The Perspective of the World* Fontana Press London UK

Campbell, E 1999 *Early Modern Europe. An Oxford History* OUP Oxford UK

Cipolla, M (ed) 1972 *The Fontana Economic History of Europe Vol I—The Middle Ages* Fontana Press London UK

Cipolla, M (ed) 1974 *The Fontana Economic History of Europe Vol II—The Sixteenth and Seventeenth Centuries* Fontana Press London UK

Cooper, JP (ed) 1970 *The New Cambridge Modern History Vol IV—The Decline of Spain and the Thirty Years War 1609–1659* Cambridge University Press Cambridge UK

Cronin, V 1974 *Louis and Antoinette* William Collins London UK

Crowley, R 2008 *Empires of the Sea—The Final Battle for the Mediterranean 1521–1580* Faber and Faber London UK

Crowley, R 2011 *City of Fortune—How Venice Won and Lost a Naval Empire* Faber and Faber London UK

Dakin, D 1973 *The Greek Struggle for Independence* Batsford London UK

Dangerfield, G 1977 *The Damnable Question—A Study in Anglo-Irish Relations* Constable London UK

Davies, RT 1937 *The Golden Century of Spain 1501–1621* MacMillan London UK

de Maartens, F 1818 *Receuil des Principaux Traites depuis 1761 jusqu'a present* Gottingen Germany

Duerloo, L 2012 *Dynasty and Piety—Archduke Albert and Hapsburg Political Culture in an Age of Religious Wars* Ashgate London UK

Eckhard, L 1992 *Het Admiralen Boek* Bataafse Leeuw Amsterdam Netherlands

Fall, B 1982 *The Two Vietnams* Praeger New York USA

Fishman, JS 1998 *Diplomacy and Revolution—The London Conference of 1830 and the Belgian Revolt* CHEV Amsterdam Netherlands

Fraser, D 2000 *Frederick the Great* Allen Lane History London UK

Fruin, R 1922 *Gescheidenis de staatsinstellingen in Nederland* The Hague Netherlands

Fuller, JFC 1985 *Decisive Battles of the Western World Vol I* Paladin Books London UK

Geyl, P 1961 *History of the Dutch Speaking Peoples 1555–1648* Phoenix Press London UK

Geyl, P 1964 *History of the Low Countries—Episodes and Problems* MacMillan London UK

Hamilton, EJ 1934 *American Treasure and the Price Revolution in Spain 1501–1650* Harvard Economic Studies Vol VIII Harvard University Press USA

Hart, M, Junker, J and van Zanden, JL 1997 *A Financial History of the Netherlands* Cambridge University Press Cambridge UK

Hastings, M 2018 *Vietnam—An Epic Tragedy 1945–1975* William Collins London UK

Houssaye, H 1896 *1815 la Premiere Restoration, le Retour de l'Isle de lElba, les Cent Jours* Perrin et Cie Paris France

Israel, J 1989 *Dutch Primacy in World Trade 1585–1740* Clarendon Press Oxford UK

Israel, J 1990 *Empire and Entrepots* Hambledon Press London UK and Rio Grande OhioUSA

Israel, J 1992 *The Dutch Republic and the Hispanic World 1606–1661* Clarendon Press Oxford UK

Israel, J 1998 *The Dutch Republic—Its Rise Greatness and Fall 1477–1806* Clarendon Press Oxford UK

Jones, C 2003 *The Great Nation* Penguin Books London UK

Kikkert, JG 2008 *Maurits van Nassau* Uitgeverij ASPEKt Soesterberg Netherlands

Kloek, E 2014 *Kenau en Magdalena—vrouwen in de Tachtigjarige Oorlog* Uitgeverij Vantilt Nijmegan Netherlands

Lessafer, R (ed) 2014 *The Twelve Years Truce 1609—Peace, Law and War in the Low Countries at the Turn of the Seventeenth Century* Brill Nijhoff Netherlands

Livermore, H 1947 *A History of Portugal* Cambridge University Press Cambridge UK

Maland, D 1880 *Europe at War 1600–1650* Macmillan London UK

Martin, C and Parker, G 1998 *The Spanish Armada* Hamish Hamilton/Guild Publishing London UK

Mattingly, G 1955 *Renaissance Diplomacy* Peregrine Books London UK

Mclean, M 1981 *Vietnam—The Ten Thousand Day War* Thames Methuen London UK

Neale, JE 1934 *Queen Elizabeth I* Penguin Books London UK

Nordmann, C 1971 *Grandeur et Liberte de la Suede* Beatrice -Nauwelaarts Paris France

Oman, C 1937 *The XVI Century* Cornell University Press New York USA

Pares, B 1965 *A History of Russia* University Paperback Methuen London UK

Parker, G 1972 *The Army of Flanders and the Spanish Road 1567–1659* Cambridge University Press Cambridge UK

Parker, G 1979 *Europe in Crisis 1598–1648* Fontana Press London UK

Parker, G 1987 *The Thirty Years War* Routledge Kegan and Paul London UK

Parker, G 1998 *The Grand Strategy of Philip II* Yale University Press Conn USA

Parker, G 2014 *Imprudent King—A New Life of Philip II* Yale University Press Conn USA

Polisensky, J 1991 *Tragic Triangle—The Netherlands Spain and Bohemia* Charles University Prague Czech Republic

Prak, M 2005 *The Dutch Republic in the Seventeenth Century* Cambridge University Press Cambridge UK

Price, JL 1974 *Culture and Society in the Dutch Republic During the 17th Century* Batsford London UK

Price, JL 1974 *The Dutch Republic in the Seventeenth Century* Batsford London UK

Price, JL 1994 *Holland and the Dutch Republic in the Seventeenth Century—The Politics of Particularism* Clarendon Press London UK

Rady, M 1988 *The Emperor Charles V* Longmans London UK and New York USA

Ridley, N 2018 *Michael Collins and the Funding of Political Violence* Routledge London UK

Rude, G 1976 *Europe Between Revolutions 1815–1848* Fontana London UK

Ryle Dwyer, T 2005 *The Squad and the Intelligence Operations of Michael Collins* Mercier Press Cork Ireland

Schama, S 1989 *Citizens—A Chronicle of the French Revolution* Alfred A. Knopf New York USA

Schmidt, B 2006 *Innocents Abroad—The Dutch Imagination and the New World 1570–1670* Cambridge University Press Cambridge UK

Stein, CR 2013 *Margaret of Parma—A Life* Koninklijke Brill Netherlands

van Cruyningen, A 2017 *De Tachtiglarige Ooorlog* Uitgeverij Omniboek Netherlands

van Deursen, A 2000 *Maurits de Nassau—de winaar de faalde* Uitgeverij Bert Bakker Amsterdam Netherlands

van Deursen, A 2004 *De last van veel Geluk—de Gescheidenis va Nederland 1555–1702* Uitgeverij Bert Bakker Amsterdam Netherlands

Van Stipriaan, R (ed) 2000 *Ooggetuigen van de Gouden Eeuw* Prometeus Netherlands

Wallerstein, I 1970 *The Modern World System II—Mercantalism and the Consolidation of the European World Economy 1600–1750* Academy Press New York USA and London UK

Wedgwood, CV 1949 *Richelieu and the French Monarchy* Hodder and Stoughton London UK

Wedgwood, CV 1964 *The Thirty Years War* Jonathan Cape London UK

Wilson, CH 1967 *Englands Apprenticeship 1603–1763* Longmans London UK and New York USA

Wilson, CH 1968 *The Dutch Republic* Weidenfeld and Nicolson London UK

Wilson, CH 1979 *Queen Elizabeth and the Revolt of the Netherlands* Martinus Nijhoff Netherlands

Wilson, PH 2009 *The Thirty Years War—Europe's Tragedy* Belknap Press Harvard USA

Zamoyski, A 2007 *Rites of Peace—The Fall of Napoleon and the Congress of Vienna* Harper Press London UK

Zamoyski, A 2014 *Phantom Terror—The Threat of Revolution and the Repression of Liberty 1798–1848* William Collins London UK

Index

Printed in Great Britain
by Amazon